COSTA RICA

TOP SIGHTS, AUTHENTIC EXPERIENCES

Mara Vorhees, Jade Bremner,
Ashley Harrell, Brian Kluepfel

Contents

COVID-19

We have re-checked every business in this book before publication to ensure that it is still open after 2020's COVID-19 outbreak. However, the economic and social impacts of COVID-19 will continue to be felt long after the outbreak has been contained, and many businesses, services and events referenced in this guide may experience ongoing restrictions. Some businesses may be temporarily closed, have changed their opening hours and services, or require bookings; some unfortunately could have closed permanently. We suggest you check with venues before visiting for the latest information.

SARAPIQUÍ VALLEY (p251)

Puerto Viejo
de Sarapiquí

POÁS

Reserva Forestal
Cordillera
Volcánica Central

SAN JOSÉ (p35)

Cartago

Parque Nacional
Tapantí-Macizo
Cerro la Muerte

San Gerardo
de Dota

Reserva
Forestal
Los Santos

San Isidro de
El General

Dominical

A BALLENA
(p149)

CARIBBEAN SEA

TORTUGUERO (p63)

Parque
Nacional
Tortuguero

Guácimo

Siquirres

Parque
Nacional
Barbilla

Turrialba

Valle de la Estrella

Puerto Limón

SOUTHERN
CARIBBEAN
(p79)

Cahuita

Puerto Viejo
de Talamanca

Bribrí

Manzanillo

TALAMANCA
MOUNTAINS
(p115)

San Gerardo
de Rivas

Rivas

Parque
Internacional
La Amistad

Buenos
Aires

Uvita

Sierpe

Bahía
Drake

Rincón

PENÍNSULA DE OSA
(p129)

Puerto
Jiménez

Parque Nacional
Corcovado

Carate

Cabo
Matapalo

Pavones

Fila Costeña

Río Claro

Zona
Protectora
Las Tablas

PANAMA

Paso
Canoas

La Concepción

Welcome to Costa Rica

Centering yourself on a surfboard or yoga mat, descending into bat-filled caves or ascending misty volcanic peaks, hiking, biking or ziplining – the only limit is your return date.

If marketing experts could draw up an ideal destination, it would look like Costa Rica. The 'rich coast' stands apart from its Central American neighbors on the cutting edge of so many trends, especially sustainable tourism.

A superlative suite of outdoor adventures offers thrills in every shape and size – from the squeal-inducing rush of a canopy zipline to a sun-dazed afternoon at the beach. National parks allow visitors to hike through rainforest, cloud forest and dry forest; simmering volcanoes offer otherworldly landscapes; and aquatic adventurers can kayak, surf, snorkel or dive on two coastlines.

Meanwhile, wildlife abounds. Keel-billed toucans eye you from treetops and scarlet macaws raucously announce their flight plans. Blue morpho butterflies flit amid orchid-festooned trees, while colorful tropical fish, sharks, rays, dolphins and whales thrive offshore – all as if in a conservationist's dream.

Developing infrastructure is balanced by green energy such as wind and hydro. One of the world's most biodiverse countries, it also protects a quarter of its wild lands through law.

Costa Rica consistently shows up at or near the top of lists of the happiest places on Earth. It's the perfect place to relax and enjoy the 'pure life' – or, as locals like to say, *pura vida, mae*.

> **If marketing experts could draw up an ideal destination, it would look like Costa Rica.**

Surfers, Tamarindo (p276)
COLIN D. YOUNG/SHUTTERSTOCK ©

Squirrel monkey (p180)
EHTESHAM/SHUTTERSTOCK ©

Plan Your Trip
Costa Rica's Top 12

Southern Nicoya

Wild ocean meets lush jungle

If you dig artsy-rootsy beach culture and lounging on sugar-white coves, find your way to southern Nicoya (p185). In the little surf towns of Mal País and Santa Teresa, the sea is replete with wildlife and the waves are near ideal in shape. There's easy access to Cabo Blanco reserve or Montezuma's triple-tiered waterfall, and some excellent restaurants await. Best of all, you're never far from the rhythm of the sea. Above: Playa Los Suecos, Mal País (p192); right: Capuchin monkey

1

MARCO LISSONI/SHUTTERSTOCK ©

VACLAV SEBEK/SHUTTERSTOCK ©

Tortuguero

Sea-turtle spotting and canal tours

Canoeing the canals of Parque Nacional Tortuguero (p72; pictured) is a boat-borne safari: thick jungle meets inky water and you can get up close to caimans, river turtles, black-crowned night herons, monkeys and sloths. Under the cover of darkness, watch the ritual of turtles building nests and laying eggs. Between wetlands and the wild Caribbean Sea, this is among the country's premier places for wildlife. Bottom: Teratohyla spinosa glass frog

2

MARTINA CLERC/SHUTTERSTOCK ©

Costa Ballena

Whale-watching, wave riding and pure deliciousness

South of Quepos, the well-trodden central Pacific trail tapers off, evoking the Costa Rica of yesteryear – surf shacks and empty beaches, roadside *ceviche* vendors and a little more space. Along the Costa Ballena (p149), intrepid travelers stumble upon great surf spots and long coconut-strewn beaches perfect for whale-watching (pictured).

3

4

Península de Osa

Immersive wilderness and arresting wildlife

Muddy and intense, the vast, largely untouched rainforest of Parque Nacional Corcovado (p132) is no walk in the park. Here, travelers with a sturdy pair of rubber boots thrust themselves into the unknown and emerge with stories of a lifetime. The further into the jungle you go, the better it gets: the best wildlife-watching, most desolate beaches and vivid adventures lie down these seldom-trodden trails. Scarlet macaws

5

Manuel Antonio

Alive with the call of birds and monkeys

Although droves of visitors pack Parque Nacional Manuel Antonio (p165), the country's most popular (and smallest) national park remains an absolute gem. Capuchin monkeys scurry across its idyllic beaches, brown pelicans dive-bomb its clear waters and sloths watch over its trails. It's a perfect place to introduce youngsters to the wonders of the rainforest; indeed, you're likely to feel like a kid yourself.

Southern Caribbean

Laid-back charm and raucous surf

By day, lounge in a hammock, cycle to uncrowded beaches and visit remote indigenous territories. By night, dip into zesty Caribbean cooking and sway to reggaetón at open-air bars cooled by ocean breezes. The villages of Cahuita, Puerto Viejo de Talamanca and Manzanillo – all outposts of this unique mix of Afro-Caribbean, Tico and indigenous culture – are perfect bases for adventures on the Caribbean's southern coast (p79). Punta Uva beach (p84)

6

Volcán Poás

A bubbling, steaming cauldron

An hour northwest of the capital, Poás (p101) is a fairy-tale land of verdant mountains and hydrangea-lined roadsides. The volcano itself is a spectacular, sulfurous behemoth – the largest and most accessible volcanic crater in the country. Driving the winding approach takes you past strawberry farms and coffee plantations, storybook waterfalls and animal rescue operations, culminating in the smoking volcano and emerald-green crater lake.

7

Volcán Arenal

An iconic volcano, bubbling springs and stunning lake

While the molten night views are gone, this mighty, perfectly conical giant is still worthy of a pilgrimage. Shrouded in mist or bathed in sunshine, Arenal (p229) has a lake to paddle (pictured), trails to explore, waterfalls to swim in and hot springs to soak in. Some of these springs are free, and any local can point the way. Others range from inexpensive Tico favorites to pricier over-the-top resorts to isolated ecstasy.

CARMELA SOTO/SHUTTERSTOCK ©

9

Monteverde

A pristine expanse of virginal forest

Monteverde Cloud Forest (p202) and its neighboring preserves provide an escape into a mysterious neverland shrouded in mist, draped with mossy vines, sprouting with ferns and bromeliads, gushing with creeks, blooming with life and nurturing rivulets of evolution. It's easier than ever to reach this cloud-covered paradise, as the main road from the Interamericana is now completely paved. From left: Birding in Monteverde (p206); Fern (tracheophyta) in Reserva Santa Elena (p215)

Talamanca Mountains

Spectacular views above the clouds

The Talamanca Mountains (p115) are Costa Rica's highest and longest mountain range, splitting the country quite dramatically. Their centerpiece is Cerro Chirripó, the tallest peak, yielding views of wind-swept rocks and icy lakes. But you don't have to climb a mountain to appreciate this mystical range, home to fantastic scenery and countless bird species, including the resplendent quetzal.

Top: Crestones. Parque Nacional Chirripó (p118); left: White-throated mountain-gem

10

WOLFGANG KAEHLER/LIGHTROCKET VIA GETTY IMAGES ©

Sarapiquí Valley

Kayaking and white-water rafting adventures

The Sarapiquí Valley (p251) rose to fame as a principal port in the nefarious old days of United Fruit dominance, only to be reborn as a paddler's paradise, thanks to the frothing serpentine magic of its namesake river. These days it's still a rafter's paradise, dotted with fantastic ecolodges and private forest preserves that will lead you into that steaming, looming, muddy jungle, and bring you up close to local wildlife.

11

DIXANA SALAS/GETTY IMAGES ©

San José

Historic neighborhoods, vibrant culture, local cuisine

The heart of Tico culture lives in San José (p35), as do university students, intellectuals, artists and politicians. While not the most attractive capital in Central America, it does have graceful neo-classical and Spanish-colonial architecture, leafy neighborhoods, museums housing pre-Columbian jade and gold, and sophisticated restaurants. Street art adds unexpected pops of color and public discourse to the cityscape. Octopus and fish *ceviche* (p295)

12

Plan Your Trip
Need to Know

When to Go

- **Tamarindo** GO Nov–Apr
- **Puerto Limón** GO Jan–Apr
- **San José** GO Dec–Apr
- **Parque Nacional Manuel Antonio** GO Dec–Feb
- **Puerto Jiménez** GO Dec–Mar

Tropical climate, rain year-round
Tropical climate, wet and dry seasons

High Season (Dec–Apr)
○ 'Dry' season still sees some rain; beach towns fill with domestic tourists on weekends.

○ Accommodations should be booked well ahead; some places enforce minimum stays.

Shoulder (May–Jul)
○ Rain picks up and the stream of tourists tapers off.

○ Many accommodations offer lower prices.

○ Muddy roads make more remote travel challenging.

Low Season (Aug–Nov)
○ Rainfall is highest; Pacific swells mean good surfing.

○ Rural roads can be impassable due to river crossings.

○ Accommodations prices lower significantly.

○ Some places close entirely; check before booking!

Currency
Costa Rican colón (₡)
US dollar ($)

Language
Spanish, English

Visas
Most nationalities do not need a visa for stays of up to 90 days. Check requirements at www.costarica-embassy.org.

Money
US dollars are accepted almost everywhere and dispensed from many ATMs; carry colones for small towns and bus fares. Credit cards are widely accepted.

Cell Phones
Cheap prepaid SIM cards are widely available. Both 3G and 4G are available; US plans require international roaming. See www.opensignal.com/networks for details of cellular providers.

Time
Central Standard Time (GMT/UTC minus six hours)

Daily Costs

Budget: Less than US$50

- Dorm bed: US$8–20
- Meal at a *soda* (inexpensive eatery): US$5–8
- DIY hikes without a guide: free
- Travel via local bus: US$2 or less

Midrange: US$50–150

- Basic room with private bathroom: US$40–80 per day
- Meal at a restaurant geared toward travelers: US$5–12
- Travel on an efficient 1st-class shuttle van like Interbus: US$50–60

Top End: More than US$150

- Upscale lodges and boutique hotels: from US$80
- Meal at an international fusion restaurant: from US$20
- Guided wildlife-watching excursion: from US$40
- Short domestic flight: from US$100
- 4WD rental for local travel: from US$60 per day

Useful Websites

Essential Costa Rica (www.visitcosta rica.com) The Costa Rica Tourism Board website has planning tips and destination details.

The Tico Times (www.ticotimes.net) Costa Rica's English-language newspaper's website.

Lonely Planet (www.lonelyplanet.com/costa -rica) Destination information, hotel bookings, traveler forum and more.

My Tan Feet (www.mytanfeet.com) Read tips and travel stories from a Tico-expat couple living in Costa Rica.

Opening Hours

The following are high-season opening hours; hours tend to shorten in the shoulder and low seasons. Generally, sights, activities and restaurants are open daily.

Banks 9am–4pm Monday to Friday, sometimes 9am–noon Saturday

Bars and clubs 8pm–2am

Government offices 8am–5pm Monday to Friday; often closed 11:30am–1:30pm

Restaurants 7am–9pm

Shops 9am–6pm Monday to Saturday

Arriving in Costa Rica

Aeropuerto Internacional Juan Santamaría (San José) Buses from the airport to central San José (US$2, 20 minutes to one hour, hourly) run all day. Taxis (from US$30, 20 minutes to one hour) depart from the official stand. Interbus runs between the airport and San José accommodations (adult/child US$19/9). Many rental-car agencies have desks at the airport; book ahead.

Getting Around

Air Inexpensive domestic flights between San José and popular destinations such as Puerto Jiménez, Quepos and Tortuguero will save you the driving time.

Bus Very reasonably priced, with extensive coverage of the country, but travel can be slow and some destinations have infrequent service.

Shuttle Private and shared shuttles such as Interbus and Gray Line provide door-to-door service between popular destinations and allow you to schedule to your needs.

Car Renting a car allows you to access remote destinations not served by buses, and frees you to cover as much ground as you like. Cars can be rented at international airports and in major tourist destinations. A 4WD vehicle is advantageous (and essential in some parts of the country); avoid driving at night.

For more on **getting around**, see p308

Plan Your Trip
Hot Spots for...

Wildlife-Watching

World-class parks, dedication to environmental protection, and mind-boggling biodiversity enable Costa Rica to harbor many rare and endangered species.

MARCO SIMONI/GETTY IMAGES ©

Península de Osa (p129) Parque Nacional Corcovado and its environs teem with wildlife, including animals rarely seen elsewhere.

Scarlet Macaws (p144) Frequently seen on the Agujitas–Corcovado Trail.

Tortuguero (p63) Witness sea-turtle nesting season at this remote Caribbean outpost.

Sea Turtles (p66) Three species nest at the Tortuguero beaches.

Parque Nacional Manuel Antonio (p168) This park may be tiny, but it's full of wild creatures that are easily encountered.

Fantastic Mammals (p168) Sloths, anteaters and monkeys inhabit the park.

Surfing

Point and beach breaks, lefts and rights, reefs and river mouths, warm water and year-round waves make Costa Rica a favorite surfing destination.

ANDRIA PATINO/GETTY IMAGES ©

Dominical (p160) Countless foreigners show up here to surf – and can't bring themselves to leave.

Costa Rica Surf Camp (p161) Established, locally owned surf school.

Southern Caribbean (p79) Salsa Brava is the country's biggest break – in December waves get up to 7m.

Caribbean Surf School (p83) The most acclaimed instructor on this coast.

Santa Teresa (p192) The best beach break in southern Nicoya, especially when there's an offshore wind.

Nalu Surf School (p193) Surf lessons that are both fun and professional.

Yoga

Something about yoga and Costa Rica go together, and beachfront studios are catering to this need, fantastic views included.

PAYTONVANGORP/SHUTTERSTOCK ©

Dominical (p160) With a popular festival and year-round counter-culture, this is a hot spot for spiritual stretching.

Danyasa (p161) Offers a variety of levels and styles of yoga.

Southern Nicoya (p185) Away from it all, southern Nicoya is an ideal place to relax, breathe and hold uncomfortable positions.

Casa Zen (p194) A lovely studio and hotel in Santa Teresa.

Montezuma (p196) This laid-back beach town attracts a wellness-seeking set with yoga studios and resorts.

Montezuma Yoga (p198) Open-air studio offering vinyasa and yin yoga.

Rafting & Kayaking

With Costa Rica's ample waterways, the opportunities for cruising gentle mangroves and rushing down frothing rapids will satisfy every thirst for adventure.

JUAN CARLOS MUNOZ/GETTY IMAGES ©

Río Sarapiquí (p254) Sparsely populated by people but crowded with wildlife, this is a great place to raft or kayak.

Sarapiquí Outdoor Center (p255) The local authority, based in La Virgen.

Golfo Dulce (p140) Discover the ecology and animals of the mysterious mangroves and glorious gulf by kayak.

Aventuras Tropicales (p140) Offers kayaking tours from Puerto Jiménez.

Río Savegre (p174) Gentle rapids that intensify in the rainy season are a great intro to rafting; trips depart from Quepos.

H2O Adventures (p174) For kayaking, rafting or tubing.

Plan Your Trip
Essential Costa Rica

Activities

Miles of shoreline, endless warm water and an array of national parks and reserves provide an inviting playground for active travelers. Whether it's the solitude of absolute wilderness, family-oriented hiking and rafting adventures, or surfing and jungle trekking you seek, Costa Rica offers fun to suit everyone. Coastal areas are sunny, hot and humid, calling for a hat, shorts and short sleeves, but you'll want to pack a sweater and lightweight jacket for high-elevation destinations. If you plan to hike up Chirripó, bring lots of layers and a hat and gloves. While hiking through the rainforest is often a hot and sweaty exercise, long sleeves and lightweight, quick-drying pants help keep the bugs away.

Shopping

Costa Rica has everything from full-on urban mall experiences to cute craft stores and stands in tourist towns featuring well-made artisanal wares. Coffee and chocolate are good consumable souvenirs, usually available at the local grocery store. Wood products are gorgeous and often made with repurposed wood; be sure to inquire about the source of the materials, so you know that forest trees were not felled for the items' production.

Avoid purchasing animal products, including turtle shells, animal skulls and anything made with feathers, coral or shells (it's illegal to export them, in addition to the bad karma).

Eating

Bordered by two oceans and heavily populated with expats, Costa Rica is a foodie's delight, on both a local and international level. It's the sort of place where you can dig into an oh-so-satisfying *casado,* the Ticos' staple platter of rice, beans and meat, or walk down the road and feast on five-star sushi. French and Italian pastry chefs sate

JOHN COLETTI/GETTY IMAGES ©

morning munchies and *taquerías* (taco stalls) and American bar food tempt nocturnal nibblers. And the regional Nicoya diet is one of the healthiest in the world. Dig in!

Drinking & Nightlife

In the more touristy areas of Costa Rica, there's no shortage of bars and nightclubs. San José has the most going on, with all the dive bars, lounges and dance clubs you could ask for. Tamarindo, Santa Teresa, Dominical and Puerto Viejo are top spots for '*un zarpe*' (just one more!), but almost every beach town in the country has at least one local bar where everybody goes.

Entertainment

Live music, dance performances, parades, soccer matches and bullfights are the primary forms of entertainment around

★ Best Restaurants

Playa de los Artistas (p198), Southern Nicoya

La Luna (p182), Manuel Antonio

Restaurante Celajes (p225), Monteverde

Selvin's Restaurant (p94), Puerto Viejo de Talamanca

Café de los Deseos (p52), San José

Costa Rica. All can be found in San José on a regular basis. The national stadium hosts big-gun touring acts, while a couple of less-stress seaside events like Envision (p22) immerse you in a mad mix of cultural cool. Nearly every town has its own festival, complete with carnival games, rides and rodeos.

From left: Chorotega pottery (p285); Coffee bean farming

Plan Your Trip
Month by Month

January

Every year opens with a rush, as North American and domestic tourists flood beach towns to celebrate. January sees dry days and occasional afternoon showers.

🎊 Las Fiestas de Palmares

In the second half of the month, the tiny town of Palmares, near Alajuela, turns into party central, with carnival rides, bullfighting (Toros a la Tica), live music, a horse parade and plenty of boozing. Note that the bull is not injured in the Toros a la Tica.

February

February is the perfect month, with ideal weather and no holiday surcharges. The skies above Nicoya are particularly clear, and it's peak season for some species of nesting turtle to do their thing.

🎊 Envision Festival

Held in Uvita in late February, this is a festival (p156) with a consciousness-raising, transformational bent, bringing together fire dancers, performance artists, yoga, music and spiritual workshops. Also takes place during the first week of March in Dominical.

March

Excellent weather continues through the early part of March, though prices shoot up during Semana Santa (the week leading up to Easter) and North American spring break, aka Holy Week and Unholy Week.

🚴 Vuelta al Lago Arenal

They say that it's virtually impossible to circumnavigate this lake – in the shadow of Volcán Arenal – under your own locomotion. But *they* have never participated in the two-day Vuelta al Lago Arenal, an annual event, when some 4000 cyclists do just that.

Above: Costa Rica Independence Day (p24)

© CYRIELLE BEAUBOIS/GETTY IMAGES ©

April

Easter and Semana Santa can fall early in April, which means beaches fill and prices spike. Nicoya and Guanacaste are dry and hot, with little rain.

🎊 Día de Juan Santamaría

Commemorating Costa Rica's national hero (the main airport is named for him), who died in battle against American colonist William Walker's troops in 1856, this day of celebration on April 11 includes parades, concerts and dances.

🎊 Festival de las Artes (FIA)

This multidisciplinary, multiday festival featuring international artists takes flight all across San José and usually happens in March or April, but the month can vary.

May

Attention, budget travelers: wetter weather begins to sweep across the country in May, heralding the country's low season. So, although conditions are pleasant, prices drop.

★ Best Festivals

Las Fiestas de Palmares, January

Envision Festival, February

Vuelta al Lago Arenal, March

Costa Rican Independence Day, September

Whale & Dolphin Festival, September

✗ Día de San Isidro Labrador

On May 15, visitors can taste the bounty of San Isidro and neighboring villages during the nation's largest agricultural fair, in honor of the growers' patron saint.

June

The Pacific coast gets fairly wet during June, though this makes for good surfing. The beginning of the 'green season,' this time of year has lots of discounted rates.

Above: Whale and Dolphin Festival (p156)

July

July is mostly wet, particularly on the Caribbean coast, but the month also occasionally enjoys a brief dry period that Ticos call *veranillo* (summer). Expect rain, particularly late in the day.

☆ Walter Ferguson Calypso Festival

One weekend each summer Cahuita hails centenarian Walter Gavitt Ferguson (b 1919), the 'Calypso King' who invented the local style of music you hear often around town. Calypso Limonese has been declared a national cultural heritage, and Walter personifies 'living legend.'

🏄 National Surfing Championship

Local surfers head to Jacó, about an hour north of Quepos, for this much publicized national competition on the waves, held in July or August.

August

The middle of the rainy season doesn't mean that mornings aren't bright and sunny. Travelers who don't mind some rain will find great hotel and tour deals.

September

The Península de Osa gets utterly soaked during September, which is the heart of the rainy season and what Ticos refer to as the *temporales del Pacífico*. It's the cheapest time to visit the Pacific.

🎉 Costa Rica Independence Day

With events all over the country, Costa Rica's Independence Day on September 15 is a fun party. The center of the action is the relay race that passes a 'Freedom Torch' from Guatemala to Costa Rica. The torch arrives at Cartago on the evening of the 14th, when the nation breaks into the national anthem.

🐋 Whale & Dolphin Festival

Uvita officially kicks off whale-watching season with a lively, responsibly organized, weeklong festival (p156), featuring dolphin- and whale-watching tours, as well as a fun run and a mountain-bike race.

October

Many roads become impassable as rivers swell and rain continues to fall in one of the wettest months in Costa Rica. Lodges and tour operators are sometimes closed until November.

November

The weather can go either way in November. Access to Parque Nacional Corcovado is difficult after several months of rain, though the skies are usually clear by month's end.

🎉 Día de los Muertos

Families visit graveyards and have religious parades in honor of the dead in this lovely and picturesque festival on November 2.

December

Although the beginning of the month is a great time to visit – with clearer skies and relatively uncrowded attractions – things ramp up toward Christmas and reservations become crucial.

🎉 Las Fiestas de Zapote

In San José between Christmas and New Year's Eve, this weeklong celebration of all things Costa Rican (rodeos, cowboys, carnival rides, fried food and booze) draws tens of thousands of Ticos to the bullring in the suburb of Zapote daily.

Plan Your Trip
Get Inspired

Read

Tropical Nature: Life and Death in the Rain Forests of Central and South America (Adrian Forsyth and Ken Miyata; 1987) Easy-to-digest natural-history essays on rainforest phenomena, written by two biologists.

Monkeys are Made of Chocolate (Jack Ewing; 2011) The author recounts his adventures and interactions over 30 years of living in Costa Rica and converting a cattle ranch back to rainforest.

Costa Rica: A Traveler's Literary Companion (Barbara Ras, foreword by Óscar Arias; 1994) Collection of stories reflecting distinct regions of Costa Rica.

Watch

Entonces nosotros (*About Us*, 2016) Directed by Hernan Jimenez, this film sees a couple trying to repair their relationship on a beach getaway. It simultaneously makes you laugh, cringe and want to be on that beach.

Presos (*Imprisoned*; 2015) Director Esteban Ramirez probes various meanings of 'imprisonment' in this film about a young woman who secretly befriends an inmate in a San José prison.

Del amor y otro demonios (*Of Love and Other Demons*; 2009) The adaptation of Gabriel García Márquez' magical-realism novel, directed by Hilda Hidalgo.

Listen

La Llorona (Chavela Vargas; 1994) The most popular album from the Costa Rican–born singer, featuring hauntingly beautiful folk ballads.

Un Día Lejano (Malpaís; 2009) Costa Rica's innovative and now defunct rock band mixes calypso, jazz and Latin American balladry.

Calypsos: Afro-Limonese Music From Costa Rica (various artists; 1991) A raucous collection that captured the heart of Costa Rica's Afro-Caribbean folk scene.

Mundo (Rubén Blades; 2002) The Panamanian superstar was backed by the Costa Rican jazz band Editus on this Grammy-winning album.

Above: Three-toed sloth, Parque Nacional Manuel Antonio (p168)

Plan Your Trip
Five-Day Itineraries

Pacific Dreams

Discover the Costa Rica capital before heading to the Pacific coast for some fun in the sun. Spend your days exploring dreamy beaches, swimming in turquoise waters and spying on playful monkeys. Spend your nights indulging in amazing seafood, sunset views and rollicking nightlife.

San José (p35) Devote a day to exploring the neighborhoods, perusing the museums and sampling the dining and drinking scene.
✈ 1 hr to Quepos

Montezuma (p196) Hike to waterfalls, ride the surf and salute the sun in open-air yoga studios.

Manuel Antonio (p165) National park hiking, swimming and kayaking, followed by sundowners at nearby bars. 🚌 to Jacó, then ⛴ 1 hr to Montezuma

Eastern Escapade

Steaming volcanoes, raging rivers, jungle-clad canals, and postcard-perfect beaches... Take a jaunt through the northern lowlands and on to the Caribbean coast for a unique sampling of adventure, culture and wildlife galore.

Tortuguero (p63) Paddle through greenery-draped canals, where birds and animals hide around every corner.
⛴ 3½ hrs to Moín, then 🚌/🚗 1 hr to Puerto Viejo

Sarapiquí Valley (p251) Prime territory for riding rapids, visiting local farms and spotting wildlife.
🚗 2 hrs to La Pavona, then ⛴ 1 hr to Tortuguero

Volcán Poás (p104) Reach the top of this mighty volcano and peer into its steaming crater. 🚗 1 hr to La Virgen

Puerto Viejo de Talamanca (p92) Relax into a hammock on the beach, hike through steaming jungles, and feast on delicious Caribbean fare.

Plan Your Trip
10-Day Itinerary

Essential Costa Rica

This is the trip you've been dreaming about: a romp through paradise, with seething volcanoes, hot-spring soaks, monkey-crowded rainforest and ghostly cloud forest, followed by relaxing and recuperating on sun-kissed beaches.

Playa Santa Teresa (p192) Next up: beach time. In this charming coastal enclave, surfing, snorkeling and swimming are at your doorstep. ③

KIKOSTOCK/SHUTTERSTOCK ©

①

Volcán Arenal (p229) Head for La Fortuna, where adventure awaits. Hike to crater lakes, swim beneath waterfalls and spot a sloth.
🚌 4 hrs to Monteverde

Monteverde (p201) Zip through the treetops on a canopy tour or learn about your favorite morning drink on a coffee tour. 🚌 5 hrs to Santa Teresa

Plan Your Trip
Two-Week Itinerary

Southern Adventure

Satisfy your adventurous spirit with a journey to the lesser-traveled southern sector. Climb the country's highest peak, then recover on its glorious beaches. Along the way, keep your eyes peeled for birds, monkeys and countless other creatures.

San Gerardo de Dota (p122) Get up early to spot the elusive but captivating resplendent quetzal.
🚌 1½ hrs to San Gerardo de Rivas

Cerro Chirripó (p118) It's a challenging 20km hike on well-marked trails to the summit of Cerro Chirripó.
🚌 to San Gerardo, then
🚗 4 hrs to Puerto Jiménez

San José (p35) Spend a day visiting museums and checking out the capital's street art. 🚗 1½ hrs to San Gerardo de Dota

San Gerardo de Rivas (p124) Stock up on supplies and get a good night's rest before your hike.
🚌 to Parque Nacional Chirripó

Parque Nacional Corcovado (p132) Undertake the ambitious two-day hike across Corcovado, or the more manageable El Tigre loop.

Puerto Jiménez (p140) Take a day or two to recover with local farm tours, mangrove kayaking and beach lounging.
🚗 30 mins to Parque Nacional Corcovado

Plan Your Trip
Family Travel

With such a stellar array of experiences and close encounters in Costa Rica – wildlife, waves, ziplines and volcanoes – the biggest challenge might be choosing where to go. Fortunately, each region has its attractions, and kids of all ages will find epic adventure awaiting them.

Eating

○ Hydration is crucial in this tropical climate; fortunately, Costa Rica's tap water is safe everywhere (except for the rare exception, usually in remote areas).

○ Kids love refreshing *batidos* (fresh fruit shakes), either *al agua* (made with water) or *con leche* (with milk).

○ Coconut water might be old news back home, but watching a smiling Tico hack open a *pipa fría* (cold young coconut) with a machete is another thing entirely.

○ Consider renting accommodations with kitchen facilities (shared or private) to avoid eating out all the time.

○ Most restaurants have high chairs available but children's menus are less common.

Accommodations

Many hostels and budget lodgings have accommodations that are suitable for families. Lodges and resorts often offer discounts up to 50% for children under 12 years old. Look also for family packages, which include activities that are appealing for children.

Transportation

○ Families with small children get expedited access through immigration and customs at the international airports.

○ Children under the age of 12 receive discounts up to 25% on domestic flights. Children under two usually fly free (provided they sit on a parent's lap).

○ By law, children under the age of 12 are required to be in car seats (up

KEVIN WELLS PHOTOGRAPHY/SHUTTERSTOCK ©

to 15kg/33lb) or booster seats (up to 36kg/79lb). The law is not often enforced. Car seats are usually (though not always) available from most car rental agencies, but they are not always in good repair.

Practicalities

Baby Products Baby products like diapers and formula are readily available throughout Costa Rica.

Breastfeeding Breastfeeding in public is acceptable and even encouraged.

Resources

Lonely Planet Kids (www.lonelyplanet.com/kids) Loads of activities and great family-travel blog content.

Book: Let's Explore Jungle (https://shop.lonelyplanet.com) An activity book for ages five and up, jam-packed with facts, puzzles and pictures about tropical rainforests.

★ Best Family Adventures

Surf Lessons (p83), Puerto Viejo de Talamanca

Parque Nacional Volcán Poás (p104), Central Valley

Canopy Tours (p210), Monteverde

Parque Nacional Tortuguero (p72), Tortuguero

Isla del Caño (p138), Bahía Drake

Book: First Words Spanish (https://shop.lonelyplanet.com) A beautifully illustrated introduction to the Spanish language for ages five to eight.

Two Weeks in Costa Rica (www.twoweeks incostarica.com) Travel tips from an expat couple and their two kids.

From left: Surf lessons (p83); Violet sabrewing, Reserva Biológica Bosque Nuboso Monteverde (p204)

Church of Our Lady
of Solitude

Mercado Central (p46)

Arriving in San José

International flights arrive at Aeropuerto
Internacional Juan Santamaría (p308)
in nearby Alajuela. An official, metered
taxi from the airport to downtown San
José costs around US$30. There are
also Interbus shuttles (US$19), and
public buses (US$2) operated by Tuasa
and Station Wagon that run between
downtown and the airport. The drive
takes 20 minutes to an hour, sometimes
longer on the bus.

Where to Stay

Accommodations in San José run the
gamut from simple but homey hostels
to luxurious boutique retreats. If you're
flying into or out of Costa Rica from
here, it may be more convenient to stay
in Alajuela, as the town is minutes from
the international airport.

For information on what each neighborhood has to offer, see p61.

Teatro Nacional

MIHAI-BOGDAN LAZAR/SHUTTERSTOCK ©

Plaza de la Cultura

This architecturally unremarkable concrete plaza in the heart of downtown is usually packed with locals slurping ice-cream cones and observing street life: juggling clowns, itinerant vendors and cruising teenagers.

Great For...

☑ Don't Miss
The Teatro Nacional's most famous painting, *Alegoría al café y el banano.*

Teatro Nacional

On the southern side of the Plaza de la Cultura resides the **Teatro Nacional** (Map p48; ☎2010-1110; www.teatronacional.go.cr; guided tours US$11; ⊘9am-5pm Mon-Fri), San José's most revered building. Constructed in 1897, it features a columned neoclassical facade that is flanked by statues of Beethoven and famous 17th-century Spanish dramatist Calderón de la Barca. The lavish marble lobby and auditorium are lined with paintings depicting various facets of 19th-century life.

The theater's most famous painting is *Alegoría al café y el banano*, an idyllic canvas showing coffee and banana harvests. It seems clear that the painter never witnessed a banana harvest because of the way the man in the center is awkwardly

Gold prawn, Museo de Oro Precolombino y Numismática

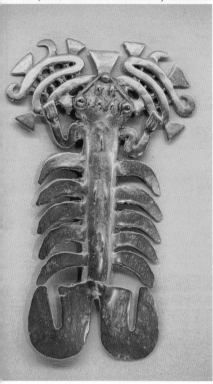

grasping a bunch (actual banana workers hoist the stems onto their shoulders).

Tours

On the fascinating hourly **tour** (ext 1114 2010-1100; www.teatronacional.go.cr/Visitenos/turismo; tours US$11, child under 12yr free; hourly between 9am-4pm), guests are regaled with stories of the art, architecture and people behind Costa Rica's crown jewel, the national theater. The best part is a peek into otherwise off-limits areas, such as the Smoking Room, which feature famous paintings, lavish antique furnishings and ornate gold trim.

Performances

Costa Rica's most important theater stages plays, dance, opera, symphony, Latin American music and other major

ⓘ Need to Know

Map p48; Avs Central & 2, btwn Calles 3 & 5

✕ Take a Break

Enjoy an espresso at the Teatro Nacional's atmospheric **Alma de Café** (Map p48; ☎2010-1119; www.teatronacional.go.cr/Cafeteria; mains US$6-11; ☺9am-7pm Mon-Sat, to 6pm Sun).

★ Top Tip

Tours of the Teatro Nacional are offered every hour on the hour in Spanish and English.

events. The main season runs from March to November, but there are performances throughout the year.

Museo de Oro Precolombino y Numismática

This three-in-one **museum** (Map p48; ☎2243-4202; www.museosdelbancocentral.org; adult/student/child US$13/8/free; ☺9:15am-5pm) houses an extensive collection of Costa Rica's most priceless pieces of pre-Columbian gold and other artifacts, including historical currency and some contemporary regional art. The museum, located underneath the Plaza de la Cultura, is owned by the Banco Central and its architecture brings to mind all the warmth and comfort of a bank vault. Security is tight; visitors must leave bags at the door.

Museo Nacional de Costa Rica

Plaza de la Democracia

Between the national museum and the Museo de Jade is the stark Plaza de la Democracia, which was constructed by President Óscar Arias Sánchez in 1989 to commemorate 100 years of Costa Rican democracy.

Great For...

☑ **Don't Miss**

Mural by César Valverde Vega in the Museo de Jade.

Museo de Jade

In its spectacular building, this **museum** (Map p48; ☎2521-6610; www.museodelja-deins.com; US$15; ☺10am-5pm) houses the world's largest collection of American jade (pronounced 'ha-day' in Spanish). The ample space (five floors offer six exhibits) allows extensive access to nearly 7000 finely crafted, well-conserved pieces, from translucent jade carvings depicting fertility goddesses, shamans, frogs and snakes to incredible ceramics (some reflecting Maya influences). A bonus is the kid-friendly videos explaining each salon.

Museo Nacional de Costa Rica

Entered via a beautiful glassed-in atrium housing an exotic butterfly garden, the

Pre-Columbian artifact, Museo Nacional de Costa Rica

ⓘ Need to Know

Plaza de la Democracia y de la Abolición del Ejército; Map p48; Avs Central & 2, btwn Calles 13 & 15

✕ Take a Break

Centrally located **El Patio del Balmoral** (Map p48; ☎2222-5022; www.balmoral.co.cr; Av Central, btwn Calles 7 & 9; mains US$8-27; ⊘4-10pm Tue-Sat) is a fine spot for lunch and people-watching after a visit to the nearby museums.

★ Top Tip

The elevated terraces provide lovely views of the mountains surrounding San José (especially at sunset).

Mercado Artesanal

The **Mercado Artesanal** (Crafts Market; Map p48; ⊘8am-7pm) is a touristy open-air market that sells everything from hand-crafted jewelry and Bob Marley T-shirts to elaborate woodwork and Guatemalan sarongs.

Asamblea Legislativa

Costa Rica's congress meets in the grand **Asamblea Legislativa** (Legislative Assembly; Map p48; Av Central, btwn Calles 15 & 17), across from Parque Nacional, in the center of San José. While this historic assembly building is two stories high and a charming pastel blue, an intimidating new 21-floor, all-white structure cost, controversially, more than US$100 million to build. One city councillor called architect Javier Salinas' monolithic design a 'concrete trash can.'

Museo Nacional de Costa Rica (Map p48; ☎2257-1433; www.museocostarica. go.cr; Calle 17, btwn Avs Central & 2; adult/student/child US$11/6/free; ⊘8:30am-4:30pm Tue-Sat, 9am-4:30pm Sun) provides a quick survey of Costa Rican history. Exhibits of pre-Columbian pieces from ongoing digs, as well as artifacts from the colony and the early republic, are all housed inside the old Bellavista Fortress, which historically served as the army headquarters and saw fierce fighting (hence the pockmarks) in the 1948 civil war.

It was here that President José Figueres Ferrer announced, in 1949, that he was abolishing the country's military. Among the museum's many notable pieces is the fountain pen that Figueres used to sign the 1949 constitution.

Casado (set meal)

GUSTAVO MIRANDA HOLLEY/GETTY IMAGES ©

San José Cuisine

Full of young, locally educated chefs and a few who've traveled abroad, the capital offers eating options from dawn to dusk. Each barrio has a distinct flavor, from old-school cantinas (canteens) to European-influenced five-star affairs.

Great For...

☑ Don't Miss

Barrio Escalante's Av 33 has enough restaurants for a week; Amón's artsy cafes are a great way to start the day.

Vegan San José

It makes sense that Costa Rica's trendy capital would be the center of vegan eats in the country. From Barrios Amón (p46) and Escalante (p46) to Escazú you'll find new vegan cafes and restaurants opening up.

De Acá (Mini Mercado y Vegan Cafe; Map p48; ✆7014-3221; Calle 3A, btwn Avs 9 & 11; desserts & smoothies US$5-6, mains US$7-9; ⏰11:30am-7pm; 🌱) is a welcoming two-level taste sensation, while Los Yoses' **Capra Vegano** (Map p48; Av Central, near Calle 35; mains US$5-6; ⏰noon-9pm Mon-Sat; 🌱) is lower key but still scrummy. Even the guide from Barrio Bird Walking Tours (p50) is a vegan pastry chef!

Real Local Food

You can return to Tico roots at places like Sikwa (p53; for indigenous cuisine) and Maxi's By Ricky (p55; for Caribbean).

Coffee brewed in a *chorreador*

VALERIJA POLLAKOVSKA/SHUTTERSTOCK ©

For a taste of old-school *cantina* grub, bend an elbow – and a fork – at **La Bohemia** (Map p48; Calle 5 near Av 12; ◷5pm-midnight).

For a modern twist on the same, **Restaurante Silvestre** (Cothnejo Fishy Cantina; Map p48; www.restaurantesilvestre.com; Av 11 near Calle 3A, Barrio Amón; mains US$20-30, tasting menu US$60; ◷6-11pm Mon-Sat) has got game.

Cafe Life

Chepeneños love, love, love their coffee, and not only in the morning. Having a cuppa with a friend is a way of life here, and you could wander from a French-style cafe near **Parque Francia** (Map p48; Cnr Av 5 & Calle 29, Barrio Escalante), naturally, to the marvelous Alma de Café (p39) in the Teatro Nacional, or to newer options in Amón such as De Acá.

For a mark of authenticity, ask for yours to be made in a *chorreador,* a filter that looks a bit like a used sock, but produces an amazing *tinto*.

Market Fresh

Totally immerse yourself in trade and Tico tastes at the city's bustling markets.

The Mercado Central (p46) and **Mercado Borbon** (Map p48; ☏2223-3512; www.facebook.com/mercadoborbon; cnr Av 3 & Calle 8; ◷5am-5pm Mon-Sat) are feasts for the eyes, ears and mouth, and the Feria Verde de Aranjuez (p51) farmers market in Aranjuez and Colón offers the chance to pick your own breakfast or lunch, straight from the tree, as it were.

San José Walking Tour

Historic Barrio Amón abounds with 19th-century *cafetalero* (coffee grower) mansions and brightly painted tropical Victorians, many of which house hotels, cafes and boutiques.

Start Parque España
Distance 1.4km
Duration Two hours

5 Stroll north on Calle 7 to find cutting-edge contemporary art gallery **TEOR/éTica** (p47).

4 Back on Av 7, **Galería Namu** (p51) has the country's best selection of indigenous handicrafts.

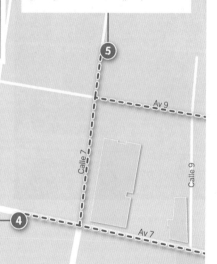

Av 9

Calle 7

Calle 9

Av 7

Parque Morazán

Calle 9

Av 3

Calle 7

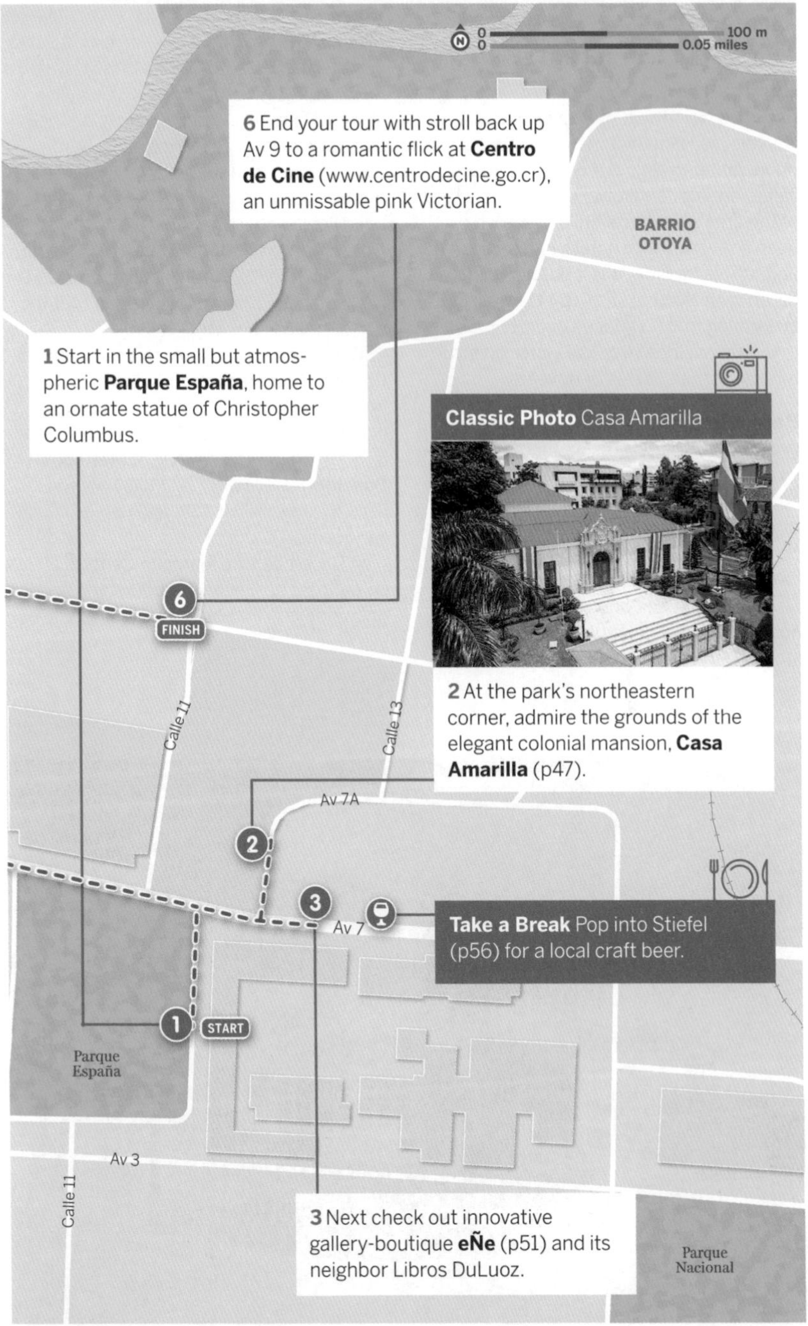

6 End your tour with stroll back up Av 9 to a romantic flick at **Centro de Cine** (www.centrodecine.go.cr), an unmissable pink Victorian.

BARRIO OTOYA

1 Start in the small but atmospheric **Parque España**, home to an ornate statue of Christopher Columbus.

Classic Photo Casa Amarilla

2 At the park's northeastern corner, admire the grounds of the elegant colonial mansion, **Casa Amarilla** (p47).

⑥ FINISH

Calle 11

Calle 13

Av 7A

②

③ Av 7

Take a Break Pop into Stiefel (p56) for a local craft beer.

① START

Parque España

Av 3

Calle 11

3 Next check out innovative gallery-boutique **eÑe** (p51) and its neighbor Libros DuLuoz.

Parque Nacional

2 GIANFRANCO VIVI/SHUTTERSTOCK © 4 LAIGLESANT/SHUTTERSTOCK © 5 PIGINKA/GETTY IMAGES ©

100 m
0.05 miles

⊙ SIGHTS

◎ Central San José

Barrio Amón   Area

(Map p48) Northwest of Plaza España lies this pleasant, historical neighborhood, home to a cluster of 19th-century *cafetalero* (coffee grower) mansions. Many of the area's historical buildings have been converted into hotels, cafes, bars and offices, making this a popular district for an architectural stroll (p44). You'll find everything from art deco concrete manses to brightly painted tropical Victorian structures in various states of upkeep.

Barrio Escalante   Area

(Map p48) Formerly a residential enclave, the streets of this increasingly hip neighborhood are now lined with dozens of restaurants, cafes, bakeries and bars. The largest concentration stretches along Calle 33 and has been dubbed Paseo Gastronómico La Luz (La Luz Restaurant Promenade) in honor of a small grocery store that used to stand on the street's corner.

Mercado Central   Market

(Map p48; www.facebook.com/Mercado-Central-de-San-José-Costa-Rica-132271433523797; Avs Central & 1, btwn Calles 6 & 8; ⊙6:30am-6pm Mon-Sat) Though *josefinos* mainly do their shopping at chain supermarkets, San José's crowded indoor markets retain an old-world, authentic feel. This main market, lined with vendors hawking everything from spices and coffee beans to *pura vida* souvenir T-shirts. It's all super cheap, and likely made in China or Nicaragua (not the coffee beans, though).

While browsing, try an ice-cream cone from **La Sorbetera de Lolo Mora** (Map p48; ☑2256-5000; www.facebook.com/Lolomora1901; desserts US$2-5; ⊙9:30am-5:30pm Mon-Sat), or a quick *ceviche* at **Mariscos Poseidon** (Map p48; ☑2221-8589; Mercado Central Annex; mains US$5-12; ⊙9am-6pm Mon-Fri, to 5pm Sat).

In December the Mercado Central sometimes has extended hours and is open on Sundays.

Barrio Amón

Museo de Arte y Diseño Contemporáneo
Museum

(MADC; Map p48; ☑2257-7202; www.madc.cr; cnr Av 3 & Calle 15; US$3, 1st Tue free; ⊙9:30am-5pm Tue-Sat) Commonly referred to as MADC, the Contemporary Art & Design Museum is housed in the historical National Liquor Factory building, which dates from 1856. It's just across from the **Parque Nacional** (Map p48; Avs 1 & 3, btwn Calles 15 & 19). Modern photography, painting and other exhibits are the norm.

TEOR/éTica
Gallery

(Arte y pensamiento; Map p48; ☑2233-4881; www.teoretica.org; cnr Calle 7 & Av 11, Casa 953, Barrio Amón; ⊙11am-6pm Wed-Fri, 10am-4pm Sat) **FREE** This contemporary-art museum is the brick-and-mortar gathering space for the TEOR/éTica Foundation, a nonprofit organization that supports Central American art and culture. Housed in a pair of vintage mansions across the street from one another, each elegant room exhibits cutting-edge works from Latin America and the rest of the world.

Casa Amarilla
Historic Building

(Map p48; Av 7, btwn Calles 11 & 13) On Parque España's northeast corner, this elegant colonial-style yellow mansion (closed to the public) houses the Foreign Affairs Ministry. The ceiba tree in front was planted by John F Kennedy during his 1963 visit to Costa Rica. If you walk around to the property's northeast corner, you can see a graffiti-covered slab of the Berlin Wall standing in the rear garden.

The building, initially the Central American Court of Justice, was built with funds donated by Andrew Carnegie in 1910. There's a nice tribute to tango legend Carlos Gardel adjacent (on the 'Paseo Argentino') as well as some cute cafes, giftshops and a groovy bookstore.

◎ La Sabana & Around

Parque Metropolitano La Sabana
Park

(Map p52) Once the site of San José's main airport, this 72-hectare green space at

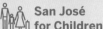

San José for Children

If you're in Costa Rica on a short vacation, chances are you'll be heading to the countryside fairly quickly. But if you're hanging out in San José for a bit, here are activities your kids will enjoy.

Museo de Ciencias Naturales La Salle (Map p52; ☑2232-1306; www.museolasalle. ed.cr; Sabana Sur; adult/child US$2/1.60; ⊙8am-4pm Mon-Sat, 9am-5pm Sun; ⊕) Ever wanted to see a spider-monkey skeleton or a herd of stuffed tapirs? This place has an extensive collection of taxidermic animals, skeletons, minerals, preserved specimens and a vast new collection of butterflies.

Museo de los Niños & Galería Nacional (Map p48; ☑2258-4929; www. museocr.org; Calle 4; adult/child US$4.50/4; ⊙8am-4:30pm Tue-Fri, 9:30am-5pm Sat & Sun; ⊕) If you want to get your kids interested in art and science, this unusual museum is an excellent place to start. In an old penitentiary, it's part children's museum and part art gallery. Small kids will love the hands-on exhibits.

Spirogyra Jardín de Mariposas (Map p48; ☑2222-2937; www.butterflygardencr. com; Barrio Amón; adult/child US$7/5; ⊙9am-2pm Mon-Fri, to 3pm Sat & Sun; ⊕; ☐to El Pueblo) Housing more than 30 species of butterfly – including the luminescent blue morpho – in plant-filled enclosures, this small butterfly garden is a great spot for kids. Visit in the morning to see plenty of fluttering.

Museo de Ciencias Naturales La Salle
MARGUS VILBAS/SHUTTERSTOCK ©

Central San José

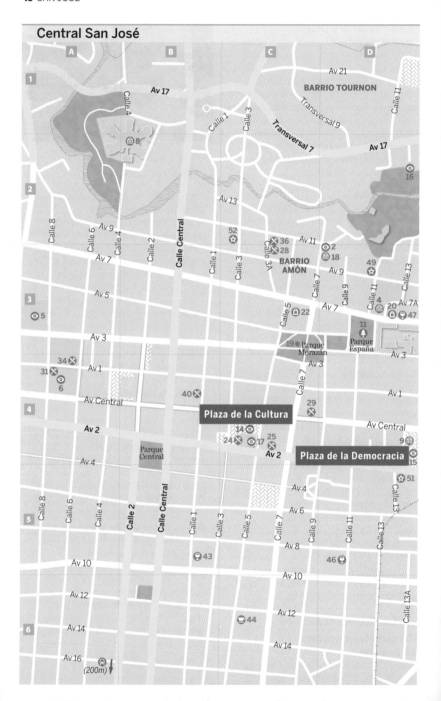

A
B
C
D

1

Av 21

BARRIO TOURNON

Av 17

Calle 4

Transversal 9

Calle 11

Calle 1

Calle 3

Transversal 7

Transversal 7

Av 17

2

16

Av 13

Calle 8

Av 9

Calle 6

Calle 4

Calle 2

Calle Central

Av 7

52

Av 11

36

2

28

18

Calle 3A

**BARRIO
AMÓN**

Calle 7

49

Calle 1

Calle 3

Av 9

Calle 9

Calle 11

Calle 13

3

5

Av 5

Calle 5

22

Av 7

4

20

47

Av 3

19

Parque
Morazán

11

Parque
España

Av 3

34

Av 1

Calle 7

Av 3

Av 1

31

6

Av Central

40

Calle 7

29

Plaza de la Cultura

4

Av 2

14

Av Central

Av 2

24

17

25

9

Parque
Central

Av 2

Plaza de la Democracia

15

Av 4

51

Calle 8

Calle 6

Calle 4

Calle 2

Calle Central

Calle 1

Calle 3

Calle 5

Calle 7

Av 4

Av 6

Calle 9

Calle 11

Calle 13

5

Av 10

43

Av 8

46

Calle 13A

Av 10

Av 12

Av 12

44

Av 14

6

Av 14

Av 16

(200m)

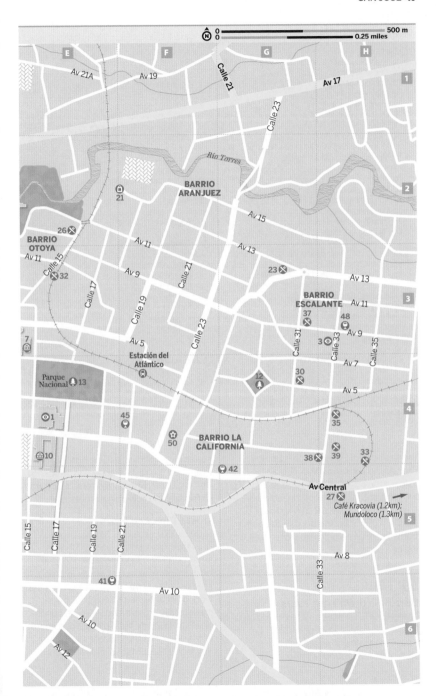

0 500 m
0 0.25 miles

E **F** **G** **H**

Av 21A Av 19 Calle 21 Av 17 **1**

Calle 23

Río Torres

BARRIO ARANJUEZ **2**

21 Av 15

Av 11 Av 13

BARRIO OTOYA
26
Av 11
Calle 15
32 Av 9 Av 13 23 Av 13

Calle 17 Calle 21 **BARRIO ESCALANTE** Av 11 **3**

Calle 19 37 48 Av 9
Calle 31 3 Calle 33 Av 9
Av 5 Calle 35

Estación del Atlántico Calle 23 Av 7

30 Av 5

Parque Nacional 13 12 **4**

35

1 45 **BARRIO LA CALIFORNIA** 38 39 33

10 50 42

Av Central
27
Café Kracovia (1.2km);
Mundoloco (1.3km) **5**

Calle 15 Calle 17 Calle 19 Calle 21 Av 8

Calle 33

41 Av 10

Av 10 **6**

Av 10

Av 12

Central San José

the west end of Paseo Colón is home to a regional art **museum** (Map p52; ☎2256-1281; www.mac.go.cr; ◎9am-4pm Tue-Sun; 🖼) FREE, a lagoon and various sporting facilities – most notably Costa Rica's National Stadium (p57). During the day, the park's paths make a relaxing place for a stroll, a jog or a picnic.

TOURS

Barrio Bird Walking Tours   Walking
(Map p48; ☎6280-6169; www.toursanjosecosta rica.com; tours from adult/child US$32/10) Knowledgeable and engaging guides show visitors San José's famous and not-so-famous sights, providing history and insight on the city's architecture, markets and urban art. Specialized tours also cater to foodies and culture enthusiasts.

Costa Rica Art Tours   Tours
(☎8359-5571, in USA 877-394-6113; www.costa ricaarttours.com; per person US$150) This small outfit conducts private tours that offer an intimate look at artists in their studios, where you can view (and buy) the work of local painters, sculptors, print-makers, ceramicists and jewelers. Lunch and San José city hotel pickup included in the price. Reserve at least a week in advance. Discounts available for groups.

Carpe Chepe — Tours

(📞8347-6198; www.carpechepe.com; guided pub crawls US$25; ⊘8pm Fri & Sat) For an insider's look at Chepe's nightlife, join one of these Friday- and Saturday-evening guided pub crawls, led by an enthusiastic group of young locals. A shot is included at each of the four bars visited. There are other offerings as well, including a hop-on, hop-off nightlife bus, food tours, a craft-beer tour and free walking tours of San José.

Note that the tours may not run on time and can feel a bit disorganized.

🔒 SHOPPING

Whether you're looking for indigenous carvings, high-end furnishings or a stuffed sloth toy, San José has no shortage of shops, from artsy boutiques to tourist traps stocked full of tropical everything. Haggling is not tolerated in stores (markets are the exception).

Feria Verde de Aranjuez — Market

(Map p48; www.facebook.com/feriaverde; Barrio Aranjuez; ⊘7am-12:30pm Sat) For a foodie-friendly cultural experience, don't miss this fabulous Saturday market, a meeting place for San José's artists and organic growers since 2010. You'll find organic coffee, artisanal chocolate, tropical-fruit ice blocks, produce, leather, jewelry and more at the long rows of booths set up in the park at the north end of Barrio Aranjuez.

Feria Verde is also held in Barrio Colón on Tuesdays from 1pm to 7pm.

Galería Namu — Arts & Crafts

(Map p48; 📞2256-3412, in USA 800-616-4322; www.galerianamu.com; Av 7, btwn Calles 5 & 7; ⊘9am-6:30pm Mon-Sat Jan-Dec, 11am-4pm Sun Dec-Apr) The Bribrí word for jaguar, Namu fair-trade gallery brings together artwork and cultural objects from a diverse popula-tion of regional ethnicities, including Boru-ca masks, finely woven Wounaan baskets, Guaymí dolls, Bribrí canoes, Chorotega ceramics, traditional Huetar reed mats, and contemporary urban and Afro-Caribbean

🏠 Biesanz Woodworks

Located in the hills of Bello Horizonte in Escazú, the workshop of **Biesanz Woodworks** (📞2289-4337; www.biesanz. com; Calle Pedrero 33; ⊘8am-5pm Mon-Fri Jan-Dec, 9am-3pm Sat Dec-Apr) can be difficult to find, but the effort will be well worth it. This shop is one of the finest woodcrafting studios in the nation, run by celebrated artisan Barry Biesanz. His bowls and other decorative containers are exquisite and take their inspiration from pre-Columbian techniques.

Rosewood bowl
 PATRICIOGB/GETTY IMAGES ©

crafts. It can also help arrange visits to remote indigenous territories in different parts of Costa Rica.

eÑe — Arts & Crafts

(Tienda eÑe; Map p48; 📞2222-7681; www. facebook.com/esquina13y7; cnr Av 7 & Calle 11A; ⊘10am-6:30pm Mon-Sat) This hip little design shop across from Casa Amarilla (p47) sells all manner of pieces crafted by Costa Rican designers and artists, including clothing, jewelry, handbags, picture frames, zines and works of graphic art.

🍴 EATING

From humble corner stands offering gut-filling *casados* (set meals) to contemporary bistros serving fusion everything, in cosmo-politan San José you'll find the country's best restaurant and cafe scene. Dedicated foodies should also check out the dining

La Sabana

options in Los Yoses and San Pedro, as well as Escazú and Santa Ana.

Top-end restaurants are often busy on weekend evenings; make a reservation.

⊗ Central San José

Café de los Deseos   Cafe $
(Map p48; ☑2222-0496; www.facebook.com/
cafedelosdeseos; Calle 15, btwn Avs 9 & 11; mains
US$5-12; ⊗11:30am-10pm Tue-Thu, to 11pm Fri &
Sat; ☎) Abuzz with artsy young bohemians,
this colorful Barrio Otoya cafe makes a
romantic spot for drinks (from sangria to
cocktails to smoothies), *bocas* (handmade

tortillas with Turrialba cheese, salads,
teriyaki chicken, individual pizzas) and
tempting desserts. Walls are hung with the
work of local artists and rooms are adorned
with hand-painted tables, beaded curtains
and branches entwined with fairy lights.

La Terrasse   French $$$
(Map p48; ☑8939-8470; www.restaurantla
terrasse.blogspot.com; Calle 15, btwn Avs 9 & 11;
mains US$17-32; ⊗noon-2pm & 7-10pm Tue-Fri,
7-10pm Sat, noon-2pm Sun) Hidden away in the
living room of a 1927 Barrio Otoya home,
this intimate French restaurant regularly
welcomes well-heeled locals with some-

thing to celebrate. Talented chef Patricia reveals her fine sensibilities in thick, creamy soups and cheeses, hearty meat dishes and imaginative presentation. Her husband, the gracious Gerald, plays host. Order French wine and a few dishes to share.

By reservation only; payment in cash or bank transfer.

ⓧ La Sabana & Around

Lubnan Lebanese **$$**
(Map p52; ☑2257-6071; www.facebook.com/lubnancr; Paseo Colón, btwn Calles 22 & 24; mains US$8-25; ☉11am-3pm & 6pm-midnight Tue-Fri, noon-4pm & 6-11pm Sat, 11am-5pm Sun; Ⓟ)
This atmospheric Lebanese place is a great date spot, with creamy hummus, flavorful tabbouleh and an array of succulent meats – some cooked, some deliciously raw. Waiters wear fezzes and a live belly-dancing performance goes down every Thursday at 8pm. A cave-like ambience with pillowy seats enhances the *1001 Nights* feeling.

ⓧ Los Yoses,
Barrio Escalante & San Pedro

Olio Mediterranean **$$**
(Map p48; ☑2281-0541; www.facebook.com/restaurante.olio; cnr Calle 33 & Av 3, Barrio Escalante; tapas from US$7, dishes US$12-22; ☉11:30am-11pm Mon-Wed, to midnight Thu & Fri, 5pm-midnight Sat; ☑) This cozy, Mediterranean-flavored gastropub in a century-old brick building serves a long list of tempting tapas (many veggie), including divine stuffed mushrooms, goat-cheese croquettes and pastas. The enticing drinks list includes homemade sangria and a decent selection of beers and wine. It's a romantic spot for a date, with imaginative, conversation-worthy quirks of decor and beautiful patrons.

Café Kracovia Cafe **$$**
(☑2253-9093; www.cafekracovia.com; Paseo del la Segunda Republica, San Pedro; snacks US$4-10, mains US$8-14; ☉10:30am-9pm Mon, to 11pm Tue-Sat; ☜) With several distinct spaces – from the low-lit, intimate basement to the outdoor garden courtyard – this hip cafe

---

★ Top Five for Foodies

Restaurante Silvestre (p43)

Sikwa

Maxi's By Ricky (p55)

Café de los Deseos

---

has something for everyone. Contemporary artwork and a university vibe create an appealing ambiance for lunching on crepes, wraps, salads, sweet and savory Polish pierogi and craft beer. It's 500m north of the Fuente de la Hispanidad, just past the university entrance.

Sikwa Costa Rican **$$**
(Map p48; cnr Calle 33 & Av 1, Barrio Escalante; appetizers US$7, mains US$10-16; ☉noon-10pm)
Pablo Bonilla's intention is no less than to rescue indigenous cuisine in his homeland. Sikwa ('outsider') is an interesting take on Costa Rican indigenous food, with an 'ancestral tasting menu' (US$50) of six courses and a fascinating blue-corn-and-ginger drink called *cichleme*. Ambient (sometimes annoying) music, simple brick facade.

Saúl Bistro Mediterranean **$$**
(Map p48; ☑2228-8685; www.saulemendez.com; cnr Av 9 & Calle 31, Barrio Escalante; appetizers US$10-16, mains US$11-25; ☉7am-10pm Mon-Thu, to midnight Fri-Sun) There are life-sized plastic zebras in the dining room at this snazzy open-air restaurant. An extension of Saúl Mendez, the Guatemala-based empire of men's fashion, the restaurant is adorned with curious art, bubbling fountains and vertical gardens. It serves delicious Mediterranean cuisine, savory crepes, fine wines and exquisite cocktails.

Saúl's clothing stores dominate the suburbs, but the only bistro is here, in ever-edible Escalante.

> *There are life-sized plastic zebras in the dining room at this snazzy open-air restaurant.*

From left: Sea bass *ceviche*; Fish taco; Churros

Lolo's
Pizza $$

(La Cava de Lolo; Map p48; ☎2283-9627; Barrio Escalante, pizzas US$14-24; ☺6pm-midnight Mon-Sat) Fans of bohemian chic will appreciate this quirky pizzeria, hidden in a mustard-yellow house (No 3396) along the railroad tracks north of Av Central. The vibrantly colorful, low-lit interior, hung with an eclectic collection of armor and other medieval bric-a-brac, creates an artsy, romantic setting for sangria and pizzas fired up in the bright-red oven out back.

> *Fans of bohemian chic will appreciate this quirky pizzeria, hidden in a mustard-yellow house*

Sofia Mediterráneo
Mediterranean $$$

(Map p48; ☎2224-5050; www.facebook.com/sofiamediterraneo; cnr Calle 33 & Av 1, Barrio Escalante; mains US$12-28; ☺6-11pm Mon &

Wed-Fri, noon-11pm Sat, noon-5pm & 6:30-9pm Sun; ☑) This gem serves a superb mix of authentic Mediterranean specialties, including house-made hummus, tortellini, grilled lamb and a rotating selection of daily specials, accompanied by sweet, delicate baklava for dessert. The restaurant doubles as a community cultural center where owner Mehmet Onuralp hosts occasional themed dinners featuring musicians, chefs and speakers from around the world.

Al Mercat
Gastronomy $$$

(Map p48; ☎2221-0783; www.almercat.com; Av 13, Barrio Escalante; mains US$15-30, bocas US$8-10; ☺noon-5pm Tue & Wed, noon-5pm & 6:30-10pm Thu-Sat, noon-3pm Sun; ☑) Inspired by Tico author Aquileo Echeverría, Cordon Bleu alumnus Jose González serves market-fresh produce, often from his own *finca* (farm). Family-style dishes of corn and sweet potato *chalupas* or grilled vegetables with smoked cheese are fresh and flavorful; both vegetarians and carnivores are well served. The service is impeccable

TERI VIRBICKIS/SHUTTERSTOCK ©

and the atmosphere is enlivened by vertical gardens.

The chef has recently added smaller and less expensive plates to the menu, such as tacos and *ceviche*.

Kalú Café
& Food Shop
International $$$

(Map p48; ☑2253-8367, 2253-8426; www.kalu. co.cr; cnr Calle 31 & Av 5; mains US$15-21; ☺noon-7pm Tue-Fri, 9am-7pm Sat-Sun; ☑) Located in Barrio Escalante, chef Camille Ratton's exceptional cafe serves a global fusion menu of soups, salads, sandwiches, pastas and unconventional delights such as the fish taco trio filled with mango-glazed salmon, red-curry prawns and macadamia-crusted tuna. Don't miss the mind-meltingly delicious passion-fruit pie (US$7, but you only live once).

🍴 Escazú & Santa Ana

Maxi's By Ricky Caribbean $$

(☑2282-8619; www.facebook.com/restaurant. maxi; Calle San Rafael, Santa Ana; appetizers US$5-8, mains US$10-20; ☺noon-10:30pm) If you can't get to the Caribbean coast, the 'yard'

vibe here is a good substitute. Manzanillo native Ricky transported his lip-smacking restaurant to the Central Valley so *josefinos* could feast on the traditional rice-n-beans, Caribbean chicken and *rondón* soup. The small plates *(bocas)* are a perfect chance for everybody to try a little of everything. Delish!

It's tricky to find: ask locally for directions. If you get too chill (literally), there's an outdoor fireplace.

Container Platz Gastronomy $$

(☑6050-1045; www.facebook.com/container platz; Calle 5, Santa Ana; mains US$6-15; ☺noon-10pm Mon-Thu, 11am-midnight Fri & Sat, 11am-8pm Sun) In this gastronomic experiment, 20 mini-businesses representing Latin American and world flavors have sprung to life in brightly painted shipping containers. It earns high marks for innovation and reasonably priced, artisanal fast food, with everything from a circus-themed nacho place to a churros factory and a 'hummuseria' that serves its house-made hummus with delectable pita triangles.

 **LGBT+
San José**

San José is home to Central America's most thriving LGBT+ scene. As with other spots, admission charges vary depending on the night and location (from US$5 to US$10). Some clubs close on various nights of the week (usually Sunday to Tuesday) and others host women- or men-only nights; inquire ahead or check individual club websites for listings.

Many clubs are on the south side of town, which can get rough after dark: take a taxi. However, a new joint inside the trendy **Steinvorth Building** (El Stein; Map p48; www.edificiosteinvorth.com; Calle 1 btwn Avs Central & 1), **BomBóm**, has opened up on the 3rd floor. Other trending spots include **Club Teatro** (Av 16 near Calle 2), **Neon Ice** near Parque Francia (Calle 31 near Av 7), plus **Venue** and **PopPop** in La California (Av 2 near Calle 19).

La Avispa (Map p48; ✆2223-5343; www.laavispa.com; Calle 1, btwn Avs 8 & 10; ⊗8pm-6am Thu-Sat, 5pm-6am Sun) is a lesbian disco bar that has been in operation for more than four decades, La Avispa (the Wasp) has a bar, pool tables and a boisterous dance floor that's highly recommended by travelers.

Pucho's Bar (Map p48; ✆2256-1147; cnr Calle 11 & Av 8; ⊗8pm-2am Tue-Sat) is more low-rent (and significantly raunchier) than some; you'll find scantily clad go-go boys and over-the-top drag shows.

LGBT pride flag
SERGIO A. SIMON/SHUTTERSTOCK ©

Communal picnic tables foster a sense of camaraderie, as does the craft-beer container and play area for kiddies. Hours vary slightly by business.

🍷 DRINKING & NIGHTLIFE

San José has plenty of venues to keep you lubricated. Students congregate along Av 21 and around; older folk hit Escalante, Escazú, or elsewhere.

Stiefel Pub
(Map p48; ✆8850-2119; www.facebook.com/stiefelpub; Av 5; ⊗11:30am-2pm & 6pm-2am Mon-Sat) Two dozen–plus Costa Rican microbrews on tap and an appealing setting in a historical building create a convivial buzz at this pub half a block from Plaza España. Grab a pint of Pelona or Maldita Vida, Malinche or Chichemel; better yet, order a flight of four miniature sampler glasses and try 'em all.

Casa House of Beers Craft Beer
(Map p48; ✆8345-4100; Av Central btwn Calles 27 & 27A; ⊗6pm-midnight Mon-Thu, to 2am Fri-Sat) On the other side of Av Central from the rowdier college bars, this two-level house has about two dozen beers on tap to satisfy the thirstiest of hop-starved pilgrims. Programmed music fills downstairs while live bands and DJs thrash away on the 2nd floor. Good, relatively cheap food (sausage, pizza) too. Magnificently decrepit.

Antik Club
(Map p48; www.antik.cr; Av 10 near Calle 21, Casa Matute; cover US$10; ⊗11:30am-3pm & 6-11pm Tue-Thu, 11:30am-3pm & 6pm-6am Fri, 6pm-6am Sat) Set in a historical mansion that once belonged to a Venezuelan general, Antik offers a tri-level experience, with a basement catering to the EDM crowd, a main level pizza restaurant and an upper floor featuring Latin dance rhythms and a sweet balcony with city views. There are a couple of bars offering craft beer and excellent, reasonably priced cocktails.

Mercado La California   Beer Garden

(Map p48; www.facebook.com/mercadola california; Calle 21; ⏲6pm-3:30am Thu-Sat, 4pm-1:30am Sun) Inspired by Madrid's 'Mercado San Miguel,' El Mercadito (as the locals say) is a recent addition to the up-and-coming Barrio La California. The line regularly snakes down the block from the entrance to this nightlife plaza's food kiosks, cocktail stands and craft-beer vendors, and the people in that line are often stunning to behold.

Wilk   Brewery

(Map p48; www.facebook.com/wilkcraftbeer; cnr Calle 33 & Av 9; ⏲4pm-1am Tue-Sat) Named Wilk (Wolf) in honor of its former life as the Polish embassy, this Escalante pub attracts a mixed Tico/gringo crowd who share an appreciation for craft brews and seriously delicious burgers (veggie included). More than a dozen craft beers include concoctions from Costa Rica Craft Brewing and Treintaycinco. On occasion, a local brewmaster invents a new beer, live.

 ENTERTAINMENT

Pick up *La Nación* on Thursday for listings (in Spanish) of the coming week's attractions. The free publication *GAM Cultural* (www.gamcultural.com) and website San José Volando (www.sanjosevolando.com) are also helpful guides to nightlife.

Mundoloco   Live Performance

(☎2253-4125; www.facebook.com/mundolocorestaurante; Av Central; ⏲4pm-2:30am Mon-Thu, from noon Fri & Sat, noon-1:30am Sun) Grab a craft beer and some vegetarian grub, such as stuffed mushrooms, at this cute San Pedro restaurant and bar. Then head to the spacious and comfortable back room for the entertainment, which rotates through stand-up comedy, dance performances and live music. There are great acoustics here: it's an ideal place to catch a local band.

Estadio Nacional de Costa Rica   Stadium

(Map p52; Parque Metropolitano La Sabana) Costa Rica's graceful, modernist 35,000-seat national soccer stadium, constructed

Estadio Nacional de Costa Rica

MARCPRO/GETTY IMAGES ©

Rainbow eucalyptus, San José

with funding from the Chinese government and opened in 2011, is the venue for international and national Division 1 *fútbol* (soccer) games. Its predecessor in the same spot in Parque Metropolitano La Sabana (p47) hosted everyone from Pope John Paul II to Bruce Springsteen and soccer legend Pelé over its 84-year history.

El Sótano   Live Music

(Map p48; ☎2221-2302; www.amonsolar.com; cnr Calle 3 & Av 11; ☺5pm-2am Mon, Tue & Thu-Sat) One of Chepe's most atmospheric nightspots, Sótano is named for its cellar jazz club, where people crowd in for frequent performances including intimate jam sessions. Upstairs in the same mansion, a cluster of elegant rooms with high ceilings have been converted into a gallery space, a stage and a dance floor where an eclectic mix of groups play live gigs.

El Lobo Estepario   Live Music

(Map p48; ☎2256-3934; www.facebook.com/loboestepariocr; Av 2; ☺4pm-1am Sun-Thu, to 2am Fri & Sat) ✔ This artsy, two-story dive attracts some of the top local talent for live music gigs. The blackboard ceiling fills with messages and drawings nightly. And for literary fans, what could be cooler than a bar with bookshelves named for a Hermann Hesse novella? Serves up good vegetarian fare too.

Jazz Café Escazú   Live Music

(☎2253-8933; www.jazzcafecostarica.com; Autopista Prospero Fernandez; cover US$6-13; ☺6pm-2am Mon-Sat) Now with only a single location in the suburb of Escazú, Jazz Café nonetheless continues to impress. Countless performers have taken to the stage here, including legendary Cuban bandleader Chucho Valdés and Colombian pop star Juanes. It's across from Hospital CIMA.

Cine Magaly   Cinema

(Map p48; ☎2222-7116, box office 2223-0085; www.cinemagaly.com; Calle 23 btwn Avs Central & 1; ☺bar noon-10pm Mon-Sat, 1-10pm Sun) Screens the latest releases in a large renovated theater, along with independent films in English. The attached Kubrick

Gastro Bar serves up delicious salads, pizza, desserts and flavored teas.

ℹ️ INFORMATION

EMERGENCY

Fire	☎118
Red Cross	☎128
Traffic Police	☎2523-3300 ☎2222-9245 ☎2222-9330

LGBT+ TRAVELERS

In recent years attitudes toward LGBT+ locals and travelers have shifted towards acceptance. Pride parades take place regularly, and the city's youth are leading the country's tolerance movement. A good site is www.gaycationscosta rica.com, which offers listings of bars, clubs and hotels that cater to the LGBT+ community.

ℹ️ GETTING THERE & AWAY

Aeropuerto Internacional Juan Santamaría (p308) Located in nearby Alajuela, handles handles international flights in its main terminal. Domestic flights on **Sansa** (☎2290-4100; www. flysansa.com) depart from the Sansa terminal.

Aeropuerto Tobías Bolaños (☎2232-2820) In the San José suburb of Pavas; services private charter and a few domestic flights.

ℹ️ GETTING AROUND

Central San José frequently resembles a parking lot – narrow streets, heavy traffic and a complicated one-way system mean that it is often quicker to walk than to take the bus. The same applies to driving: if you rent a car, try to avoid downtown. If you're in a real hurry to get somewhere that's more than 1km away, take an Uber or a taxi; note that Uber is technically illegal here, but everyone uses it.

If traveling by bus, you'll arrive at one of several bus terminals sprinkled around the western and southern parts of downtown. Some of this area is walkable provided you aren't hauling a lot of luggage and are staying nearby. But if

Santa Ana

you're arriving at night, take a taxi, since most terminals are in dodgy areas.

CAR

It is not advisable to rent a car just to drive around San José. The traffic is heavy, the streets are narrow and the meter-deep curbside gutters make parking nerve-wracking. In addition, break-ins are frequent, and leaving a car – even in a guarded lot – might result in a smashed window and stolen belongings.

If you are renting a car to travel throughout Costa Rica, there are more than 50 car-rental agencies – including many of the global brands – in and around San José. Travel agencies and up-market hotels can arrange rentals; you can also arrange rentals online and at the airport. Note: If you book a rental car online and the low cost seems too good to be true, it is. Rental agencies are notorious for tacking on hundreds of dollars in mandatory insurance when you arrive. They are also known to lie about this over the phone.

One excellent local option is **Wild Rider** (Map p52; ☑2258-4604, in USA/Canada 800-721-9821; www.wild-rider.com; Diagonal 16 near Calle 34; ☺8am-6pm). It has a fleet of reasonably priced 4WD vehicles (from US$380 per week in high season, including all mandatory insurance coverage). There's a discount of up to 40% for long-term rentals (four weeks or more). Reserve well in advance.

TAXI

Red taxis can be hailed on the street day or night, or you can have your hotel call one for you.

Marías (meters) are generally used, though a few drivers will tell you they're broken and try to charge you more – especially if you don't speak Spanish. Not using a meter is illegal. The rate for the first kilometer should appear when the meter starts up (at the time of research, the correct starting amount was 610 colones). Make sure the *maría* is operating when you get in, or negotiate the fare up front. Short rides downtown cost US$2 to US$4. There's a 20% surcharge after 10pm that may not appear on the *maría*.

You can hire a taxi and a driver for half a day or longer; it is best to negotiate a flat fee in advance. Uber has also become popular (though technically illegal), and some savvy Ticos use a third level of transport, the *pirata* (pirate taxi), when in a jam.

Where to Stay

Reservations are recommended in the high season (December through April), in particular the two weeks around Christmas and Semana Santa (Holy Week, the week preceding Easter).

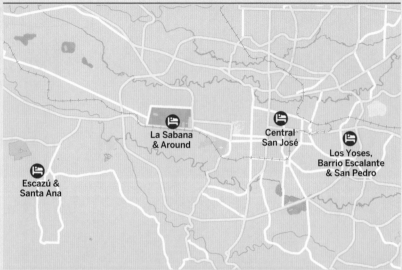

Neighborhood	Atmosphere
Central San José	The best hotels are east of Calle Central, many of which are housed in historic Victorian and art-deco mansions; close to sights, restaurants and nightlife; nonstop traffic jams and street noise.
La Sabana & Around	West of the city center; great variety of accommodations, from hostels to vintage B&Bs; pleasant setting around Parque Metropolitano La Sabana; some good dining venues, though budget options are limited.
Los Yoses, Barrio Escalante & San Pedro	Lively university area, replete with restaurants and nightlife; walking distance to city center; excellent choices for budget travelers.
Escazú & Santa Ana	Affluent suburbs with mostly upscale accommodations ranging from sleek boutique inns to homey B&Bs; innovative dining scene; 20-minute drive or bus ride from city center; challenging to navigate.

TORTUGUERO

Tortuguero at a Glance...

Located within the confines of Parque Nacional Tortuguero, accessible only by air or water, this bustling little village with strong Afro-Caribbean roots is best known for attracting hordes of sea turtles (tortuguero means 'turtle catcher') – and the hordes of tourists who want to see them. While peak turtle season is in July and August, the park and village have begun to attract travelers year-round. Even in October, when the turtles have pretty much returned to the sea, families and adventure travelers arrive to go on jungle hikes, take in the wild national park and canoe the area's lush canals.

One Day in Tortuguero

If you only have one day in Tortuguero, it's going to be a busy one. Start early with breakfast from **Dorling Bakery** (p75), then hit the (aquatic) trails on a **boat tour** (p70), keeping your eyes peeled for wildlife. Rest up in the afternoon so you're ready for a (seasonal) **turtle tour** (p66) at sunset.

Two Days in Tortuguero

With an extra day, you can spread out the action. On the first day, take a **boat tour** (p70), followed by a few hours' relaxing at the lodge.

On day two, follow the short **hiking trail** (p72) behind Cuatro Esquinas ranger station in the morning, before taking a **turtle tour** (p66) in the evening.

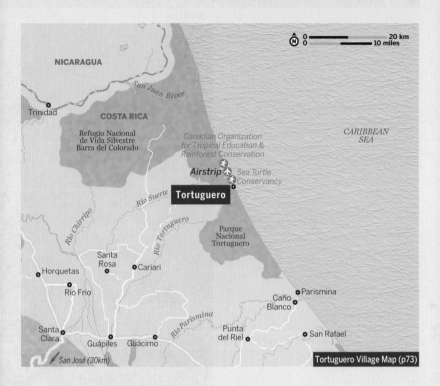

Tortuguero Village Map (p73)

Arriving in Tortuguero

If you're coming from San José, the two most convenient ways to get to Tortuguero are by air or all-inclusive bus-boat shuttles – though budget travelers can save money by taking public transportation.

If you're coming from the southern Caribbean, your best bets are with private boat operators from Moín or shuttle deals from Cahuita and Puerto Viejo.

Where to Stay

There are two main areas of Tortuguero where travelers stay. The village itself has the largest variety and selection of accommodations, catering especially to budget and midrange travelers. The higher-end lodges are north of the village (and across a canal, meaning that guests can only access the village by water taxi).

Sea turtle nesting

Turtle Tours

One of the most moving experiences is turtle-watching on these wild beaches. Witnessing a massive turtle return to its natal beach and perform its laborious nesting ritual feels both solemn and magical.

Great For...

ⓘ Need to Know

Arrange tours at local hotels and at the official Asociación de Guías de Tortuguero (p74) kiosk.

★ Top Tip

Four species of sea turtle nest in Tortuguero – green, leatherback, hawksbill and loggerhead.

Turtle Nesting

Most female turtles share a nesting instinct that drives them to return to the beach of their birth (their natal beach) in order to lay their eggs. (Only the leatherback returns to a more general region instead of a specific beach.) During their lifetimes, they will usually nest every two to three years and, depending on the species, may come ashore to lay eggs 10 times in one season. Often, a turtle's ability to reproduce depends on the ecological health of this original habitat.

The female turtle digs a perfect cylindrical cavity in the sand using her flippers, and then lays 80 to 120 eggs. She diligently covers the nest with sand to protect the eggs, and may even create a false nest in another location to confuse predators. She then makes her way back to sea – after which the eggs are on their own. Incubation

ranges from 45 to 70 days, then hatchlings – no bigger than the size of your palm – break out of their shells using a caruncle, a temporary tooth. They crawl to the ocean in small groups, moving as quickly as possible to avoid dehydration and predators. Once they reach the surf, they must swim for at least 24 hours to get to deeper water, away from land-based predators.

Tours

Because of the sensitive nature of the habitat and the critically endangered status of some species, tours to see this activity are highly regulated. It is important not to alarm turtles as they come to shore (a frightened turtle will return to the ocean and dump her eggs). In high season, tour groups gather in shelter sites close to the beach and a spotter relays a turtle's

Green sea turtle hatchling

location via radio once she has safely crossed the high-tide mark and built her nest. At this time, visitors can then go to the beach and watch the turtle lay her eggs, cover her nest and return to the ocean. Seeing a turtle is not guaranteed, but licensed guides will still make your tour worthwhile with the wealth of turtle information they'll share. By law, tours can only take place between 8am and midnight. Some guides will offer tours after midnight; these are illegal.

Visitors should wear closed-toe shoes and rain gear. Tours cost US$25. Nesting season runs from March to October, with July and August being prime time. The

next-best time is April, when leatherback turtles nest in small numbers. Flashlights and cameras (including cell-phone cameras) are not allowed on the beach. Wear nonreflective, dark clothing.

Save the Turtles

The area attracts four of the world's seven species of sea turtle, making it a crucial habitat for these massive reptiles – it's little surprise that these hatching grounds gave birth to the sea-turtle conservation movement. The Caribbean Conservation Corporation, the first program of its kind in the world, has continuously monitored turtle populations here since 1955. Today green sea turtles are increasing in numbers along this coast, but the leatherback, hawksbill and loggerhead are in decline.

The **Canadian Organization for Tropical Education & Rainforest Conservation** (COTERC; ☏2709-8052; www.coterc.org; dm per week incl 3 meals per day US$310) is a not-for-profit organization operating the Estación Biológica Caño Palma, 8km north of Tortuguero village. This small biological research station runs a community program and a volunteer program in which visitors can assist with upkeep of the station and ongoing research projects, including sea-turtle, bird, mammal, caiman and snake monitoring.

About 200m north of the village, **Sea Turtle Conservancy** (STC; ☏2297-5510, in USA 352-373-6441; www.conserveturtles.org; museum US$2.50; ◷10am-noon & 2-5pm), Tortuguero's original turtle-conservation organization (founded in 1959), operates a research station, visitor center and museum. Exhibits focus on all things turtle related, including a video about the local history of turtle conservation. STC also runs a highly reputable volunteer program. During nesting season volunteers can observe turtle tagging and assist with egg counts and biometric-data collection.

☑ **Don't Miss**

The scurry of the hatchlings as they set off on their journey to the sea.

KENCANNING/GETTY IMAGES ©

✕ **Take a Break**

Taylor's Place (p75) will feed you if watching turtles has made you hungry.

Boating the canals of Parque Nacional Tortuguero

KEVIN WELLS PHOTOGRAPHY/SHUTTERSTOCK ©

Boat Tours

Tortuguero teems with wildlife. You'll find howler monkeys in the treetops, green iguanas scurrying among buttress roots, and endangered manatees swimming in the canals – all visible from the seat of a guided motorboat, or rental canoe or kayak.

Great For...

☑ Don't Miss

The great green macaw (though you'll need a good guide and some luck).

Aquatic Trails

Four aquatic trails wind their way through Parque Nacional Tortuguero, inviting waterborne exploration. **Río Tortuguero** acts as the entranceway to the network of trails. This wide, beautiful river is often covered with water lilies and is frequented by aquatic birds such as herons, kingfishers and anhingas – the latter is known as the snakebird for the way its slim, winding neck pokes out of the water when it swims.

Caño Chiquero and **Canõ Mora** are two narrower waterways with good wildlife-spotting opportunities. According to park regulations, only kayaks, canoes and silent electric boats are allowed in these areas. Caño Chiquero is thick with vegetation, especially red guacimo trees and epiphytes. Black turtles and green iguanas like to hang out here. Caño Mora

Green macaw

KENNETH VARGAS TORRES/SHUTTERSTOCK ©

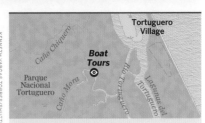

ℹ Need to Know

To see the most wildlife, be on the water early or go out following heavy rain.

✕ Take a Break

Grab a yummy breakfast from Dorling Bakery (p75) before you set out.

★ Top Tip

Going out *after* the 6am rush may be a bit more tranquil.

is about 3km long but only 10m wide, so it feels as if it's straight out of *The Jungle Book*. **Caño Haroldas** is actually an artificially constructed canal, but that doesn't stop the creatures – such as Jesus Christ lizards and caimans – from inhabiting its tranquil waters.

Tour Guides

Leonardo Tours (p72) and Tinamon Tours (p72) are recommended for canoeing and kayaking tours.

Wildlife-Watching

More than 400 bird species, both resident and migratory, have been recorded in Tortuguero – it's a birdwatchers' paradise. Due to the wet habitat, the park is especially rich in waders, including egrets, jacanas and 14 types of heron, as well as species such as kingfishers, toucans and the great curassow (a type of jungle peacock known locally as the *pavón*). The great green macaw is a highlight, most common from December to April, when the almond trees are fruiting. In September and October, look for flocks of migratory species such as eastern kingbirds, barn swallows and purple martins. The Sea Turtle Conservancy (p69) conducts a biannual monitoring program in which volunteers can help scientists take inventory of local and migratory species.

Certain species of mammal are particularly evident in Tortuguero, especially mantled howler monkeys, the Central American spider monkey and the white-faced capuchin. If you've got a reliable pair of binoculars and a good guide, you can usually see both two- and three-toed sloths. In addition, normally shy neotropical river otters are reasonably habituated to boats. Harder to spot are timid West Indian manatees and dolphins, which swim into the brackish canals looking for food. The park is also home to big cats such as jaguars and ocelots, but these are savvy, nocturnal animals – sightings are very rare.

Tortuguero Village

⊙ SIGHTS

Parque Nacional
Tortuguero   National Park

(📞2709-8086; www.acto.go.cr; US$15; ⊙6am-6pm, last entry 4pm) This misty, green coastal park sits on a broad floodplain parted by a jigsaw of canals. Referred to as the 'mini-Amazon,' Parque Nacional Tortuguero is a place of intense biodiversity that includes more than 400 bird species, 60 known species of frog, 30 species of freshwater fish and three monkey species, as well as the threatened West Indian manatee. Caimans and crocodiles can be seen lounging on riverbanks, while freshwater turtles bask on logs.

More than 150,000 visitors a year come to boat the canals and see the wildlife, particularly to watch turtles lay eggs. This is the most important Caribbean breeding site of the green sea turtle, 40,000 of which arrive every season to nest. Of the seven species of marine turtle in the world, six nest in Costa Rica, and four nest in Tortuguero. Various volunteer organizations address the problem of poaching with vigilant turtle patrols.

Park headquarters is at **Cuatro Esquinas** (📞2709-8086; www.acto.go.cr; ⊙6am-4pm), just south of Tortuguero village.

Strong currents make the beaches unsuitable for swimming.

> *This is the most important Caribbean breeding site of the green sea turtle, 40,000 of which arrive every season to nest.*

✪ ACTIVITIES

Most visitors come to watch sea turtles lay eggs on the wild beaches. The area is more than just turtles, though: Tortuguero teems with wildlife. You may find sloths and howler monkeys in the treetops, tiny frogs and green iguanas scurrying among buttress roots, plus mighty tarpons, alligators and endangered manatees swimming in the waters.

HIKING

Behind Cuatro Esquinas ranger station, the main well-trodden trail is a muddy, 2km out-and-back hike that traverses the tropical humid forest and parallels a stretch of beach. Green parrots and several species of monkey are commonly sighted here. The short trail is well marked. Rubber boots are required and can be rented at hotels and near the park entrance.

A second hiking option, **Cerro Tortuguero Trail**, is also available. To reach the trailhead, guests have to take a boat to the town of San Francisco, north of Tortuguero village, where they will disembark at another ranger station and buy a ticket (US$7, plus US$4 for the 15- to 20-minute round-trip boat ride). The trail then takes visitors 1.8km up a hill for a view of the surrounding lagoon, forest and ocean. Any of the hotels in Tortuguero village can help guests organize the details and even arrange a local guide (from US$35) to take you on the trip.

⊕ TOURS

Leonardo Tours   Outdoors

(📞8577-1685; www.leonardotours.wordpress. com; nature walks from US$20, canoe/kayak tours US$30/40; ⊙9am-7pm) With more than a decade of experience guiding tours in the area, Leonardo Estrada brings extensive knowledge and infectious enthusiasm to his turtle, canoeing, kayaking and hiking tours. He can arrange pick-ups in San José and Cahuita.

Tinamon Tours   Tours

(📞8842-6561; www.tinamontours.de; 2½hr hikes from US$25) Zoologist and 20-plus-year Tortuguero resident Barbara Hartung offers hiking, canoeing, cultural and turtle tours in German, English, French or Spanish. Tour packages, including two nights'

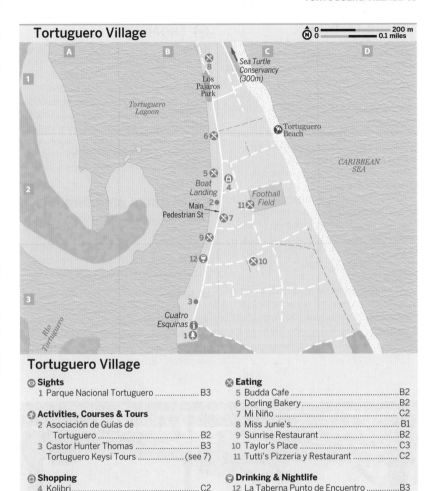

Tortuguero Village

accommodations, breakfast, a canoe tour and a hike, start at US$100 per person. Note that you'll need to pay the US$15 entrance fee for park hikes.

Castor Hunter Thomas Tours

(📞8870-8634; www.castorhunter.blogspot.com; nature tours per person from US$35) Excellent local guide and lifelong Tortuguero resident Castor Hunter Thomas has led hikes, turtle tours and canoe tours for more than 20

years. There's also a cool restaurant right next to his house.

Riverboat Francesca Nature Tours Fishing

(📞2226-0986; www.tortuguerocanals.com; 2-day nature packages from US$225, per hour US$65-75) A highly recommended company run by Modesto and Fran Watson, Riverboat Francesca offers sportfishing (river and ocean) as well as wildlife-viewing tours through the national park.

Asociación de Guías de Tortuguero
Tours

(☎2767-0836; www.asoprotur.com; ⏰6am-7pm)
The most convenient place to arrange tours
is at the official Asociación de Guías de
Tortuguero kiosk by the boat landing. Made
up of scores of local guides, the association
offers tours in English, French, German
and other languages. Although guides are
all certified to lead tours in the park, the
quality of the tours can vary.

Note that tour departure times can
change with the weather.

Rates at the time of research were
US$30 per person for a two-hour turtle
tour and US$25 for a canoe tour. Other
options include two-hour walking (US$20
to US$25), birdwatching (US$35) and
fishing (from US$80, minimum two
people) tours.

Tours also involve an extra US$15 admis-
sion fee to the park (not required for the
fishing tour). A newish tour (US$35) offers
a view from Cerro Tortuguero, the highest
point on the Caribbean coast.

🛍 SHOPPING

Kolibri
Design

(☎2767-0010; tiendakolibri@hotmail.com; small
art pieces from US$40; ⏰11am-1pm & 3-6pm)
Colorful artworks made of recycled driftwood, jicaro fruit and the flower pods of coconut trees are housed in this sleek white
gallery space on Tortuguero's main street.
Most creations are by Austrian resident
Tina Lindner, but other pieces are made by
locals. Find handmade jewelry here, too.

🍴 EATING & DRINKING

One of Tortuguero's unsung pleasures is its
cuisine: the homey restaurants lure you in
with steaming platters of Caribbean-style
food, plus international options including
pizza and pasta. Most use local produce.

Mi Niño
Caribbean $

(☎8460-5262; mains US$3.50-9, smoothies
US$3-4; ⏰7am-10pm; 🍴) Juan and Carole
are getting high marks for their vegetarian
and vegan offerings, as well as coastal
specialties such as pasta in Caribbean

Budda Cafe

sauce and garlic shrimp. To capitalize on their success, they're also offering a more romantic setting uptown, in the former Tutti locale, called Mi Niño Spot II, with the same menu.

Tutti's Pizzeria y Restaurant
Italian $

(www.facebook.com/admintuttis; mains US$5.50-9; ⊘noon-9pm) The site has changed but it's still the place to come for an Italian fix: Tutti's lasagna and spaghetti dishes remain a hit. There are also plenty of pizzas and loaded calzones – the Caribbean flavor comes with tomato sauce infused with coconut and shrimps. Happy hour (two selected drinks for US$10) from 3:30pm to 5:30pm. The only joint in town with artisanal beers.

Taylor's Place
Caribbean $

(☑8319-5627; mains US$7-14; ⊘6-9pm) Low-key atmosphere and high-quality cooking come together beautifully at this back-street eatery southwest of the soccer field. The inviting garden setting, with chirping insects and picnic benches spread under colorful paper lanterns, is rivaled only by friendly chef Ray Taylor's culinary artistry. House specialties include beef in tamarind sauce, grilled fish in garlic sauce, and avocado-and-chicken salad.

Dorling Bakery
Bakery $

(☑2767-0444; pastries US$2, breakfast US$4-5; ⊘5am-8:30pm Mon-Sat, to noon Sun) Thanks to its predawn opening time, this is a good spot to pick up homemade banana bread, lemon-and-orange cake or cinnamon rolls before an early-morning flight or canal tour.

Budda Cafe
European $

(☑2709-8084; www.buddacafe.com; mains US$7-9, pizzas US$7-9; ⊘1-9pm Tue-Sun; 🛜🍴) Ambient club music, Tibetan prayer flags and a river view give this trendy cafe a tranquil vibe. It's a pleasant setting for pizzas, salads, cocktails and crepes (savory and sweet). Grab a table outside for a prime view of the boats going by and, if you're

🍽️ Afro-Caribbean Cuisine

Thanks to the Afro-Caribbean influence, the food here has more of a kick than that of other regions. Even rice-and-beans becomes something special in the Costa Rican Caribbean, with the simple additions of coconut milk, Panamanian peppers, thyme and ginger. Mouthwatering lobster and whole fish are ubiquitous, as is the staple *pollo caribeño* (Caribbean chicken). Pair these delights with *agua de sapo* (lemonade with ginger and sugar-cane juice).

Rice, beans and *pollo caribeño*
ARNOLDO ROBERT/GETTY IMAGES ©

lucky, the yellow-bellied flycatchers zipping across the water.

Miss Junie's
Caribbean $$

(☑2709-8029; www.iguanaverdetours.com/lodge.htm; mains US$11-16; ⊘7-9am, noon-2:30pm & 6-9pm) Over the years, Tortuguero's best-known and most delicious Caribbean eatery has grown from a personal kitchen to a full-blown restaurant. Prices have climbed accordingly, but the menu remains true to its roots: jerk chicken, filet mignon, whole snapper and coconut-curry mackerel with rice and beans. It's at the northern end of the main street.

> *...the menu remains true to its roots: jerk chicken, filet mignon, whole snapper and coconut-curry mackerel...*

Red-eyed tree frog, Parque Nacional Tortuguero (p72)

Sunrise Restaurant   Caribbean $$

(mains US$10-12; ⏱11am-9pm) Between the dock and the national park, this cozy log-cabin-like place will lure you in with the delicious smoky aroma of grilled chicken and pork ribs. It also serves seafood pasta, fajitas, salad, breakfast and a full Caribbean menu at lunch and dinnertime, plus a handful of luscious cocktails (caipirinha, piña colada).

ℹ INFORMATION

There's no longer an ATM here: stock up on cash in La Pavona, Guápiles or Puerto Limón.

ℹ GETTING THERE & AWAY

The small airstrip is 4km north of Tortuguero village. Sansa (www.flysansa.com) has regular high-season flights, and charter flights land here regularly.

The classic public-transit route to Tortuguero is a bit of a faff, taking four to six hours, but is by far the cheapest option. You'll travel by bus from San José to Cariari and then La Pavona, and then by boat from La Pavona to Tortuguero. Alternatively, Tortuguero is easily accessible by private boat from Moín (three to four hours).

SHUTTLE TRIPS

If you prefer to leave the planning to someone else, convenient shuttle services can whisk you to Tortuguero from San José, Arenal-La Fortuna or the southern Caribbean coast in just a few hours. Shuttle companies typically offer minivan service to La Pavona or Moín, where waiting boats take you the rest of the way to Tortuguero. This is a relatively inexpensive, hassle-free option, as you only have to buy a single ticket, and guides help you negotiate the van-to-boat transfer.

All Rankin's Tours (☎2709-8101, WhatsApp 8815-5175; www.allrankinslodge.com; round trips to Tortuguero from US$70) Round-trip shuttles to Tortuguero from Moín, including excellent nature guides.

Caribe Shuttle (☎2750-0626; www.caribe shuttle.com) Shuttles from Puerto Viejo (US$75, five hours), San José (US$50, six hours) and Arenal-La Fortuna (US$60, six hours).

Exploradores Outdoors (Map p93; ☎2222-6262; www.exploradoresoutdoors.com; 1-day rafting trips incl lunch & transportation from US$99) More-expensive package deals that include transport from San José, Puerto Viejo or Arenal-La Fortuna, a mid-journey Río Pacuare rafting trip, and accommodations in Tortuguero.

Jungle Tom Safaris (☎2221-7878; www.jungle tomsafaris.com) Offers one-way shuttles between Tortuguero and San José (US$62). All-inclusive one- and two-night packages (US$135 to US$206) can also include shuttles from Cahuita (US$70), Puerto Viejo (US$70) and Arenal-La Fortuna (US$70), as well as optional tours.

Pleasure Ride (Map p93; ☎2750-0290, 2750-2113; www.pleasureridecr.com) Shuttles from Puerto Viejo (from US$75, around 1½ hours) and Cahuita (from US$70, around one hour).

Ride CR (☎2469-2525; www.ridecr.com) Shuttles from Arenal-La Fortuna (US$55). Minimum two passengers.

Riverboat Francesca Nature Tours (p73) Shuttles from San José to Tortuguero via Moín (from US$75, including lunch) as well as package deals including accommodations.

Terraventuras (p92) Overnight shuttle packages from Puerto Viejo (US$99) or daily departure shuttle (US$65).

Willie's Tours (☎8917-6982, 2755-1024; www.williestourscostarica.com; tours from US$30; ⏱8am-6pm Mon-Sat) Shuttles from Cahuita (from US$60; two-person minimum).

SOUTHERN
CARIBBEAN

In this Chapter

Southern Caribbean at a Glance...

The southern coast is the heart and soul of Costa Rica's Afro-Caribbean community. Jamaican workers arrived in the middle of the 19th century, and stayed to build the railroad and work for the United Fruit corporation. Then in the 1980s the southern coast began to welcome surfers, backpackers and adventurous families on holiday – many of whom have stayed, adding Italian, German and North American flavors to the cultural stew. For the traveler, it's a rich and rewarding experience – with lovely beaches to boot.

Two Days in the Southern Caribbean

When in the southern Caribbean, go **surfing** (p82)! Remember that Salsa Brava is for experts only; otherwise, head to Playa Cocles. After riding the waves, enjoy a seafood feast at **Miss Lidia's** (p96). On day two, explore **REGAMA** (p84) with an early-morning hike, followed by lunch at the **Cool & Calm Cafe** (p99), and an afternoon of swimming and snorkeling at Manzanillo beach.

Four Days in the Southern Caribbean

Rent a bicycle and spend a day beach-hopping from Playa Cocles to Playa Chiquita to Punta Uva, with a stop at the **Jaguar Centro de Rescate** (p92). Have dinner at one of the southern Caribbean's phenomenal restaurants, such as **La Pecora Nera** (p94) or **Selvin's** (p94). Your final day is free for the **Chocolate Forest Experience** (p92). How's that for dessert?

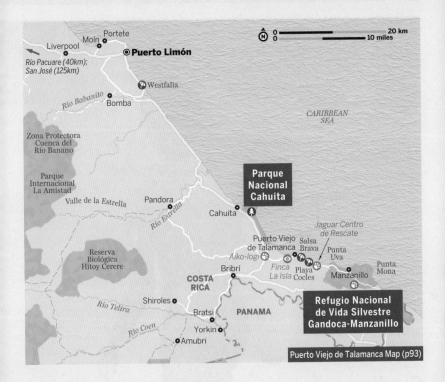

Puerto Viejo de Talamanca Map (p93)

Arriving in the Southern Caribbean

It's about a four-hour drive from San José to Puerto Viejo de Talamanca, on paved (but not always well-maintained) roads. Shuttle companies like Grayline and Interbus (p97) make this run, as do the public buses.

Where to Stay

Here you'll find everything from inventive tree houses to laid-back B&Bs and raucous hostels. What you won't find are chain hotels: the southern Caribbean prides itself on inspired and independent lodgings.

In Puerto Viejo, many budget spots have private hot-water bathrooms and wi-fi. Rates are generally discounted slightly if you pay in cash.

JAMES DOBERMAN/SHUTTERSTOCK ©

Surfing

The town of Puerto Viejo was built on waves – specifically, the infamous Salsa Brava that breaks on the sharp, shallow reef offshore. But there are other, more forgiving places to surf, even for beginners.

Great For...

☑ Don't Miss

Riding one of the most celebrated (and feared) waves in the country.

Where to Surf

Find one of the country's most notorious waves at Salsa Brava – a shallow reef break that's most definitely for experts only. It's a tricky but thrilling ride over sharp coral. Salsa Brava offers both rights and lefts, although the right is usually faster. Conditions are best with a south-easterly swell.

For a softer landing, try the beach break at **Playa Cocles**, where the waves are consistent, the white water is abundant for beginners, and the wipeouts are more forgiving. Cocles is about 2km east of town. Conditions are usually best early in the day, before the wind picks up.

Salsa Brava

One of the best breaks in Costa Rica, Salsa Brava is named for the heaping helping

Playa Cocles

CARIBBEAN SEA

Salsa Brava

Puerto Viejo de Talamanca

Playa Cocles

ⓘ Need to Know

Waves peak from November to March, with a surfing miniseason from June to July.

✕ Take a Break

Sip a cold one and enjoy the view of the namesake break at Salsa Brava (p97).

★ Top Tip

The nearest medical facility is **Hospital Tony Facio** (☎2758-2222) in Puerto Limón.

Surf Lessons

Several surf schools around town charge US$40 to US$50 for two-hour lessons. Locals on Playa Cocles rent boards from about US$20 per day.

Caribbean Surf School (☎8357-7703; 2hr lesson US$55) offers lessons by super-smiley surf instructor Hershel Lewis and are widely considered the best in town. He also teaches paddleboarding.

Julie Hickey and her surfing sons, Cedric and Solomon, from **One Love Surf School** (☎8719-4654; www.onelovecostarica.wordpress. com; 2hr surf lesson US$50) specialize in beginners' surf lessons, Reiki and Thai massage.

of 'angry sauce' it serves up on the sharp, shallow reef, continually collecting its debt of fun in broken skin, boards and bones. The wave makes its regular, dramatic appearance when the swells pull in from the east, pushing a wall of water against the reef and generating a thick and powerful curl in the process. There's no gradual build-up here: the water is transformed from swell to wave in a matter of seconds. Ride it out and you're golden. Wipe out and you may rocket into the reef. Some mordant locals have dubbed it 'the cheese grater.'

Salsa Brava wipeouts, drug running, and other adventures are related in Allan Weisbecker's *In Search of Captain Zero: A Surfer's Trip Beyond the End of the Road*. Captain Zero still lives in the area.

Plumed basilisk in REGAMA

MR JAMES KELLEY/SHUTTERSTOCK ©

Refugio Nacional de Vida Silvestre Gandoca-Manzanillo

This little-explored refuge protects nearly 70% of the southern Caribbean coast, extending from Manzanillo all the way to the Panamanian border.

Great For...

☑ **Don't Miss**

Swimming and snorkeling off the gorgeous beach in Manzanillo village.

REGAMA encompasses 50 sq km of land plus 44 sq km of marine environment. The peaceful, pristine stretch of sandy white beach – one of the area's main attractions and the center of village life in Manzanillo – stretches from **Punta Uva** in the west to Punta Mona in the east. Offshore, a 5-sq-km coral reef is a teeming habitat for lobsters, sea fans and long-spined urchins.

Hiking

A coastal trail heads 5.5km east out of Manzanillo to **Punta Mona**. The first part of this path, which leads from Manzanillo to Tom Bay (about a 40-minute walk), is well trammeled and clearly marked and doesn't require a guide. Once you pass Tom Bay, however, the path gets murky and it's easy to get lost, so ask about conditions before you set out, or hire a local guide. It's

Dolphin-watching trip

MARGUS VILBAS/SHUTTERSTOCK ©

❶ Need to Know

REGAMA; ☑2759-9100; US$6; ⊙8am-4pm

✕ Take a Break

Enjoy the hot food and cool vibe at Cool & Calm Cafe (p99).

★ Top Tip

Refugio Nacional de Vida Silvestre Gandoca-Manzanillo is an excellent photo book by Juan José Puccí.

a rewarding walk with amazing scenery, as well as excellent (and safe) swimming and snorkeling at the end.

Recommended Guides

Local guide and former park ranger **Florentino Grenald** (☑8841-2732; 4hr tours per person from US$40) is one of the most knowledgeable naturalists in the Caribbean. Since 1992 he's been handing out rubber boots and escorting guests through his yard, a veritable tropical Eden, before taking them into the Gandoca-Manzanillo reserve, where he quickly spots caimans, frogs, snakes and whatever else is nearby.

Other recommended guides include **Omar Cook Campbell** (☑8932-0030; 4-5hr hikes per person US$40) and **Abel Bustamante** (☑2759-9043).

Snorkeling & Diving

The undersea portion of the park cradles one of the two accessible living coral reefs in the country. Comprising five types of coral, the reefs begin in about 1m of water and extend 5km offshore to a barrier reef. **Punta Mona** is a popular destination for snorkeling, though it's a trek so you may wish to hire a boat. Otherwise, you can snorkel offshore at Manzanillo (p97) at the eastern end of the beach (the riptide can be dangerous; inquire about conditions). Also check out the Coral Reef Information Center at Bad Barts (p97) in Manzanillo.

Dolphin-Watching

In 1997 a group of local guides in Manzanillo identified tucuxi dolphins, a little-known species previously not found in Costa Rica, and began to observe their interactions with bottlenose dolphins. A third species – the Atlantic spotted dolphin – is also common in this area. For dolphin-watching trips in the reserve (from US$50 for three hours), contact Bad Barts (p97), and keep in mind that it is illegal to swim with dolphins.

Rafting on the Río Pacuare

Rafting the Río Pacuare

From family-friendly riffles to nearly unnavigable rapids, this river offers highly varied but always thrilling experiences. All white-water rafting requires a certified guide, so book trips through a reputable tour agency. No matter the run, you'll get totally soaked and tossed about, so pack a sense of humor.

Great For...

☑ Don't Miss

A cool, invigorating dip in the river during one of the calmer stretches.

Traditionally the two most popular rafting rivers have been Río Reventazón and Río Pacuare, but the former has been dramatically impacted by a series of hydroelectric projects, including a huge 305-megawatt dam currently under construction. As a result, most organized expeditions from Turrialba now head for the Río Pacuare, which arguably offers the most scenic rafting in Central America. The river plunges down the Caribbean slope through a series of spectacular canyons clothed in virgin rainforest, through runs named for their fury and separated by calm stretches that enable you to stare at near-vertical green walls towering hundreds of meters above.

● Lower Pacuare – With Class II–IV rapids, this is the more accessible run: 28km through rocky gorges, past an indigenous village and untamed jungle.

PAFNUTY/SHUTTERSTOCK ©

ⓘ Need to Know

Tour operators can transport you to the launch site from anywhere in Costa Rica.

✕ Take a Break

After braving the rapids, reward yourself with a passion-fruit coffee drink at **Maracuyá** (📞2556-2021; www.facebook. com/maracuya2012; Calle 2; frozen coffee from US$2, mains from US$8; ⏱2-9:30pm Wed-Mon; 🅿) in Turrialba.

★ Top Tip

When the guide says paddle hard, or get down, just do it.

• Upper Pacuare – Classified as Class III–IV, but a few sections can go to Class V, depending on conditions. It's about a two-hour drive to the put-in, then you'll have the prettiest jungle cruise on earth all to yourself.

When to Go

The Pacuare can be run year-round, though June to October are considered the best months. The highest water is from October to December, when the river runs fast with huge waves. March and April are when the river is at its lowest, although it's still challenging.

Trips & Prices

Rafting trips are offered by several Turrialba-based agencies as well as reputable national companies such as **Exploradores Outdoors** (p77) and **Ríos Tropicales** (Map p52; 📞2233-6455, in USA 866-722-8273; www.riostropicales.com; Calle 38 btwn Avs 3 & 5, San José; day tours from $96).

Day trips usually raft the Class II–IV Lower Pacuare, thanks to its relative ease of access. A tamer alternative for beginners and families is the Class I–II Río Pejibaye. Other runs – such as the Upper Pacuare and/or remaining navigable segments of Río Reventazón – require more time spent in a van and tend to be more expensive.

For day trips (many of which originate in San José), expect to pay from US$100 to US$150 depending on transportation, accessibility and amenities. It is generally less expensive to leave from Turrialba (day trips around US$80). Children must be at least nine years old for most trips, and older for tougher runs.

Brown-throated three-toed sloth

Parque Nacional Cahuita

This is one of the smallest and most accessible of Costa Rica's national parks. Its 9km of hiking trails have vistas of dangling sloths (pictured) and monkeys, waterbound caimens and lizards and, at the end, white-sand beaches to loll on. When the green flags are up, jump into the ocean, or hire a boat for an unforgettable snorkeling experience.

Great For...

☑ Don't Miss

Snorkeling the reefs when the water is clear, checking out otherworldly coral shapes and brilliantly colored fish.

ℹ Need to Know

☏ 2755-0302, 2755-0461; US$5; ⊘ Kelly Creek entrance 6am-5pm, Puerto Vargas entrance 8am-4pm

Hiking

On the Trails

You can hike an approximately 7km loop through various habitats: Sendero Punto Cahuita goes just 1.5km, from the Cahuita park entrance to the Río Suarez (obey red flags – the tides can literally carry you away). From the river it's another 2.4km to Punta Cahuita. From Punta Cahuita to the Puerto Vargas entrance it's another 2.1km.

Cahuita is meteorologically typical of the entire coast (that is to say: very humid), which results in dense tropical foliage, you'll walk through a forest of trees such as the sangregado ('bleeding' tree), a traditional curative; sea grape (papaturros); sangrillo (mahogany); and mangrove.

The area includes the swampy Punta Cahuita, which juts into the sea between two stretches of sandy beach. Often flooded, the point is covered with cativo and mango trees and is a popular hangout for birds such as the green ibis, the yellow-crowned night heron, the boat-billed heron and the rare green-and-rufous kingfisher.

Red land and fiddler crabs live along the beaches, attracting mammals such as crab-eating raccoons and white-nosed pizotes (coatis). White-faced capuchins, southern opossums and three-toed sloths also live in these parts. The mammal you are most likely to see (and hear) is the mantled howler monkey, which makes its bellowing presence known.

Hiking in Parque Nacional Cahuita

Real wildlife lovers may want to start their hike at the southern entrance to the park, from **Puerto Vargas Ranger Station** (☏2755-0302; US$5; ⏰8am-4pm), which is less well known.

Recommended Guide

Richard Robinson (☏8750-9261) is one of the few government-registered guides in the area, meaning he's taken a few years of coursework studying Costa Rican natural history, as well as guiding intrepid tourists for two decades.

✗ Take a Break

A short walk from the park entrance, **Soda Kawe** (☏2755-0233; casados US$6; ⏰5:30am-7pm) has rejuvenating fresh juices and coffee.

DUDAREV MIKHAIL/SHUTTERSTOCK ©

Snorkeling

Parque Nacional Cahuita contains one of the last living coral reefs in Costa Rica. While the reef represents some of the area's best snorkeling, it has suffered damage over the years from earthquakes and tourism-related activities. In an attempt to protect the reef from further damage, snorkeling is only permitted with a licensed guide. The going rate to accompany one person is about US$35.

Conditions vary greatly, depending on the weather and other factors.

On the Reef

After donning fins and mask, you might spy French angelfish, blue parrotfish, barracuda, sea cucumber and, less frequently, manta rays, sharks, and turtles. It's a color-splashed living aquarium out there on a good day.

When to Go

September and October are the most agreeable and driest months here on the coast.

Trips & Prices

A walk in the national park with a guide should cost from US$15 to US$25 per person for 1½ to 2½ hours. A two-hour basic snorkeling outing should be about US$30 per person.

★ Top Tip

The Playa Blanca entrance (near town) has wheelchair-accessible paths that are flat or covered with planks.

Puerto Viejo de Talamanca

This burgeoning party town is no longer a destination for intrepid surfers only; it's bustling with tourist activity. Street vendors tout Rasta trinkets and Bob Marley T-shirts, stylish eateries serve global fusion, and rustic bamboo bars pump dancehall and reggaetón. It can get downright hedonistic, attracting revelers wanting to marinate in ganja and *guaro* (a local firewater made with sugarcane). Despite its reputation, Puerto Viejo manages to hold onto an easy charm. If you're looking to chill a little, party a little and eat a little, you've come to the right place.

◎ SIGHTS

Jaguar Centro de Rescate
Wildlife Reserve

(☏2750-0710; www.jaguarrescue.foundation; 1½hr tours adult/child under 10yr US$20/free; ☺tours 9:30am & 11:30am Mon-Sat; 🚼) 🌿 Named in honor of its original resident, a jaguar, this well-run wildlife-rescue center in Playa Chiquita now focuses mostly on other animals, including sloths, crocodiles, anteaters, snakes and monkeys. Founded by zoologist Encar and her late partner Sandro, a herpetologist, the center rehabilitates orphaned, injured and rescued animals for reintroduction into the wild whenever possible (40% success rate).

Volunteer opportunities (US$350 including accommodation) are available with a one-month minimum commitment. You can also tour the Punta Uva release center, where many of the center's success stories are returned to their natural habitat.

Aiko-logi
Wildlife Reserve

(☏8997-6869, 2750-2084; www.aiko-logi-tours. com; day tours incl transportation & lunch US$60, overnight stays per person incl meals US$120; 🅿) 🌿 Nestled into the Cordillera de Talamanca, 15km outside Puerto Viejo, this private 135-hectare reserve is centered on a former *finca* (farm), on land fringed with dense primary rainforest. It's ideal for birdwatching, hiking and splashing around

in swimming holes. Day tours from Puerto Viejo (or Cahuita) can be arranged, as can overnight tent-platform stays and yoga classes. Reserve in advance.

Finca La Isla
Gardens

(☏8886-8530, 2750-0046; www.costaricaorganicsfarm.com; self-guided/guided tours US$6/12; ☺10am-4pm Fri-Mon; 🅿) 🌿 West of town, this farm and botanical garden has long produced organic pepper and cacao, along with more than 150 tropical fruits and ornamental plants. Birds and wildlife, including sloths, poison-dart frogs and toucans, abound. Informative guided tours (minimum three people) include admission, fruit tasting and a glass of fresh juice; alternatively, buy a booklet (US$1) and take a self-guided tour. The farm also makes its own chocolate (three-hour workshop US$32).

ⓖ TOURS

Chocolate Forest Experience
Tours

(☏8341-2034, 2750-0504; www.caribeanscr. com; tours US$28; ☺8:30am-6pm Mon-Sat, tours 10am Mon, 10am & 2pm Tue, Thu & Fri, 2pm Sat) 🌿 Playa Cocles–based chocolate producer Caribeans leads tours of its sustainable cacao forest and chocolate-creation lab, accompanied by gourmet chocolate tastings. There's also a shop with a refrigerated chocolate room where visitors can try several varieties of chocolate flavor. This is a 1.5km walking tour of moderate difficulty.

Terraventuras
Tours

(☏2750-0750; www.terraventuras.com; ☺7am-7pm) Offers overnight stays in Tortuguero (US$99), a cultural tour to an indigenous reserve (US$75) and a Caribbean cooking class (US$55), along with the usual local tours. It also has its very own 23-platform, 2.1km-long canopy tour (US$59), complete with Tarzan swing.

Gecko Trail Costa Rica
Tours

(☏2756-8159, in USA & Canada 415-230-0298; www.geckotrail.com; ☺tours per adult from US$28) This full-service agency arranges

Puerto Viejo de Talamanca

Puerto Viejo de Talamanca

local tours as well as transportation, accommodations and excursions throughout Costa Rica, including horseback riding, hikes, rafting, hot-spring visits and spa days. It has an administrative office in Puerto Viejo, inside the Pleasure Ride (p77) building, but bookings are made by phone and online.

🔘 SHOPPING

Lulu Berlu Gallery Arts & Crafts
(☑2750-0394; ⊙9am-9pm) On a backstreet parallel to the main road, this gallery carries folk art, jewelry, ceramics, embroidered purses and mosaic mirrors, among many other one-of-a-kind, locally made items.

🍽️ Out of Town Eating

Selvin's Restaurant (Blanca and Selvin's Cabinas y Restaurante; ☑2750-0664; www. selvinpuntauva.com; Punta Uva; mains US$12-18; ⊙noon-8pm Thu-Sun) Selvin has been serving Caribbean food since 1982. His place is considered one of the region's best, specializing in shrimp, sautéed lobster in butter, garlic and onion, T-bone steak, a terrific *rondón* (seafood gumbo) and a succulent chicken *caribeño* (chicken stewed in a spicy Caribbean sauce). Those with a sweet tooth will enjoy the organic chocolate bar and coconut candy.

Pita Bonita (☑2756-8173; Playa Chiquita; dishes US$7.50-13.50; ⊙noon-9pm Mon-Sat) For Turkish coffee, hummus and the best pita bread in the Caribbean, this Israeli-owned spot is the place. There's also *moutabal* (a roasted-aubergine and tahini dip), spicy *shakshuka* (a Middle Eastern dish with poached eggs and tomato sauce) and fresh tabbouleh (tomatoes, parsley, mint, bulgur, lemon and onion).

La Pecora Nera (☑2750-0490; Playa Cocles; mains US$20-30; ⊙5:30-10pm Tue-Sun; ☑) If you're looking to enjoy a fancy meal during your trip, do it at this romantic eatery run by Ilario Giannoni. On a lovely candlelit patio, deftly prepared Italian seafood and pasta dishes are served alongside unusual offerings such as the delicate *carpaccio di carambola*: transparent slices of starfruit topped with shrimp, tomatoes and balsamic vinaigrette.

Spicy *shakshuka* dish
ISTETIANA/SHUTTERSTOCK ©

Choco Chocolate

(☑6363-4274; www.cho.co.cr; Calle 217) Québécois partners Martin and Nelson have turned this tidy air-conditioned shop into a must-stop for local Talamanca chocolates (five different brands). There are chocolate-making classes, tours of local cacao *fincas*, and pairings of beer, wine or Costa Rican rums and chocolates...yum. To call this a mere chocolate shop would be to call Willy Wonka's place a factory.

Organic Market Market

(⊙6am-noon Sat) Don't miss the weekly organic market, where local vendors and growers sell snacks typical of the region, particularly tropical produce and chocolate. Arrive before 9am or the best stuff will be long gone.

✖️ EATING

With the most diverse restaurant scene on the Caribbean coast, Puerto Viejo has the cure for *casado* overkill. You'll find everything from sushi to homemade pizza.

Bread & Chocolate Cafe $

(☑2750-0723; www.breadandchocolatecr.com; cakes US$3.50-4, meals US$7-11; ⊙6:30am-6:30pm Wed-Sat, to 2:30pm Sun; ☑) Ever had a completely homemade PB&J, with bread, peanut butter and jelly all made from scratch? That and more can be yours at this dream of a cafe, serving sandwiches, soups and salads, and (of course) the treat that gives it its name: chocolate. Served as truffles, bars, cakes, tarts and covered nuts, and in cookies (gluten-free available).

Café Rico Cafe $

(☑2750-0510; caferico.puertoviejo@yahoo. com; breakfast US$6-8; ⊙7am-noon Sat-Wed; ☑) Roger from Hounslow West, England, will sort you out with house-roasted coffee, homemade ginger-lemonade, and a massive concoction called the Ana Rosa which features a fried egg, Canadian bacon, fried potatoes, avocado and cheese. This cozy garden cafe, which could double as a library, also serves healthier breakfasts (yogurt and strawberries, omelets). Other services include wi-fi, book exchange, laundry and bike rentals.

Soda Riquisimo Caribbean $

(☎2750-0367; dishes US$4.50-9; ⊙7am-10pm; 🛜) Typical Caribbean dishes, such as jerk chicken served with salad, beans, rice and plantain, are done well at this simple *soda* off the main strip. A musical mélange fills in the background and the atmosphere is friendly enough, but in this touristy town you can't beat these prices. Packs out on weekends. Also serves toast, omelets and fruit for breakfast.

Como en mi
Casa Art Café Vegetarian $

(☎6069-6337; www.facebook.com/comoen micasaartcafe; mains US$3.50-6; ⊙8am-4pm Wed-Mon, kitchen to 2:30pm; 🍴) Owned by a friendly bohemian expat couple, this charming vegetarian cafe champions the slow-food movement and makes everything from scratch, from the jams and the hot sauces to the gluten-free pancakes. Popular items include raw

cakes, homemade lentil-bean burgers, and gluten-free avocado wraps, smoothies and chocolate brownies. The walls are covered in local art.

De Gustibus Bakery $

(☎2756-8397; www.facebook.com/degustibus bakery; baked goods from US$1; ⊙6:45am-6pm Thu-Tue) This bakery on Puerto Viejo's main drag draws a devoted following with its fabulous focaccia, along with slices of pizza, apple strudels, profiteroles and all sorts of other sweet and savory goodies. Eat in or grab a snack for the beach.

Sel & Sucre French $

(☎2750-0636; meals US$4-10; ⊙noon-9:30pm Tue-Sun; 🍴) Dark coffee and fresh-fruit smoothies offer a nice complement to the menu of savory and sweet crepes. These delights are all prepared by chef Sebastien Flageul, who also owns the hostel next door (dorm US$12, double US$30 to US$35). Service can be slow, but it's worth it; use the cash machine across the street while you wait.

KOKi Beach restaurant (p96)

Soda Shekiná   Caribbean $

(🖉2750-0549; mains US$6-10; ⏰breakfast 7:30-11:30am, lunch & dinner 11:30am-9pm Thu-Sun) Delicious pancake and fruit breakfasts and Caribbean home cooking can be found at this backstreet eatery with wooden slab tables on an open-air terrace. Lunch and dinner mains are served with coconut rice and beans, salad and caramelized fried bananas. It's just west of the soccer field.

It may close earlier on Sunday (5pm) if there's not a crowd.

Mopri   Seafood $$

(🖉2756-8411; mains US$9-20; ⏰noon-10pm; 🧒) You'd never know it from Mopri's dingy facade and cheap plastic tables, but this place serves some of the best seafood in Puerto Viejo. Choose your star ingredient – whole snapper, calamari, lobster or prawns – then choose your sauce – Caribbean, Mopri's garlic butter, curry, jalapeño or lip-smacking salsa. Last, pile on the sides: rice, fried potatoes, plantains, salad, veggies or beans.

Stashu's con Fusion   Fusion $$

(🖉2750-0530; mains US$10-16; ⏰5-10pm Thu-Tue; 🧒) Stroll 250m out of town toward Playa Cocles to this romantic low-lit patio cafe serving creative cuisine that combines elements of Caribbean, Indian, Mexican and Thai cooking. Tandoori chicken and macadamia- and coconut-encrusted tilapia are just a couple of standouts. Excellent vegetarian and vegan items. Owner-chef Stash Golas is an artist in the kitchen and out.

The Lotus Garden hotel, behind the restaurant, has two nice pools and cozy rooms; readers will gravitate to David's Library, adjacent to the main dining area.

Miss Lidia's Place   Caribbean $$

(🖉2750-0598; dishes US$7-20; ⏰1-9pm Tue-Sat, 11:30am-8pm Sun) A long-standing favorite for classic Caribbean flavors, Miss Lidia's is in its third decade of pleasing palates and satisfying the stomachs of locals and tourists alike. Lidia's rice-and-beans with anything on the side (chicken, shrimp) is excellent. The *hiel* (Jamaican lemon-ginger drink) will cool the fieriest of souls.

Bikini Restaurant & Bar   Fusion $$

(🖉2750-3061; mains US$5.50-14; ⏰5.30-11pm; 🧒) If frozen mojitos (US$3.50) are your thing, get thee to Bikini. This hip restaurant and bar attracts a crowd of revelers with its affordable cocktails and varied menu. Caribbean dishes, pasta, salads, curries and sushi all pair well with strong drinks and a convivial atmosphere. There are also 32 vegan and vegetarian options.

KOKi Beach   Latin American $$$

(🖉2750-0902; www.kokibeach.blogspot.com; mains US$10-43; ⏰5-11pm Tue-Sun; 🐾) 🍴 A high-end favorite for drinks and dinner, this sleek restaurant at the eastern end of town cranks up the lounge music and sports an interior furnished almost entirely from local river stones and an abandoned Hone Creek house. The yucca fries are a nice starter, and you can pick your own lobster. Produce comes from local organic suppliers when possible. Sometimes closed in the low season.

🍷 DRINKING & NIGHTLIFE

Restaurants often metamorphose into rollicking bar scenes after the tables are cleared.

Johnny's Place   Club

(🖉2750-2000; www.facebook.com/johnnys placepuertoviejo; ⏰11am-7pm Mon, Thu & Fri, to 2am Wed, Sat & Sun) The place shut down briefly and reopened under new ownership as a high-end attempt at selling *ceviche*, salads, mixed rice and grilled fish (meals US$5 to US$18). There's a bar with fancy cocktails. There are still DJs, dancing and occasional revelry: it's an expat must-stop on Wednesdays.

Salsa Brava
Bar

(www.facebook.com/salsabravabeachbar; ⊘9am-2am Fri-Sun) Specializing in tacos, Caribbean bowls and sweet plantain fries, this popular spot is the perfect end-of-day cocktail stop – hit happy hour from 4pm to 6pm and you'll also catch two-for-one mojitos to enjoy while taking in the sunset over the Salsa Brava surf break. On Friday and Sunday the bar brings in DJs for popular reggae nights. Cocktails from US$5.

GETTING THERE & AWAY

If you're driving your own vehicle, Puerto Viejo de Talamanca is a straight shot down the paved coastal highway from Puerto Limón.

An ever-growing number of companies offer convenient van shuttles from Puerto Viejo to other tourist hot spots around Costa Rica and down the coast to Bocas del Toro (Panama). For an exhaustive list, see Gecko Trail's very helpful website (www.geckotrail.com). The following companies operate out of Puerto Viejo.

Caribe Shuttle (☑2750-0626; www.caribe shuttle.com; tours from US$55) Serves Bocas del Toro (Panama), San José and Tortuguero.

Gecko Trail Costa Rica (p92) Standard shuttle service to San José and Tortuguero; also offers good-value Adventure Connection packages.

Interbus (☑4100-0888, WhatsApp 6050-6500; www.interbusonline.com; ⊘Mon-Sat) Serves Arenal-La Fortuna, San José, Siquirres and Puerto Viejo de Sarapiquí.

Pleasure Ride (p77) Operates tours and transportation in the Caribbean, as well as reliable private vans to the rest of the country. It also runs an Airport Express to and from San José.

GETTING AROUND

A bicycle is a fine way to get around town, and pedaling out to beaches east of Puerto Viejo is one of the highlights of this corner of Costa Rica. You'll find rentals all over town for about US$10 per day.

 Safety First

Be aware that though the use of marijuana (and harder stuff) is common in Puerto Viejo, it is nonetheless illegal.

When going for a swim, always obey the flags as the tides are very strong.

As in other popular tourist centers, theft can be an issue. Stay aware, use your hotel safe, and if staying outside town avoid walking alone late at night.

Playa Cocles, Puerto Viejo de Talamanca (p92)
JURATEBUIVIENE/SHUTTERSTOCK ©

Manzanillo

The chilled-out village of Manzanillo has long been off the beaten track, even after the paved road arrived in 2003. This little town is still a vibrant outpost of Afro-Caribbean culture and has also remained pristine, thanks to the 1985 establishment of the Refugio Nacional de Vida Silvestre Gandoca-Manzanillo (p84), which includes the village and imposes strict regulations on regional development. Activities are of a simple nature, in nature: hiking, snorkeling and kayaking reign supreme. As elsewhere, ask about riptides before heading out.

ACTIVITIES

Bad Barts
Snorkeling

(Dive Shop & Adventures; ☑8333-9688, 2750-3091; www.facebook.com/badbartsmanzanillo; ⊘8am-5pm Tue-Sun) Near the bus stop in Manzanillo, this outfit rents kayaks, body boards and bicycles. Hours vary; call ahead.

Manzanillo beach (p85)

EATING

Cool & Calm Cafe   Caribbean $$

(mains US$12-26; 11am-10pm Thu-Tue) Directly across from Manzanillo's western beachfront, this front-porch eatery plies visitors with fine Caribbean cooking – from snapper to shrimp to chicken to lobster, roasted over coconut husks – with extras such as veggie curry thrown in for good measure. Owner Andy offers Caribbean cooking classes and a 'reef-to-plate' tour where, in certain seasons, you dive for your own lobster or fish.

Andy catches the lobster and prepares his outrageous lobster *caribeño* daily.

Maxi's Restaurant   Caribbean $$

(Mr. Maxie's; 2759-9086; mains US$10-19, lobster US$20-60; noon-10pm;) Manzanillo's most famous restaurant draws a tourist crowd with large platters of grilled seafood, *pargo rojo* (whole red snapper), *ceviche*, pork-and-rice, steak and pricey

Caribbean-style lobster. Service can be slow, but the open-air upstairs dining area is a wonderful seaside setting for a meal and a beer with views of the beach and the street below.

DRINKING & NIGHTLIFE

You may find the occasional party at Maxi's Restaurant.

ℹ️ GETTING THERE & AWAY

A 13km road winds east from Puerto Viejo, through rows of coconut palms, alongside coastal lodges and through lush lowland rainforest before coming to a dead end at the sleepy town of Manzanillo. The road was paved for the first time in 2003, dramatically shortening the amount of time it takes to travel this route. The roadway is narrow, however, so if you're driving, take your time and be alert for cyclists and one-lane bridges.

VOLCÁN POÁS

Volcán Poás at a Glance...

Just 37km north of Alajuela by a winding and scenic road is the home of Poás, an impressive 2708m active volcano. Violent eruptions hadn't taken place for more than 60 years when rumblings began in 2014; there were further significant eruptions in April and June 2017, and the park did not open again until August 2018.

It's now once again possible to peer into the 260m-deep crater with a turquoise lake at its center, and see the steaming, bubbling cauldron belching sulfurous gases into the air.

One Day in Volcán Poás

Perhaps you have just flown into Juan Santamaría International Airport, or perhaps you're on your way out. Either way, **Parque Nacional Volcán Poás** (p104) is a perfect place to begin or end your Costa Rican adventure. Just be sure to get there early. In Alajuela, treat yourself to dinner at **Xandari** (p112) and go out (or in) in style.

Two Days in Volcán Poás

On your second day, make a beeline for **La Paz Waterfall Gardens** (p106), perhaps en route to your next destination, for rushing waterfalls and magnificent wildlife. Spend the day exploring the trails, admiring the waterfalls and ogling the animals. Then head to Alajuela for dinner at **Pesqueria da Limonta** (p111) in an atmospheric villa.

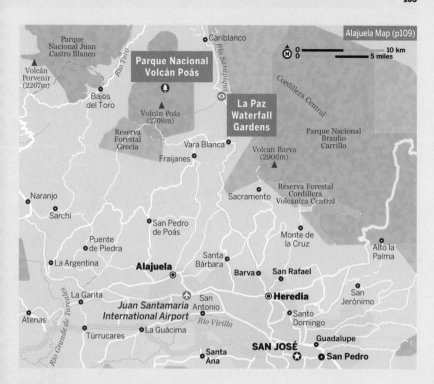

Parque Nacional Juan Castro Blanco

Volcán Porvenir (2267m)

Cariblanco

Parque Nacional Volcán Poás

Alajuela Map (p109)

N

0 — 10 km
0 — 5 miles

Cordillera Central

Bajos del Toro

Volcán Poás (2708m)

La Paz Waterfall Gardens

Reserva Forestal Grecia

Vara Blanca

Parque Nacional Braulio Carrillo

Fraijanes

Volcan Barva (2906m)

Naranjo

Sacramento

Reserva Forestal Cordillera Volcánica Central

Sarchi

San Pedro de Poás

Monte de la Cruz

Alto la Palma

Puente de Piedra

Santa Bárbara

La Argentina

Alajuela

Barva

San Rafael

San Jerónimo

La Garita

Juan Santamaría International Airport

San Antonio

Heredia

Atenas

Río Grande de Tárcoles

Santo Domingo

Túrrucares

La Guácima

Río Virilla

SAN JOSÉ

Guadalupe

Santa Ana

San Pedro

Arriving in Volcán Poás

The downside of taking a tour or local bus to Poás is that you'll typically reach the summit at around 10am – right when the clouds start rolling in. To beat the clouds and crowds, hire a car or a taxi and arrive around the park's 8am opening time (don't forget to book in advance). The road from Alajuela to the volcano is well signed.

Where to Stay

There are no accommodations inside the park itself, but the area offers a range of options. About 10km before the entrance to the national park, a winding, paved road heads east through bucolic high pastureland. This scenic, uncluttered countryside is an ideal place to stay. Alajuela (p108) is also close enough to be a convenient base for visiting Poás, with a variety of hostels and guesthouses.

Volcán Poás crater

ATLANTIDE PHOTOTRAVEL/GETTY IMAGES ©

Parque Nacional Volcán Poás

Here's your chance to get frighteningly close to an active volcano without exerting serious energy to climb it. You can drive right up, which makes this an exciting outing for families.

Great For...

☑ Don't Miss

Gazing out over one of the world's most acidic lakes, known as Laguna Caliente.

Views & Clouds

At an elevation of 2708m, the mighty Poás is clasped by 7540-year-old lava. It's possible to peer right into the mighty 260m-deep crater, with a striking turquoise lake at its center.

It's common to see dramatic smoke plumes rising from the crater. Be aware that cloud cover is also common – many travelers make the winding drive up to the summit (roughly an hour from Alajuela) only to find they can't see a thing through the mist, and there are no refunds for bad weather conditions. Your best chance of seeing a clear crater is early in the morning. It can get chilly at the crater, so bring warm clothes. You'll also need comfortable walking shoes and water.

Bangs's mountain squirrel, Parque Nacional Volcán Poás

KARIN WASSMER/SHUTTERSTOCK ©

Sendero Principal

A 750m, self-guided, uphill trail (wheelchair accessible) goes from the parking lot to the viewpoint (roughly 20 minutes' walk). It's here you get to look into the whopping 360m-diameter crater. There's a strong eggy smell of sulfur in the air and some may find that the gases irritate their throat. Officials explain that the gases in the air are checked regularly, and if they rise to a certain level your group will be asked to leave the viewpoint. Those who wish to may use one of the masks provided, but if you are struggling for breath, walk back to the visitor center. Trails around the volcano are now off-limits.

Visits take roughly 45 minutes. On arrival, guests are given a hard hat, in case of debris and ash spewing from the volcano (look for the brick-sized impact marks on the viewing platform, where fragments have hit and chipped the concrete).

Registration & Booking

Daily visitor numbers are strictly controlled at Volcán Poás, and each person is required to do an initial registration with ID at www.sinac.go.cr. Tickets should be paid for in advance on the same website. Those without bookings may be turned away at the gate.

Upon purchasing a ticket, you sign a waiver of liability outlining the increase in toxic volcanic gases at the crater (sulfur dioxide, sulfuric acid, hydrochloric acid and carbon dioxide). The booking system has been known to crash so book well in advance of your visit, and download your confirmation beforehand as wi-fi on the volcano is patchy.

Coppery-headed emerald hummingbird

La Paz Waterfall Gardens

This polished storybook garden complex offers family-friendly, digestible snippets of Costa Rica's best bits. Enjoy well-maintained trails and five jaw-droppingly scenic waterfalls, plus a sloth enclosure and interactive hummingbird and toucan experiences.

Great For...

☑ Don't Miss

Getting up close to more than 20 species of Costa Rica's exotic frogs at the ranarium.

Wildlife & Bird Feeding

If you've got kids in tow, or don't have enough time for a long trek in one of the national parks, this is where you can get up close to more than 100 species of birds. The enormous aviary is an awesome experience, acting as a refuge for wild birds that were captured illegally by hunters or donated by their past owners. The highlight is hand-feeding the toucans in a side aviary. La Paz claims its hummingbird garden is the only place in the world with 26 species. Some of these high-energy beauties feed every 10 minutes, meaning they come right up to the feeders to pose for photo opportunities.

There are also enclosures with monkeys, sloths and rescued jungle cats. The latter include jaguars, ocelots, margays, pumas

Waterfall trail

REIMAR/SHUTTERSTOCK ©

❶ Need to Know

☎2482-2720, reservations 2482-2100; www.
waterfallgardens.com; Ruta National 126;
adult/under 13yr US$45/29; ⏱8am-5pm;
🅿♿🌿

✕ Take a Break

Cast a line, catch your own lunch, then
eat it at **The Big Trout Bar** (11am to
4:30pm).

★ Top Tip

Get there before 9am or stay until
after 4pm to feed hummingbirds with
hand-feeding flowers.

jungle-clasped waterfalls. The largest are
the 37m-high Magia Blanca and 34m La
Paz waterfalls. Swimming is forbidden
in the pools beneath, but those looking
to cool down can feel the spray of these
powerful cascades from the viewing platforms. This walk is suitable for all abilities,
but bear in mind there are hundreds of
steps, mostly going down but also up in
a few places. The trail ends at a gift shop
and restroom stop, where a free vintage
shuttle bus gives rides back up the hill to
the park entrance.

and jaguarundi but, despite the rescue
efforts, these are close quarters compared
to the wild. The cats are most active around
3:30pm and are fed around this time by the
park's handlers.

Trails & Waterfalls

Save time for the trails (spanning 3.5km),
which snake in and out of 16 hectares of
cloud and rainforests. The most atmospheric and least-trafficked path is the
short and easy **Fern Trail**, along a narrow,
moss-lined concrete path and up shallow
steps, through thick jungle by the river,
with the melodic sounds of wild Costa Rica
all around.

The most popular trail follows a
boardwalk that descends 300m into the
valley, with viewing platforms looking onto

Fueling Up

There are half a dozen places to eat inside
the park. **Tortillas** does a decent cup of
locally grown coffee. **Colibries**, next to the
hummingbird garden, is the place for a
filling local and international buffet lunch.
La Terraza, at the end of the waterfall trail,
is a snack stop for a sandwich or pastry.
Want to make a night of it? Grab a cocktail
at **Las Tucas Bar** before a gourmet meal at
restaurant **Vista Poás**.

Alajuela

Alajuela is home to one of the country's most famous figures: Juan Santamaría, the humble drummer boy who died putting an end to William Walker's campaign to turn Central America into a slave territory in the Battle of Rivas in 1856. Now it's a busy agricultural hub where farmers bring their products to market.

Costa Rica's second city is by no means a tourist 'destination'. Much of the architecture is unremarkable, the streets are often crowded and there isn't a lot to see. But it's a superb base for exploring the Northern Valley and Volcán Poás, and is an inherently Costa Rican city. In its more relaxed moments, it reveals itself as such – a place where families have leisurely Sunday lunches and teenagers steal kisses in the park.

With plenty of amenities, shops, restaurants, supermarkets and banks, Alajuela makes an excellent base from which to explore the countryside to the north.

◎ SIGHTS

Museo Histórico Cultural Juan Santamaría Museum

(📞2441-4775; www.museojuansantamaria.go.cr; Av 1, btwn Calles Central & 2; ◎10am-5:30pm Tue-Sun) FREE In a century-old structure that has served as both jail and armory, this museum chronicles Costa Rican history from early European settlement through the 19th century, with special emphasis on Juan Santamaría and the pivotal mid-1850s battles of Santa Rosa, Sardinal and Rivas. Exhibits include videos, vintage maps, paintings and historical artifacts related to the conflict that ultimately safeguarded Costa Rica's independence.

Parque Central Park

(Avs Central & 1 btwn Calles Central & 2) The shady Parque Central is a pleasant place to relax beneath the mango trees or people-watch in the evenings.

Parque Juan Santamaría Plaza

(Calle 2 btwn Avs 2 & 4) Two blocks south of Parque Central, this plaza features a statue of Juan Santamaría in action, flanked by cannons. Across the way, the **Parque de los Niños** has a more park-like scene going on, and has a big play area with slides.

Cathedral Church

(Calle Central btwn Avs Central & 1) East of Parque Central is this 19th-century Roman Catholic church, which suffered severe damage and was reconstructed after earthquakes in 1941 and 1991. Two presidents are buried here and it has one of the tallest domes in Costa Rica. Take a peek inside during Sunday service to see ornate concave paintings on the ceiling.

✪ ACTIVITIES

Corso Dairy Farm Food & Drink

(📞4002-1430; Ruta Nacional 120; tours incl lunch adult/child US$11/8; ◎tours 9am, 11am & 1:30pm) With a farm-to-table restaurant, shop and dairy-farm tour, families and cheese fans will enjoy this stop before or after visiting Volcán Poás. Tours navigate 2km of trails, as a guide teaches about local geology and the methods of growing crops like strawberries, blackberries and blueberries. Kids can have a go at milking the cows.

Big groups get to ride around the farm on a tractor-trailer. Tours last 1¾ hours. The rustic restaurant is open for breakfast and lunch, serving farm-fresh eggs and bacon, plus traditional Tico dishes, *casados* and salads, all using fresh ingredients. The shop sells ice cream, bread, eggs and other delights, including delicious varieties of the farm's cheese: cheddar, mozzarella, plus herby and chili flavors.

Hacienda Alsacia Food & Drink

(📞2103-4282; www.starbuckscoffeefarm. com; tour adult/child under 6yr US$30/free; ◎8:30am-6pm Mon-Fri, 8am-6pm Sat & Sun) The only farm in the world owned by coffee giants Starbucks is at the bottom of Volcán Poás. Visitors can join a 90-minute tour to

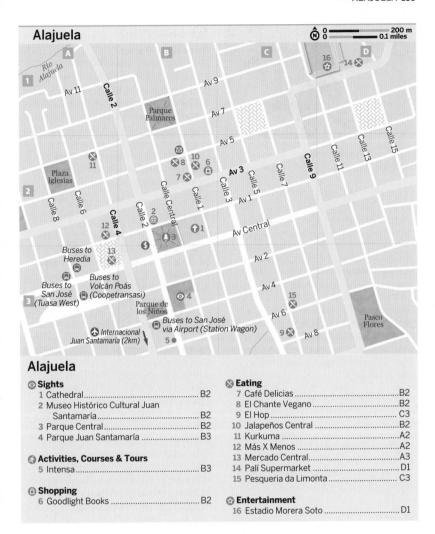

Alajuela

learn the processes from crop to cup on this 240-hectare property, before sampling coffee in a flashy tasting room and cafe. It's 15km north of Alajuela on the way to Volcán Poás.

Tours take place every half hour from 8am to 4:30pm. The cafe menu (items from US$8) includes pastries, salads and sandwiches, plus sweet treats from local artisan chocolate makers Sibu. The beautiful views of a crashing waterfall and the lush rolling hillside beyond are simply superb.

Ojo de Agua Springs   Water Park

(📞2441-0655; www.facebook.com/balnearioojo-deagua; off Ruta 111; US$2.70; ⏰7:30am-4:30pm; 🛝) About 6km south of Alajuela, this kitschy water park is packed with local families on weekends. Approximately 20,000L of water gushes from the spring every minute, powering a small waterfall and filling

Costa Rica's Soccer Town

The perennial Costa Rican soccer team, Alajuela's own La Liga (Liga Deportiva Alajuelense) has been around for more than 100 years. Over its lifetime, the club has won 29 national championships. The team plays at **Estadio Morera Soto** (2289-0909; www.lda.cr; Av Parque; tickets from US$8) at the northeastern end of town. Watch games with the locals on Sundays during soccer season (January to May and July to December). Book your tickets in advance online or at the shop (open 8am to 6pm Monday to Saturday) at the stadium.

La Liga soccer player
EZEQUIEL BECERRA/AFP VIA GETTY IMAGES ©

various pools (including an Olympic-sized lap pool complete with diving tower) and an artificial boating lake.

It's a seven-minute drive south of Juan Santamaría International Airport, just off Ruta 111.

Intensa
Language

(2442-3843, WhatsApp 8866-1059, in USA & Canada 866-277-1352; www.intensa.com; cnr Av 6 & Calle 2; 1 week group tuition 4-6hr per day US$270, with homestay US$475, private 1 week tuition 3hr per day $370, with homestay US$575; 8am-8pm Mon-Fri) Schools in Alajuela and Heredia teach everything from medical to business Spanish. Prices drop when students study for longer periods. Private or group classes available.

🔒 SHOPPING

Goodlight Books
Books

(2430-4083; Av 3 btwn Calles 1 & 3; noon-6:30pm Tue-Sat) Bookaholics, rejoice! Alajuela has one of the best English-language bookstores in the country (if not Central America). Well-organized Goodlight offers thousands of used and new books, a worthwhile stock of difficult-to-find volumes on Costa Rica, a growing supply of Spanish-language titles and a sizable array of books in other European languages.

⊗ EATING

For the cheapest meals, head to the enclosed Mercado Central. Self-caterers can stock up on groceries at the Palí or **Más X Menos** (2443-4041; www.masxmenos.cr; Av 1 btwn Calles 4 & 6; 7am-9pm Mon-Sat, to 8pm Sun) supermarkets. There are plenty of major fast-food chains in town and a couple of excellent restaurants.

Jalapeños Central
Mexican $

(Comida Tex-Mex; 2430-4027; www.facebook. com/jalapenoscentralig; Calle 1, btwn Avs 3 & 5; mains US$6-8; 11:30am-9pm Mon-Sat, to 8pm Sun) Offering the best Tex-Mex in the country, this popular, cozy spot will introduce some spice to your diet. The simple and fresh burritos, chimichangas and enchiladas come in a meal deal or on their own, and regardless should be devoured with some of the house-made guacamole and salsa, and washed down with a salty margarita or a giant Coronarita.

El Chante Vegano
Vegetarian $

(2440-3528; Av 5 btwn Calles 1 & Central; mains US$7-11; noon-8pm Tue-Sat, to 4pm Sun;) This healthy eatery specializes in organic food. Vegan treats include Buffalo cauliflower tacos, falafel pitas and portobello-mushroom burgers, plus there are many other delights such as acai bowls, pasta, pizzas and veggie sandwiches. All are served on an open-air, street-facing patio and all the decoration inside is recycled.

Café Delicias   Cafe $

(📞2431-4722; www.cafedelicias.com; cnr Calle 1
& Av 3; mains US$5-10; ⏰7am-8pm; 🛜🅿️) For
breakfast, *bocas* (appetizers), and a variety
of *típico* (traditional Costa Rican dishes),
centrally located Café Delicias is a reliably
good place to dine or enjoy a coffee accompanied by one of its rich desserts.

Palí Supermarket   Supermarket $

(Av Parque; ⏰8am-9pm Mon-Sat, to 8pm Sun)
Self-caterers can stock up on groceries at
this supermarket next to the Estadio Alejandro Morera Soto football stadium.

Kurkuma   Burgers $

(📞4080-2300; cnr Calle 4 & Av 7; mains US$6-12;
⏰noon-9:30pm Tue-Sun; 🛜) Thick, juicy tuna
or beef burgers are served up with herby
fries in this casual and welcoming place in
the north of the city, with red booths and
world flags decorating the walls. Those on
a budget should order the excellent value
casados (set meals). It stocks two dozen
imported beers, from Samuel Adams and
Estrella to Voll-Damm strong lager.

Mercado Central   Market $

(Calles 4 & 6 btwn Avs 1 & Central; ⏰8am-6pm
Mon-Sat) Head to the enclosed Mercado
Central for bargain *sodas* (cheap eateries),
and fresh produce stands.

Pesqueria da Limonta   Seafood $$

(📞2430-3572; cnr Av 6 & Calle 5; mains US$12-
16; ⏰noon-4pm Sun, noon-9pm Mon, 11:30am-
9pm Tue-Thu, 11:30am-10pm Fri, noon-10pm Sat)
Set in an atmospheric villa with a sophisticated patio lit by fairy lights, Pesqueria
da Limonta is the best dining experience
in town, serving up fresh and beautifully
presented seafood dishes with Costa Rican
and Italian flair. Mains include Parmigiano
gratin shrimps, perfectly tangy *ceviche* and
Caribbean salmon. The seafood salads are
superb, and there are succulent beef cuts
for non-seafood-eaters.

El Hop   American $$

(📞2101-0264; www.facebook.com/elhopcr; El
Patio, Calle 5 btwn Avs 8 & 6; dishes US$8-12;
⏰5pm-10pm Tue, noon-3pm & 6pm-10pm Wed &
Thu, noon-11pm Fri & Sat, noon-9pm Sun) Open-
plan gastropub serving top grub and

Alajuela's cathedral (p108)

Fish *casado*

FERTNIG/GETTY IMAGES ©

🍽️ Eating Options Near Volcán Poás

The road up to Parque Nacional Volcán Poás is lined with stands selling fruit (especially local strawberries), cheese and snacks – as well as countless touristy eateries serving typical Tico fare – so you won't go hungry. Bring your own bottled water, though, as the tap water here is undrinkable.

Colbert Restaurant (Restaurante Frances Colbert; 📞8301-1793, 2482-2776; www.colbert.co.cr; Vara Blanca; mains US$8-32; ⏰noon-7pm Fri-Tue) At this charming restaurant 6km east of Poasito, the menu is loaded with traditional French items such as onion soup, house-made pâté, beef fillet, rabbit in mustard sauce and chocolate mousse (a French recipe using chocolate from Costa Rica). A good wine list is strong on vintages from South America and France.

El Churrasco Hotel Restaurante (📞2482-2135; www.hotelelchurrasco.com; Ruta Nacional 120; mains US$8-12; ⏰8am-8pm; 🅿️🛜) On the way up to Volcán Poás, this rustic restaurant serves tasty, authentic Costa Rican cuisine. Ingredients are sourced locally and the *casados* and mixed rice dishes are full of flavor. The house specializes in steak, with nine cuts on offer. Pair your succulent slab with everything from creole tomato sauce to Roquefort cheese.

beer. The kitchen rustles up adventurous dishes like seafood cocktails (with poached octopus and shrimp), plus ultra-thin-crust pizzas that will keep you coming back. Bases come topped with classic pepperoni or more unusual toppings like mozzarella cheese with caramelized red onion and avocado. The drinks list has good craft beers and cocktails. Sit back and relax in the hip setting, with views onto Alajuela's trendy El Patio food garden.

Xandari International $$$
(📞2443-2020; www.xandari.com; Xandari Resort Hotel & Spa, Calle Burios; mains US$12-32; ⏰7-10am, noon-4pm & 6-8pm; 🍴) 🌿 If you want to impress a date, you can't go wrong at this elegant restaurant with incredible views. The menu is a mix of Costa Rican and international dishes, with plenty of vegetarian options. The restaurant uses the resort's homegrown organic produce, supplemented by locally grown organic produce whenever possible – it all makes for tasty *and* feel-good gourmet meals.

🍷 DRINKING & NIGHTLIFE

Alajuela isn't known for its nightlife; aside from dive bars, local hotels and restaurants are the best bet for a nightcap. There's a couple of good craft beer joints – Kurkuma (p111) in north Alajuela and El Hop (p111), which sits in the trendy El Patio area of town. Meanwhile, Jalapeños Central (p110) pours a decent giant salty margarita.

ℹ️ INFORMATION

Banco Nacional (Calle 2; ⏰8:30am-3:30pm Mon-Fri) The most centrally located ATM can be found in the main square opposite the church.

Hospital San Rafael (📞2436-1001; Alameda Tomás Guardia; ⏰24hr) Alajuela's hospital is a three-story building south of Av 10.

Post office (📞2443-2653; cnr Av 5 & Calle 1; ⏰8am-5pm Mon-Fri, to noon Sat)

Arabica coffee beans, Alajuela plantation

ⓘ GETTING THERE & AROUND

Taxis charge between US$6 and US$10 (depending on destination) for the five- to 10-minute drive from Juan Santamaría International Airport into Alajuela.

There is no central bus terminal; instead, a number of small terminals and bus stops dot the southwestern part of the city. Note that there are two Tuasa terminals – **east** (☑2442-6900; Calle 8 btwn Avs Central & 1) and **west** (Calle 8 btwn Avs Central & 1) – right across the street from each other. From there, **buses to Volcán Poás** (☑2442-6900; Calle 8 btwn Avs Central & 2) are a block south. **Buses to San José via the airport** (Av 4 btwn Calles 2 & 4) leave from in front of the Parque de los Niños, on the opposite side of the street.

Coopetransasi (☑2449-6040, 2449-5141) offers routes around Costa Rica. Check with local bus companies for up-to-date schedules before your journey.

TALAMANCA
MOUNTAINS

Talamanca Mountains at a Glance...

The Cordillera de Talamanca is the highest, longest and most remote mountain range in the country. Here you'll find the high-altitude Parque Nacional Chirripó and the eponymous highest peak, Cerro Chirripó (3820m). Lush cloud forest dominates the mountain slopes, providing refuge to countless bird species, including the sought-after resplendent quetzal. Birders flock to San Gerardo de Dota to catch sight of the feathered beauty. Above 3400m, the landscape is páramo (scrubby trees and grasslands). Rocky outposts punctuate barren hills and feed the glacial lakes that earned the peak its iconic name: Chirripó means 'Eternal Waters.'

Two Days in the Talamanca Mountains

You certainly shouldn't plan for any less than two days to visit **Cerro Chirripó** (p118), as that's the bare minimum for the hike. Be sure to arrive early enough to check in at the ranger station the day before. **Antojos de Maíz** (p126) is a good lunch stop on your way in.

Four Days in the Talamanca Mountains

Three days in Parque Nacional Chirripó allows time for exploration of the trails near the summit. And, there's still time to stop in **San Gerardo de Dota** (p122) to stalk the resplendent quetzal, to explore the trails and waterfalls at **Cloudbridge Nature Reserve** (p124), or to recover from your hike with a soak in **thermal hot springs** (p125).

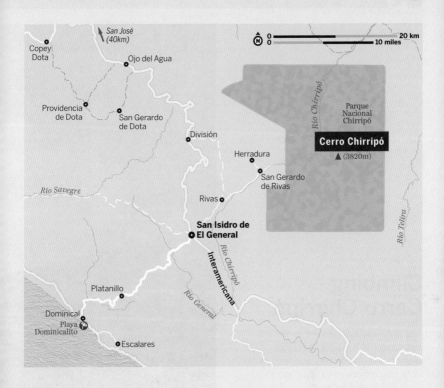

San José
(40km)

Copey
Dota

Ojo del Agua

Providencia
de Dota

San Gerardo
de Dota

División

Herradura

San Gerardo
de Rivas

Rivas

Río Savegre

Río Chirripó

Parque
Nacional
Chirripó

Cerro Chirripó

▲ (3820m)

Río Telira

**San Isidro de
El General**

Río Chirripó

Interamericana

Platanillo

Río General

Dominical
Playa
Dominicalito

Escalares

0   20 km
0   10 miles

Arriving in the Talamanca Mountains

San Gerardo de Dota is just off the Interamericana, about halfway between San José and San Isidro de El General. The gateway to Parque Nacional Chirripó is the delightful village of San Gerardo de Rivas, which is about 18km northeast of San Isidro de El General on Rte 242. Arriving by public transportation requires a bus transfer in San Isidro.

Where to Stay

If you're visiting Parque Nacional Chirripó, you'll spend at least one night in San Gerardo de Rivas, which has accommodations strung out along its narrow main road and clustered around the trailhead. The only lodging in the park itself is Crestones Base Lodge (p121). For quetzal spotting, it's worth spending a night in San Gerardo de Dota or one of the nearby mountain lodges.

Parque Nacional Chirripó

Climbing Cerro Chirripó

The only way up Chirripó is on foot. Although the trekking routes are challenging, watching the sunrise from such lofty heights is one of the country's undeniable highlights.

Great For...

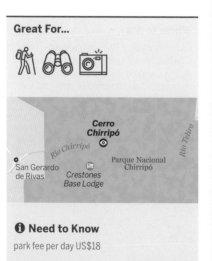

ⓘ Need to Know

park fee per day US$18

★ **Top Tip**
You must register your permit with the ranger office before you hike.

Planning Your Hike

Make arrangements well in advance (especially during the dry season).

• You'll need to purchase park permits via Sinac (www.sinac.go.cr) for each day you'll be in the park. This can be done up to six months in advance.

• You'll get an email from Consorcio Aguas Eternas. Follow the link to book your bed and meals at Crestones Base Lodge.

• Don't forget to check in at Chirripó ranger station (p127) and at the Consorcio Aguas Eternas (p127) office in San Gerardo de Rivas before you start your hike. Ideally do it the day before you hike. Otherwise, you'll get a late start, as the offices don't open until 8am.

Seasons & Weather

The dry season (from late December to April) is the most popular time to visit Chirripó. February and March are the driest months with the clearest skies. The park is open year-round, and the early months of the rainy season are good for climbing as it usually doesn't rain in the morning. In any season, temperatures can drop below freezing at night, so warm clothes (including hat and gloves) and rainwear are necessary. Wear sturdy boots and bring good second-skin blister plasters.

Timing

It takes five to 10 hours to cover the 14.5km trail to Crestones Base Lodge. From the lodge it's another 5.1km to the summit, which takes around two hours one way. For

Cuesta de los Arrepentidos

most, a minimum of two days is needed to climb from the ranger station in San Gerardo to the summit and back. During peak season you can book a maximum of two nights at the lodge. Otherwise the maximum is three nights, allowing extra time to explore the trails around the summit and/ or Crestones.

Getting Started

The park entrance is at San Gerardo de Rivas, which lies 1219m above sea level; the altitude at the summit is 3820m, which makes it 2.6km straight up! A well-marked 19.6km trail leads to the top, with trail

☑ Don't Miss

Watching the sun rise over Costa Rica from the country's highest peak.

RAUL COLE/SHUTTERSTOCK ©

markers every kilometer; no technical climbing is required.

Altitude sickness can be an issue as you get higher up. Watch out for nausea, shortness of breath, headaches and exhaustion. If you start feeling unwell, rest for a little while; if the symptoms persist, descend immediately.

The Route

Most hikers start the hike between 4am and 5am. The trailhead is in San Gerardo de Rivas just past Casa Mariposa (and about 4km from the ranger station). The actual entrance to the park is a further 4km along the trail.

The first 6km or so are mostly uphill, over uneven, rocky ground, with some relatively flat stretches. Then there's a gentle descent toward the shelter at **Llano Bonito** (7.5km). Here you can stock up on drinking water, use the flushing toilets and buy snacks and even aspirin.

Just beyond begins the **Cuesta de los Arrepentidos** (Hill of the Repentants). It's a steep uphill slog until you reach the top of **Monte Sin Fe** (Mountain Without Faith), a preliminary crest that reaches 3200m at around Km 10. By then you're on exposed ground, flanked by stunted tree growth, with gorgeous mountain views around you. The trail descends gently for around 1.5km, before the last interminable, steep ascent to **Crestones Base Lodge** (3400m).

The hike to the **summit** is 5.1km on relatively flatter terrain. Most hikers leave for the summit at around 3am the next morning to arrive in time to watch the sunrise. There is one tricky spot where it's possible to lose the trail if you're hiking in the dark, so look for painted arrows to point you in the right direction. The last couple hundred meters is very steep, requiring scrambling on all fours.

✕ Take a Break

Book in advance to eat and sleep at **Crestones Base Lodge** (☎2742-5097; www.chirripo.org/hospedaje; dm US$37; ☎).

ONDREJ PROSICKY/SHUTTERSTOCK ©

Quetzal Spotting

To spot the rare resplendent quetzal, keep your eyes peeled in the cloud forests of Chirripó and especially in the bucolic mountain village of San Gerardo de Dota and nearby forests.

Great For...

★ Did You Know?

The resplendent quetzal was considered divine by pre-Columbian cultures.

Where to Spot a Quetzal

There are many places to go birdwatching and hiking in the **San Gerardo de Dota** area. Most accommodations offer early-morning quetzal walks, on which you are likely to spot at least one of these beauties. There are a few well-known quetzal hangout spots along the river and right in the village: ask at your lodging for details or look for signs along the road.

Parque Nacional Los Quetzales

(☎2514-0403; US$10; ☺7:30am-3:30pm) True to the park's name, the quetzal is here (best spotted during the March to June nesting season), along with trogons, hummingbirds and sooty robins. Located on the Interamericana, just north of the San Gerardo turnoff.

JORY F/SHUTTERSTOCK ©

Paraíso Quetzal Lodge (☑2200-0241; www.paraisoquetzal.com; Interamericana Km 70; d incl breakfast US$116-145, half-board US$157-189) Birders rave about this lodge, surrounded by 13km of walking trails and viewing platforms that provide an excellent chance of spotting the resplendent quetzal. The lodge offers **quetzal tours** three times a day (open to nonguests, US$60 per couple), cooperating with local farmers who monitor and report on the birds' whereabouts. Located on the Interamericana, about 10km north of the San Gerardo turnoff.

Batsù Garden (☑8395-0115; www.batsucr. com; US$20; ☹5am-8pm) A garden designed specifically for birdwatching and photography. Feeders and fruits attract the birds to viewing platforms, while trails wind through the blooming gardens. The quetzal sometimes shows up during breeding season. Pay admission at the restaurant Alma de Árbol.

Savegre Hotel (☑2740-1028, in USA & Canada 866-549-1178; www.savegre.com; d from US$162; P@⊛) Operated by the Chacón family since 1957, this lodge is beautifully landscaped and hugely popular with birdwatchers, since quetzals nest along the 20km of trails on the 400-hectare property. Trails are open to nonguests.

Getting There & Away

The turnoff to San Gerardo de Dota is near Km 80 on the Interamericana. From here, the steep road down into the valley alternates between paved and dirt; you'll appreciate your 4WD. Take it slowly, as two-way traffic necessitates a bit of negotiation.

San Gerardo de Rivas

If you plan to climb Chirripó (p118), you're in the right place – the tiny, tranquil, spread-out town of San Gerardo de Rivas is at the doorstep of the national park. Here you can get supplies, have a good night's rest and take a hot shower before and after the trek. Be aware that all arrangements for hiking permits and accommodations must be made well in advance, using the park's online reservation system.

For those who don't have the time or energy to summit Chirripó, there are also lovely, less difficult hikes in private nature reserves, and rural tourism aplenty, from the local trout farm to producers of cheese and chocolate in nearby Canaán. San Gerardo's bird-filled alpine scenery makes it a beautiful place to linger, hike or no hike.

The road to San Gerardo de Rivas winds its way 22km up the valley of the Río Chirripó from San Isidro.

◉ SIGHTS

Cloudbridge Nature Reserve   Nature Reserve

(☑in USA 917-494-5408; www.cloudbridge. org; admission by donation, tours from US$35; ⊗6am-6pm) About 2km past the trailhead to Cerro Chirripó you will find the entrance to the mystical, magical Cloudbridge Nature Reserve. Covering 283 hectares on the side of Cerro Chirripó, this private reserve is an ongoing reforestation and preservation project founded by Genevieve Giddy and her late husband Ian. A network of trails traverses the property, which is easy to explore independently. Even if you don't get far past the entrance, you'll find two waterfalls, including the magnificent Catarata Pacifica.

Talamanca Reserve   Nature Reserve

(☑2742-5080; www.talamancareserve.com; US$15) With over 1600 hectares of primary and secondary cloud forest, this private reserve has miles of hiking trails to explore. Visitors will be rewarded with spectacular mountain vistas, 10 different waterfalls and sightings of countless bird species.

From left: Green honeycreeper; Clerodendrum ugandense in Jardines Secretos; San Gerardo de Rivas

Bordering the Parque Nacional Chirripó, Talamanca is a viable alternative for hikers who do not care to summit the mountain.

Jardines Secretos   Gardens
(✆2742-5086, 8451-3001; https://jardines
-secretos.negocio.site; US$5; ⏰8am-4pm)
These not-so-secret gardens make for a tranquil pre- or post-Chirripó pastime as the owners talk you through their collection of orchids and other tropical plants. Find the turnoff just after the ranger station but before the first bridge.

⚙ ACTIVITIES

Truchero Los Cocolisos Fishing, Food
(✆2742-5054; www.facebook.com/trucherolos.
cocolisos; ⏰9am-6pm Sat & Sun & by appoint-
ment) Just before the Quebrada Chispa bridge, uphill from the ranger station, take the left fork in the road to this lovely family-run trout farm. Catch your own fish from the trout pools or take in the celebrated orchid collection. Naturally, the fish is the best part; matronly Garita puts

together a homemade feast of trout and home-cooked sides (meal US$5 to US$9).

Thermal Hot Springs   Hot Springs
(Gevi Aguas Termales; ✆2742-5210; Herra-
dura; US$8; ⏰7am-5:30pm) After climbing a mountain, what could be more enticing than soothing your tired muscles in thermal pools, naturally heated to 37°C (98.6°F)? Two pools provide ample space for soaking.

Just north of the ranger station, take the left-hand turnoff (before the first bridge) and continue 700m on the paved road. Look for a signed turnoff on the right and cross the suspension bridge over the river. A steep switchback road climbs for another 1km to a small house and the entrance to the hot springs.

✕ EATING

Garden House Observatory   Cafe $
(✆8524-6857; www.facebook.com/garden
housecr; mains US$6-8; ⏰7am-6pm; ⚲) Come for breakfast or lunch and while away the day, sipping coffee, sampling baked

ARNOLDO ROBERT/GETTY IMAGES ©

Chorreada – a sweet pancake made with corn

goodies and watching the feathered friends flitting about the grounds. A short trail meanders through the gardens, but there's plenty to keep your attention if you prefer to sit still on the delightful terrace. The menu is short (juices, snacks, salads) but it's all fresh and delicious.

Antojos de Maíz   Costa Rican $

(☑2772-4381; chorreadas US$3; mains US$5; ⏱7:30am-7:30pm Wed-Mon) For all things corn, stop at this traditional roadside restaurant on your way to or from the mountain. Our favorite here is the *chorreada,* a traditional sweet pancake made with fresh white or yellow corn and served with sour cream. Pairs very well with strong, organic coffee.

Batsú Gastropub   Gastropub $$

(www.facebook.com/batsugastropub; Canaán; mains US$8-26; ⏱11am-9pm; ☑) The tiny village of Canaán is not the type of place you would expect to find a 'gastropub' yet here it is. The menu is eclectic and delicious, featuring items like sesame-crusted tuna, grilled chicken with Gruyère and figs, sandwiches served on homemade bread, and an extremely tasty veggie burger.

🔒 SHOPPING

Samaritan Xocolata   Food & Drinks

(☑8820-7095; www.samaritanxocolata.com; Canaán; ⏱10am-4pm Mon-Sat) This artisanal chocolatier transforms Costa Rican cocoa beans into rich, dark, creamy, spicy, nut- and fruit-filled temptations. Its secret is organic ingredients, small-batch processing and high cocoa content. If you're crazy about chocolate, sign up for a chocolate-making workshop (US$55 per person) or just stop by to sample the goodness.

Queso Canaán   Food & Drinks

(☑2742-5125; www.quesoscanaan.com; Canaán; ⏱9am-5pm Mon-Sat) After a trip to Switzerland, Wilberth and Katia Mata turned their Canaán dairy farm into an artisanal cheese facility, specializing in the creamy, holy, Swiss style. If you visit the shop, you can meet the cows, see the production and ageing process, and sample (and buy!) the goods.

❶ INFORMATION

Chirripó Ranger Station (Sinac; ☎905-244-7747, in USA 506-2742-5348; ⏰8am-noon & 1-4:30pm) The Chirripó Ranger Station is 1km south of the soccer field at the entrance to San Gerardo de Rivas. If you've made reservations at Crestones Base Lodge and to hike up Cerro Chirripó, you must stop by the day before to confirm your permit and obtain a wrist band. If you haven't booked your park permit in advance, there's a very slim chance of next-day availability.

Consorcio Aguas Eternas (Consortium Office; ☎2742-5097, 2742-5200; www.chirripo.org; ⏰8am-5pm Mon-Sat, from 9am Sun) By the soccer field, this is the office responsible for the Crestones Base Lodge bookings, as well as other services including meals, porters and equipment rental. Meals and lodging must be reserved in advance through the consortium website, but you still have to check in at this office on the day before or morning of your hike.

❶ GETTING THERE & AWAY

Driving from San Isidro, head south on the Interamericana and cross Río San Isidro south of town. About 500m further on, cross the unsigned Río Jilguero and take the first, steep turn up to the left, about 300m beyond the Jilguero. Note that this turnoff is not marked (if you miss the turn, it is signed from the northbound side).

The ranger station is on this road at the start of San Gerardo de Rivas, about 18km from the Interamericana. Past the ranger station, the road passes through the village and continues up to the Chirripó trailhead and Cloudbridge Nature Reserve. The road is passable for ordinary cars, but a 4WD is recommended if you are driving to Hotel Urán or to Cloudbridge Nature Reserve, as the unpaved road is steep and truly hideous.

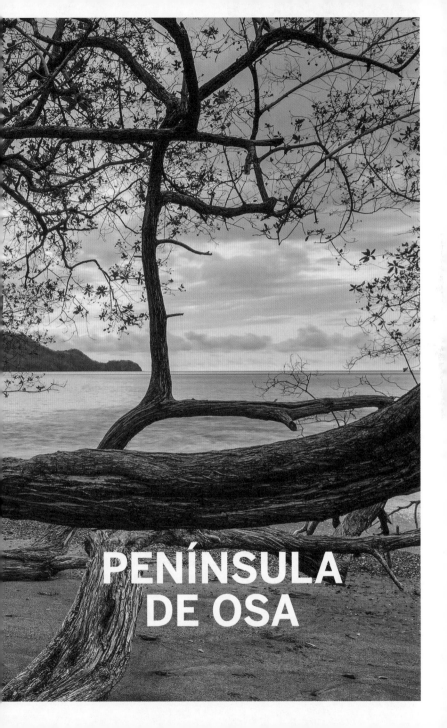

PENÍNSULA
DE OSA

Península de Osa at a Glance...

The steamy coastal jungles of the Península de Osa encompass some of the country's wildest and most tantalizing territory. Monkeys, sloths and coatis roam the region's abundant parks and reserves, and scarlet macaws soar overhead. In Parque Nacional Corcovado there's the rare chance to spy on a slumbering tapir. Meanwhile, the rugged coast captivates travelers with abandoned wilderness beaches, world-class surf and mainland Costa Rica's best snorkeling and diving. The Osa also offers opportunities to get away from it all and live off the grid, in rustic simplicity or in the lap of luxury, but always surrounded by glorious nature.

Two Days in the Península de Osa

Hire a guide for a day of hiking and wildlife-watching in **Parque Nacional Corcovado** (p132) or explore the **Agujitas–Corcovado coastal trail** (p144) along Bahía Drake. Spend your second day snorkeling or diving at **Isla del Caño** (p138) or relaxing at one of the local beaches.

Four Days in the Península de Osa

You'll spend two days hiking across **Parque Nacional Corcovado** (p132) and tallying up the animal sightings. On day three, return to Puerto Jiménez for a celebratory breakfast at **Cafetería Monka** (p140) then retreat to **Playa Platanares** (p140) for recovery. Your fourth day is free to spend waterfall rappelling with **Psycho Tours** (p140) or learning about the cultivation of chocolate at **Finca Köbö** (p142).

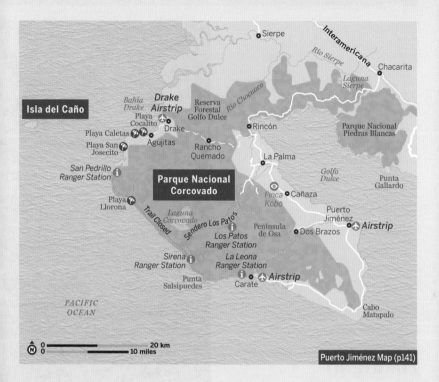

Isla del Caño

Sierpe

Río Sierpe

Interamericana

Chacarita

Laguna
Sierpe

Bahía
Drake

Drake
Airstrip

Playa
Cocalito

Reserva
Forestal
Golfo Dulce

Río Chocuaco

Rincón

Parque Nacional
Piedras Blancas

Playa Caletas

Drake

Playa San
Josecito

Agujitas

Rancho
Quemado

La Palma

San Pedrillo
Ranger Station

Parque Nacional
Corcovado

Golfo
Dulce

Punta
Gallardo

Playa
Llorona

Laguna
Corcovado

Finca
Kóbo

Cañaza

Puerto
Jiménez

Airstrip

Trail Closed

Sendero Los Patos

Península
de Osa

Dos Brazos

Los Patos
Ranger Station

Sirena
Ranger Station

La Leona
Ranger Station

Punta
Salsipuedes

Carate

Airstrip

PACIFIC
OCEAN

Cabo
Matapalo

N
0   20 km
0   10 miles

Puerto Jiménez Map (p141)

Arriving in the Península de Osa

The easiest way to reach the Osa is to
fly directly to Puerto Jiménez or Bahía
Drake. It's also possible to take a boat
from Sierpe, through the mangroves
and down the Río Sierpe, to your lodging
in Bahía Drake. If you drive, you'll need
a 4WD and plenty of confidence: many
roads in the Osa are extremely poor and
there are river crossings involved.

Where to Stay

The widest selection of lodging is in
the town of Puerto Jiménez and in the
village in Bahía Drake, although budget
options are limited in the latter. Some of
the country's best wilderness lodges are
found in Bahía Drake (along the beach
south of the village), as well as Cabo
Matapalo and Carate (south of Puerto
Jiménez).

Hiking in Parque Nacional Corcovado

Hiking in Corcovado

Parque Nacional Corcovado's amazing biodiversity as well as the park's demanding, multiday hiking trails attract a stream of visitors who descend from Bahía Drake and Puerto Jiménez to experience a bona fide jungle adventure.

Great For...

ⓘ Need to Know

Área de Conservación Osa, ACOSA; Osa Conservation Area Headquarters; ☏2735-5036; Corcovado park fee per person per day US$15; ⊘8am-4pm Mon-Fri

★ **Top Tip**

All visitors to Corcovado must be accompanied by a Costa Rican Tourism Board (ICT)–certified guide.

Hiking Trails

There are three main trails in the park that are open to visitors, as well as shorter trails around the ranger stations.

One trail traverses the park from La Leona to Sirena (or vice versa); another trail leads from Sirena to Los Patos (or vice versa). Completed in either direction, these two legs allow hikers to make a sort of loop, beginning and ending their journey in or near Puerto Jiménez, which offers easy access to both La Leona and Los Patos.

The most popular single-day hike is La Leona to Sirena. Many hikers opt to complete this one-day route, spend the night at Sirena and then boat out the next day.

At times, high water makes it impossible for vehicles to reach Los Patos to drop or retrieve hikers. In this case, hikers must tag on an additional 5km to or from the village of **La Tarde**. This results in the toughest day trek – from the village of La Tarde to Sirena via Los Patos (or vice versa) – a whopping 30km.

Hiking is best in the dry season (December to April), when there is still regular rain but all of the trails are open. It remains muddy, but you won't sink quite as deep. Carry plenty of snacks, water and insect repellent.

La Leona to Sirena   Hiking

The largely flat 16km hike (five to seven hours) follows the shoreline through coastal forest and along deserted beaches. Take plenty of water, a hat and sunscreen. It involves one major river crossing at Río Claro, just south of Sirena, and there's an excellent chance of seeing monkeys, tapirs and scarlet macaws en route.

Baird's tapir

This leg requires an additional 3.5km hike between La Leona and Carate, which is the closest access for vehicles. Some hot and sandy beach trekking is required, but much of the hike takes place on a parallel forest trail, which allows you to avoid the sizzling sun for part of the time.

Sirena to Los Patos   Hiking

This trail goes 24km through the heart of Corcovado, passing through primary and secondary forest, and is relatively flat for the first 12km. After you wade through two river tributaries before reaching the Laguna Corcovado, the route undulates steeply (mostly uphill!) for the second half. It's less

punishing to do this trek in the opposite direction, from Los Patos to Sirena.

Sendero El Tigre   Hiking

Originating in the village of Dos Brazos, part of this 7km loop trail passes through Parque Nacional Corcovado, so a guide is mandatory. It's a fairly rugged trail, part of which passes through an ancient indigenous burial ground; be prepared to spend six to seven hours completing the hike. It's doable as a day trip yet gives you a good taste of the park.

Tour Guides

Guides can be hired through the Área de Conservación Osa park office (p142) in Puerto Jiménez, or through hotels and tour operators. Prices vary considerably depending on the season, availability, size of your party and type of expedition you want to arrange. The price should include park fees, meals and transportation.

Osa Wild (☑2735-5848; www.osawildtravel. com; tours from US$40, 1-day Corcovado tour US$85-105; ☺8am-noon & 2-7pm Mon-Fri, 9am-noon & 1-4pm Sat & Sun) ✔ is the way to connect with Corcovado park and the Osa. It's just what the area so desperately needed: a resource for travelers to connect with community-oriented initiatives that go to the heart of the real Osa through homestays, farm tours and sustainable cultural exchanges. It also offers more typical stuff like kayaking tours and guided trips through Corcovado.

A team of excellent guides make **Surcos Tours** (☑8550-1089, 2235-5355; www.surcos tours.com) ✔ a great option, especially for wildlife and birdwatching tours. Surcos offers all the options for multiday treks in Corcovado, as well as shorter wildlife outings at Cabo Matapalo or around La Leona.

☑ **Don't Miss**

The chance to see a rare Baird's tapir in its natural habitat near Sirena Ranger Station.

ONDREJ PROSICKY/SHUTTERSTOCK ©

✘ **Take a Break**

Make reservations in advance to camp and eat at **Sirena Ranger Station** (dm US$30).

Scarlet macaw

SIVELSTRESELVA/GETTY IMAGES ©

Wildlife-Watching

The Península de Osa is a bastion of biological diversity, home to half of Costa Rica's species. Corcovado is legendary for its animal life, but you can spot creatures galore outside the park as well.

Great For...

☑ Don't Miss

The hard-to-spot silky anteater frequents the beachside forests between the Río Claro and Sirena Ranger Station.

What to See

The Península de Osa is home to a staggering 370 species of bird, 140 species of mammals and thousands of insect species, with more still waiting to be discovered.

Birds

The coastal trails inside and outside the park produce an endless pageant of birds. Sightings of scarlet macaws are guaranteed, as the tropical almond trees lining the coast are a favorite food.

Primates

The Osa is one the few places in Costa Rica with all four of the country's primate species. Spider monkeys, mantled howlers and white-faced capuchins can be encountered anywhere. The Central American

White-nosed coati

TODD SOWERS PHOTOGRAPHY/SHUTTERSTOCK ©

ℹ Need to Know

Visitors to Corcovado must be accompanied by an ICT-certified guide.

✘ Take a Break

Refuel at the festive **Martina's Bar** (Buena Esperanza Bar; 📞8360-9979; road to Carate, Km 17; mains US$8-18; 🕐 9am-9pm Sat-Thu, to 1am Fri) near the Matapalo turnoff.

★ Top Tip

The Osa is the only place in Costa Rica with all four of the country's primate species.

both species of peccary (collared and white-lipped). Even if you don't make it to Sirena, you have the chance to see sloths (two- and three-toed), anteaters (Mexican tamandua), tayras, coatis and agoutis, especially near the coast.

Where to See It

The best wildlife-watching in Corcovado is around Sirena Ranger Station and along the trail between La Leona and Sirena. But birds and animals do not recognize park boundaries. There is plenty of wildlife to see outside the park, including on the Agujitas–Corcovado Trail (p144; near Bahía Drake) and around Cabo Matapalo (p143; near Puerto Jiménez).

How to See It

All visitors to Corcovado must be accompanied by an ICT-certified guide (available through hotels and tour operators). Outside the park, guides are not required, of course, but they can be helpful. Besides their intimate knowledge of the trails, local guides are amazingly informed about flora and fauna. Most guides also carry telescopes, allowing for up-close views of wildlife.

squirrel monkey (the most endangered) is frequently spotted at Cabo Matapalo and along the La Leona–Sirena trail.

Wild Cats

Jaguars are rarely spotted, as their population in the Osa is suspected to be in the single digits. Pumas represent your best chance for observing a cat (the only diurnal species), but again, don't get your hopes up.

Other Mammals

For dedicated wildlife-watchers, a stay at Sirena Ranger Station is a must. On early-morning walks, a sighting of a Baird's tapir is almost guaranteed – a statement that can be made at few other places in the world. Sirena is excellent for other herbivores, particularly red brocket and

School of spottail grunts

DANIEL LAMBORN/SHUTTERSTOCK ©

Isla del Caño

Frolic with the fish in the waters surrounding Isla del Caño, a marine park with an impressive concentration and diversity of coral. The reefs attract abundant marine life, including several species of sea turtles.

Great For...

☑ Don't Miss

Keep your eyes peeled for frolicking dolphins and migrating whales, occasionally sighted from Caño-bound boats.

The Waters

About 20km off the coast of Bahía Drake, Isla del Caño is one of Costa Rica's top spots for diving and snorkeling, with intricate rock and coral formations and an amazing array of underwater life.

Some 15 different species of coral are here, as well as threatened species including the Panulirus lobster and giant conch. The sheer numbers of fish attract dolphins and whales, as well as hammerhead sharks, manta rays and sea turtles. Divers report that the schools of fish swimming overhead are often so dense that they block the sunlight from filtering down.

There are no rivers on the island and it's far enough from shore that the clarity of the water is not normally affected by seasonal rains.

Isla del Caño

DUARTE DELLAROLE/SHUTTERSTOCK ©

Bahía Drake

◎ *Isla del Caño*

Drake ●

Playa San Josecito ● ⊙ Agujitas

❶ Need to Know

www.sinac.go.cr/ES/ac/acosa/Paginas/IsladelCaño.aspx; adult/child US$15/5, diving charge US$4

✖ Take a Break

Most snorkel and dive outings stop for a picnic lunch at Playa San Josecito.

★ Top Tip

Isla del Caño is a marine reserve, so it's prohibited to take or touch anything!

The Island

Isla del Caño is a 326-hectare island – the tip of numerous underwater rock formations. On the island, at about 110m above sea level, the evergreen trees consist primarily of milk trees (also called 'cow trees' after the drinkable white latex they exude), believed to be the remains of an orchard planted by pre-Columbian indigenous inhabitants. Near the top of the ridge there are two pre-Columbian granite spheres. Archaeologists speculate that the island may have been a ceremonial or burial site for the same indigenous tribes.

The island itself is not open to recreational visitors, beyond the boat-landing beach. There is a short trail up to an observation deck.

Snorkel Tours & Dive Shops

Drake Divers   Diving

(☏2775-1818; www.drakediverscr.com; snorkeling US$85, 2-tank dive US$140; ⊙7am-7pm) This friendly outfit takes divers and snorkelers to Isla del Caño. Experienced dive masters point out the resident sharks, turtles, eels and more, while the onboard crew is helpful with setting up equipment. The outing is followed by a tasty picnic lunch at Playa San Josecito. Prices include equipment.

Caño Divers   Diving

(☏8995-0174, 2234-6154; www.canodiverscostarica.com; 2-tank dive US$140, snorkel tour US$90) Based at Pirate Cove Resort, this recommended diving outfit is competent and competitively priced. Offers the requisite trips to Isla del Caño, as well as PADI certification courses.

Puerto Jiménez

Sliced in half by the swampy, overgrown Quebrada Cacao, and flanked on one side by the emerald waters of the **Golfo Dulce**, the vaguely Wild West outpost of Puerto Jiménez is shared by local residents and wildlife. While walking through the dusty streets of Jiménez (as it's known to locals), it's not unusual to spot scarlet macaws roosting on the soccer field, or white-faced capuchins traversing the treetops along the main street.

On the edge of Parque Nacional Corcovado, Jiménez is the preferred jumping-off point for travelers heading to the famed Sirena Ranger Station, and a great place to organize an expedition, stock up on supplies and get a good night's rest before hitting the trails.

And even besides Corcovado, there are beaches to swim and sun, mangroves to kayak and fish to catch. This is a Tico town with tourist appeal, and an adventure to fit every palate.

◎ SIGHTS

Playa Platanares   Beach
About 5km southeast of town, the long, secluded – and often deserted – Playa Platanares is excellent for swimming, sunning and recovering from too much adventure. The nearby mangroves of Río Platanares are a paradise for kayaking and birdwatching. Take the road that runs parallel to the airstrip.

⊙ TOURS

Psycho Tours   Adventure
(Everyday Adventures; ☑8428-3904; www.psychotours.com; tours US$55-130) Witty, energetic naturalist Andy Pruter runs Psycho Tours, which offers high-adrenaline adventures in Cabo Matapalo. His signature tour is tree climbing (US$65 per person): scaling a 60m ficus tree, aptly named 'Cathedral.' Also popular – and definitely adrenaline-inducing – is waterfall rappelling (US$95)

down cascades ranging from 15m to 30m. The best one? The tree-climbing/waterfall combo tour (US$130).

Aventuras Tropicales   Kayaking
(☑2735-5195; www.aventurastropicales.com) Aventuras Tropicales is your specialist in water-based adventures. Its main thing is kayak tours, which might include mangrove exploration, fishing or bioluminescent paddling. Located 2km east on the road to Platanares.

🔒 SHOPPING

Jagua Arts & Crafts   Arts & Crafts
(☑2735-5267; ◷7am-3pm Mon-Sat) A terrific, well-stocked crafts shop, featuring local art and jewelry, a wonderful collection of colorful Boruca masks and black-and-ocher Guaitil pottery, as well as woven goods by the Emberá and Wounaan people. Kuna weavings technically belong across the border in Panama, but they make excellent gifts.

🍴 EATING

Cafetería Monka   Costa Rican $
(☑2735-5051; www.facebook.com/monkascafe; mains US$6-10; ◷6am-8pm; 🛜🍴) The best breakfast spot in town, Monka makes excellent coffee drinks and smoothies, as well as extensive breakfast platters, ranging from tropical French toast topped with fruits to tasty breakfast burritos. The rest of the day you can fill up on sandwiches, salads and inexpensive *casados* (set meals).

Hellen's Chill House   International $
(☑8359-5203; www.facebook.com/hellens chillhouse; mains US$5-10; ◷5am-8pm; 🛜🍴) Hellen's is supremely popular with pretty much everyone, for wake-me-up coffee drinks, filling breakfasts, excellent burgers (including veggie options) and more. The homemade bread means the sandwiches are hard to beat. Order one to go and you've got a perfect picnic for your hike or beach outing.

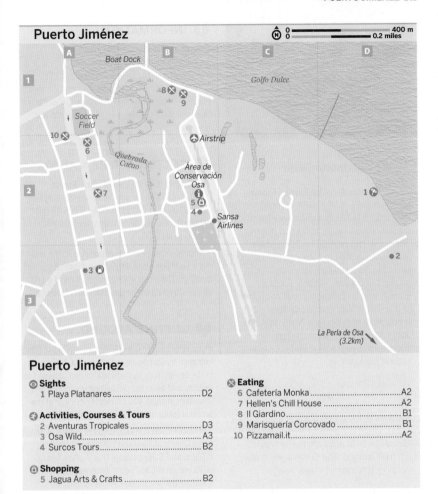

Puerto Jiménez

La Perla de Osa International $$

(☏8829-5865; mains US$10-17; ⊗11am-8pm; ⓟ🛜🅿) On the grounds of Iguana Lodge, this jungle-fringed restaurant-bar is locally (and justifiably) famous for its cocktails, accompanied by such delectable nibbles as pulled-pork tacos, grilled Asian-style tuna and shrimp plates. This is a sweet spot for a snack after a day on Playa Platanares.

Pizzamail.it Pizza $

(☏2735-5483; pizzas US$10-20; ⊗4-10:30pm; 🛜🅿) While this pizzeria's name sounds more like a website, all doubts will be cast aside when a server at Pizzamail.it brings out the pie: a thin-crust, wood-fired piece of Italy in the middle of the jungle. From its small patio diners can watch squawking macaws in the trees over the soccer pitch. Several pizza options are meat-free. *Bellissimo!*

Marisquería Corcovado Seafood $$

(☏2735-5659; mains US$8-20; ⊗11am-9pm) A spacious, covered, waterfront deck – ceiling fans spinning overhead – is the perfect place to feast on fresh grilled tuna, whole red snapper or tangy *ceviche* served with

🍴 Tour a Chocolate Farm

About 8km south of La Palma, **Finca Köbö** (☎8398-7604; www.fincakobo.com; 2hr tour US$32; 🅿) is a chocolate lover's dream come true (in fact *köbö* means 'dream' in Ngöbere). The 20-hectare *finca* is dedicated to the organic cultivation of fruits and vegetables and – the product of choice – cacao. Tours in English give a comprehensive overview of the life cycle of cacao plants and the production of chocolate (with degustation!). More than half of the territory is dedicated to protecting and reforesting natural ecosystems.

Cacao pod
JOSEPHJACOBS/GETTY IMAGES ©

patacones (fried green plantains cut in thin pieces). There is a selection of cocktails and craft beer, in addition to the typical fresh fruit *batidos*. The servers are quite charming, though not in any hurry!

Il Giardino   Italian $$

(☎2735-5129; www.ilgiardinoitalianrestaurant. com; meals US$11-16; ⊙7am-10pm) A sweet Italian restaurant with a romantic candlelit ambience. The rather long menu features pizza, pasta and other exquisite Italian dishes. Especially tantalizing are the house inventions such as Loreto pizza (with guacamole and mozzarella) and crab ravioli. Be forewarned that the Ranalli family subscribes to the 'slow food' movement: there's no rushing good cooking, especially when it's on Tico time.

ℹ INFORMATION

Área de Conservación Osa (ACOSA; Osa Conservation Area Headquarters; ☎2735-5036; Corcovado park fee per person per day US$15; ⊙8am-4pm Mon-Fri) provides information about Parque Nacional Corcovado, Isla del Caño, Parque Nacional Marino Ballena and Golfito parks and reserves.

ℹ GETTING THERE & AWAY

The **airstrip** is to the east of town. **Sansa** (☎2735-5890; www.flysansa.com), Skyway and Aerobell all have flights to/from San José (50 minutes); one-way flights are anywhere from US$80 to US$150.

Puerto Jiménez is now connected to the rest of the country by a beautifully paved road. If you're driving to Carate or Matapalo, you'll need a 4WD; be sure to fill up at the **gas station** in Jiménez.

ℹ GETTING AROUND

If you're driving to Cabo Matapalo or Carate (the entrance to Corcovado) you'll need a 4WD, even in the dry season, as there are several streams to ford, as well as a river. Assuming you don't have valuables in sight, you can leave your car at the *pulpería* (minimart; US$5 per night).

The *colectivo* (US$10) departs Puerto Jiménez for Carate at 6am and 1:30pm, returning at 8:30am and 3:30pm. Note that it often fills up on its return trip to Puerto Jiménez, especially during the dry season. Arrive at least 30 minutes ahead of time or you might find yourself stranded. Alternatively, catch a taxi from Puerto Jiménez (US$80).

Bahía Drake

One of Costa Rica's more isolated destinations, Bahía Drake (*drah*-kay) is a veritable Lost World, bordered by Parque Nacional Corcovado to the south. In the rainforest canopy, howler monkeys greet the rising sun with their haunting bellows, while pairs of macaws soar between the treetops, filling the air with their cacophonous squawking. Offshore in the bay, pods of migrating dolphins glide through turquoise waters near the beautiful Isla del Caño marine reserve.

One of the reasons Bahía Drake is brimming with wildlife is that it remains largely cut off from the rest of the country. Life is centered on the sedate village of **Agujitas**, the area's transportation hub, which attracts increasing numbers of backpackers and nature lovers with inexpensive digs and plenty of snorkeling, diving and wildlife-watching opportunities. The more remote corners of Bahía Drake are home to some of Costa Rica's best (and priciest) wilderness lodges.

◎ SIGHTS

Playa Cocalito   Beach
Just west of Punta Agujitas, a short detour off the main trail leads to the picturesque Playa Cocalito, a secluded cove perfect for sunning, swimming and body surfing.

Playa Caletas   Beach
A recommended spot for snorkeling, situated in front of Las Caletas Lodge.

Playa San Josecito   Beach
South of Río Claro, Playa San Josecito is one of the longest stretches of white-sand beach on this side of the Península de Osa. It is popular with swimmers, snorkelers and sunbathers, though you'll find it crowded at lunchtime since it's the favorite post-snorkeling picnic spot for tour companies coming back from Isla del Caño. Watch out for capuchin monkeys!

Playa Rincon de San Josecito   Beach
Just past Playa San Josecito is the less famous but more impressive beach, Playa Rincon de San Josecito. It's a vast stretch of sand – 1km or more – backed by palm trees swaying in the breeze. There's one lodge fronting the beach, and little else. Picturesque rocky outcrops punctuate either end, completing the idyllic scene. Fabulous spot to watch the sunset, with the added advantage that it's accessible by car.

 Cabo Matapalo

If you didn't know that it was here, you would hardly suspect that the jungle-obscured community of Matapalo existed. There isn't much to the southern tip of the Península de Osa save some surfing digs and homes at the entrance to the Golfo Dulce. Matapalo lies just 17km south of Puerto Jiménez, but this heavily forested and beach-fringed cape is a vastly different world. A network of trails traverses the foothills, uninhabited except for migrating wildlife from the Reserva Forestal Golfo Dulce. Along the coastline, miles of beaches are virtually empty, except for a few surfers in the know.

Cabo Matapalo is home to wilderness lodges that cater to travelers searching for seclusion and wildlife. Scarlet macaws, brown pelicans and herons are frequently sighted on the beaches, while all four species of Costa Rican monkey, several wildcat species, plus sloths, coatis, agoutis and anteaters roam the woods.

Surfers often head to Cabo Matapalo for its righteous breaks:

Playa Matapalo There are three excellent right point breaks off this beach, not far from Encanta La Vida. If there's a south or west swell, this is the best time to hit the waves.

Playa Pan Dulce Good for beginners and intermediate surfers, Pan Dulce gets some nice longboard waves most days. You can also go swimming here, but be careful of rip tides.

Playa Matapalo

 ### Sir Francis Drake Slept Here

During his 1579 circumnavigation of the globe in the *Golden Hind,* Sir Francis Drake visited this area and left his mark (or at least his name). History has it that he stopped on the nearby Isla del Caño, but locals speculate that he probably landed on the continent as well. A monument at Punta Agujitas, located on the grounds of the Drake Bay Wilderness Resort, states as much.

Portrait of Sir Francis Drake
GEORGIOSART/GETTY IMAGES ©

😊 ACTIVITIES

Agujitas–Corcovado Trail · Hiking
This 17km public trail follows the coastline from Agujitas to the San Pedrillo Ranger Station for the entire spectacular stretch, and it's excellent for wildlife-spotting (particularly early in the morning), beach-hopping and canoe tours with Río Claro Tours. Tour operators can drop you off by boat at a point of your choosing and you can walk back to Agujitas.

Río Agujitas · Kayaking
The idyllic Río Agujitas attracts a huge variety of birdlife and lots of reptiles. The river conveniently empties out into the bay, which is surrounded by hidden coves and sandy beaches ideal for exploring in a sea kayak, best done at high tide. Some accommodations have kayaks and canoes for rent; or else kayaks can be rented along Agujitas beach (around US$15 per hour).

🌏 TOURS

Pacheco Tours · Outdoors
(☑8906-2002; www.pachecotours.com) Very competent all-rounder organizing snorkeling tours to Isla del Caño, day trips to Corcovado, daylong tours combining jungle trekking with waterfall swimming (the Floating Tour, US$65), and whale-watching excursions.

Tracie the Bug Lady · Wildlife
(☑8701-7356, 8701-7462; www.thenighttour.com; tours per person US$45; ⊙7:30-10:15pm) Tracie the 'Bug Lady' has created quite a name for herself with this fascinating nighttime walk in the jungle that takes in bugs, reptiles and birds. Tracie is a walking encyclopedia on bug facts – one of her fields of research is the military use of insects! Her naturalist-photographer husband Gian also leads the night tours; reserve in advance.

Río Claro Tours · Canoeing
(☑8450-7198; www.lifeforlifehosteldrakebay.com; 2/4hr tours US$28/45) A 20-minute walk east from Playa San Josecito, a man called Ricardo (aka 'Clavito') lives by the Río Claro and runs hugely entertaining canoeing tours. The adventure starts with a rope-swing plunge in the river and continues to some waterfalls with refreshing plunge pools. Various tour operators can drop you off by boat, leaving you to walk back to Agujitas afterward.

Drake Bay Birdwatching · Birdwatching
(www.drakebaybirdwatching.com; tours from US$45) Let the experts help you spot that one special species. Tours range from morning and evening bird walks (US$45) to avian-focused boat trips, mangrove tours and Corcovado hikes.

Corcovado Canopy Tour · Canopy Tour
(www.corcovadocanopytour.com; tours US$73; ⊙7:30am, 10:30am, 1:30pm & 4pm) With 11 cables and two suspension bridges, this is the biggest and best canopy tour in the

area. Zip through primary and secondary rainforest at this excellent facility that borders the national park.

😣 EATING

Heladería Popis — Ice Cream $

(📱8529-6750; ice cream US$2-4; ⏱1-9pm) In hot and dusty Bahía Drake, there isn't a more refreshing midday treat than a vanilla milkshake from this open-air ice-cream parlor. It also does banana splits, coffee and ice cappuccinos, as well as tacos and other fast food.

Drake's Kitchen — Costa Rican $

(Casa el Tortugo; 📱6161-3193, 2775-1405; mains US$8-12; ⏱noon-9pm; 🅿) This small, friendly local restaurant is along the main dirt road from Agujitas to the airstrip. The capable and passionate chef prepares tasty *casados* featuring the catch of the day with fried plantains and avocado. Wash it down with a *fresco* (fresh juice) and soak up the mellow ambience.

Bahía Azul — Caribbean $$

(📱8360-5715; mains US$8-16; ⏱11am-8pm) It's not much to look at, but your mouth and stomach will thank you after a meal of fresh fish served Caribbean style. A selection of mojitos and margaritas washes it down nicely. The diverse menu also includes pizza, pasta and some mouthwatering desserts.

Soda Mar y Bosque — Costa Rican $$

(📱5002-7554, 2775-1639; mains US$5-16; ⏱6am-9pm; 🕾) This restaurant up the hill in Agujitas serves typical Tico cuisine on Tico time. The downstairs bakery is perfect for an early-morning breakfast or an afternoon snack. From the spacious terrace and upstairs seating area, it's possible to catch a cool breeze and spot pairs of scarlet macaws coasting over the sea.

Kalaluna Bistró — Latin American $$$

(📱6030-2615, 8355-8237; www.kalalunabistro.com; mains US$18-30; ⏱11am-8pm) Located at the Hotel Jinetes de Osa, Kalaluna is a gourmet affair that uses fresh local ingredients and highlights them with artistic flair.

Suspension bridge over the Río Agujitas

From left: Kingfisher; Bahía Drake (p142); Boat trip through the mangroves, Sierpe

Go for a filet of pork with coffee sauce, fish filet cooked in coconut milk, or the famous guacamole made with black olives and fresh basil. There's also homemade pasta, several *ceviche* options and cocktails.

🛈 GETTING THERE & AWAY

AIR

Departing from San José, Sansa, Skyway and Aerobell all have daily flights to the **Drake airstrip**, which is 6km north of Agujitas. Prices vary according to season and availability, though you can expect to pay around US$100 to US$140 one way.

Most lodges provide transportation to/from the airport or Sierpe, which involves a jeep or a boat or both, but advance reservation is necessary.

BOAT

An exhilarating boat ride from Sierpe is one of the true thrills of visiting Bahía Drake. Boats travel along the river through the rainforest and the mangrove estuary. Captains then pilot boats through tidal currents and surf the river mouth

into the ocean. All of the hotels offer boat transfers between Sierpe and Bahía Drake with prior arrangements. Most hotels in Drake have beach landings, so wear appropriate footwear.

If you have not made advance arrangements with your lodge for a pickup, two *colectivo* boats depart daily from Sierpe at 11:30am and 4:30pm, and from Bahía Drake back to Sierpe at 7:15am (US$15) and 2:30pm (US$20).

🛈 GETTING AROUND

Once you reach Bahía Drake, the only way to get around is on foot or by boat.

Sierpe

This sleepy village on the Río Sierpe is the gateway to Bahía Drake. If you've made a reservation with any of the jungle lodges further down the coast, you will be picked up here by boat. Otherwise, there is little reason to linger, except to catch a glimpse of a Unesco-recognized archae-ological artifact. You can see some of the pre-Columbian stone spheres in the main

CL-MEDIEN/SHUTTERSTOCK ©

square, or visit the excellent museum at Sitio Arqueológico Finca 6 nearby.

If you're not continuing on to Bahía Drake, this is your chance to take a boat trip through the mangroves with La Perla del Sur or **Kokopelli** (☏8897-1678; www.sierpemangrovetour.com; tour US$68).

◎ SIGHTS

Sitio Arqueológico
Finca 6   Archaeological Site
(☏2100-6000; finca6@museocostarica.go.cr; US$6; ⊗8am-4pm Tue-Sun) This site, 4km north of Sierpe, offers the best opportunity to view the mysterious pre-Columbian spheres created by the Diquís civilization between 300 BCE and 1500 CE, in their originally discovered locale, near culturally significant mounds 30m in diameter. In their original setting, one can really appreciate their size and perfect sphericity. The onsite museum screens an informative video on the spheres' significance and purpose, and there are other fascinating artifacts on display here, such as stone sculptures.

❶ INFORMATION

La Perla del Sur (☏2788-1082; info@perladelsur.net; ⊗6am-10pm; ☎) This info center and open-air restaurant next to the boat dock is the hub of Sierpe – arrange your long-term parking (US$6 per night), book a tour and use the free wi-fi before catching your boat to Drake.

❶ GETTING THERE & AWAY

Scheduled flights (Sansa, Skyway and Aerobell) and charters fly into Palmar Sur, 14km north of Sierpe. If you are heading to Bahía Drake, most upmarket lodges will arrange the boat transfer. Regularly scheduled *colectivo* (shared) boats depart Sierpe for Drake at 11:30am (US$15) and 4:30pm (US$20). If things go awry or if you're traveling independently, there's no shortage of water taxis milling about – be ready to negotiate.

Buses to Palmar Norte (US$0.70, 40 minutes) depart from in front of Pulpería Fenix six times a day between 5:30am and 6pm. A shared taxi to Palmar costs about US$10 per person.

COSTA BALLENA

In this Chapter

Costa Ballena at a Glance...

South of Quepos, this strecth of coastline evokes the feel of old Costa Rica – surf shacks and empty beaches, roadside ceviche vendors and space. Travelers can have their pick of deserted beaches and great surf spots. Known as the Costa Ballena, the beauteous length of coastline between Dominical and Ojochal focuses on three things: surfing (Dominical), whale-watching (Uvita) and gourmet cuisine (Ojochal). For the time being, the area largely retains an easygoing, unjaded allure despite the growing numbers discovering its appeal.

One Day on the Costa Ballena

Settle in and head for **Parque Nacional Marino Ballena** (p152), a national marine park with a sandbar shaped like a whale's tail at low tide. Swim, snorkel, frolic about and then grab a delicious late breakfast or lunch at **Sibu Cafe** (p158). In the afternoon, get your waterfall on at **Cascada Verde** (p156) or **Cataratas Nauyaca** (p154). Do dinner at **Sabor Español** (p158).

Two Days on the Costa Ballena

Get your dose of Dominical counter-culture. Start by fueling up on *gallo pinto* at **Cafe Mono Congo** (p162) before braving a **surf lesson** (p161) or a **yoga class** (p161). In the afternoon, check out the local rescues at **Alturas Wildlife Sanctuary** (p160) and then feast in foodie beach town Playa Ojochal. Top choices include **Exotica** (p162) and **Citrus** (p162).

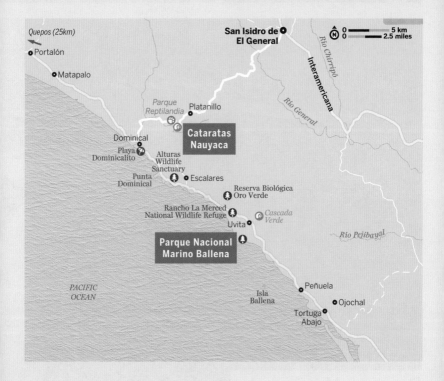

Quepos (25km)

Portalón

Matapalo

Parque Reptilandia

Platanillo

Dominical

Playa Dominicalito

Alturas Wildlife Sanctuary

Punta Dominical

Escalares

Cataratas Nauyaca

Reserva Biológica Oro Verde

Rancho La Merced National Wildlife Refuge

Uvita

Cascada Verde

Parque Nacional Marino Ballena

San Isidro de El General

Río Chirripó

Interamericana

Río General

Río Pejibayal

0 — 5 km
0 — 2.5 miles

PACIFIC OCEAN

Isla Ballena

Peñuela

Ojochal

Tortuga Abajo

Arriving on the Costa Ballena

This stretch of the coast is well served by frequent buses heading toward the border with Panama and the Península de Osa in the south, and Quepos and Jacó in the north. Private and shared shuttles also abound. If you're looking to stay up in the hills, you'll need a 4WD for the rough, steep roads.

Where to Stay

Dominical proper is home to the majority of the area's budget accommodations, while midrange and top-end places are popping up in and around town. There are some terrific, more remote lodges in Uvita and the jungle-clad hills above the coast, plus a few pristine proposal-worthy romantic spots.

Punta Uvita's 'Whale Tail'

Parque Nacional Marino Ballena

It's appropriate that this stunning national park is shaped like a whale's tail; from its beaches it's possible to spot the migrating giants as they swim near shore.

Great For...

☑ Don't Miss

In the fall and spring, migrating humpback whales can be viewed here.

Created in 1989, this marine park protects coral and rock reefs surrounding several offshore islands. Its name, Ballena, meaning 'whale' in Spanish, comes not only from the humpback whales that breed here but also because of the Punta Uvita 'Whale Tail,' a distinctive sandbar extending into a rocky reef that, at low tide, forms the shape of a whale's tail. The importance of this area cannot be overstated, especially since it protects migrating humpback and pilot whales, three types of dolphin and nesting sea turtles, not to mention colonies of seabirds and several terrestrial reptiles.

Activities

Swimming

The beaches at Parque Nacional Marino Ballena are a stunning combination of golden sand and polished rock. All of them

U. EISENLOHR/SHUTTERSTOCK ©

estuaries and rocky headlands. In the early morning, before other visitors arrive, you'll have the best opportunity for good birdwatching.

The park is home to, or frequently visited by, a number of wildlife species, including dolphins and a variety of lizards. The offshore islands are important nesting sites for frigate birds, brown boobies and brown pelicans and, from May to November (peaking in September and October) olive ridley and hawksbill turtles bury their eggs in the sand nightly. But the star attractions are the pods of humpback whales that pass through the national park from July to November and December to April, as well as occasional pilot whales.

are virtually deserted and many spots are perfect for peaceful swimming and sunbathing. Check with the ranger for current conditions and the safest spots to swim.

Diving & Snorkeling

The coral reefs around the offshore islands are a good place to experience the park's underwater world, unlike the coral reefs near the shore that were heavily damaged by sediment runoff from the construction of the coastal highway. To delve into the underwater beauty of the park, go on a diving or snorkeling trip with local providers like Mad About Diving (p157).

Wildlife-Watching

Heading southeast from Punta Uvita, the park includes mangrove swamps,

Information

There are four entrances to the park, the most commonly used being the one by the **ranger station** (☏2743-8141; Calle Playa Bahía) in Playa Uvita (follow the main road through Uvita). Park entrances are open from 7am to 4pm.

Cataratas Nauyaca

DUARTE DELLAROLE/SHUTTERSTOCK ©

Cataratas Nauyaca

Reached by a 12km hike or horseback-ride, secluded Nauyaca waterfalls are spectacular, surrounded by a protected reserve of primary and secondary forest.

Great For...

☑ Don't Miss

Cooling off in the lower pool and swimming right up to the refreshing cascade.

Home to the central Pacific coast's prettiest waterfalls, this land is owned and operated by a Costa Rican family who offer self-guided or guided access for a fun morning or afternoon of adventure. These 61m-high twin cascades tumble through a quiet and protected reserve with plenty of wildlife-spotting opportunities. Visitors can also swim in the inviting natural water at the lower falls. The area can only be reached by hiking or, from the entrance, the family runs horseback-riding tours and tours by pickup truck to the falls.

Activities

Walking

The 12km round-trip hike to Cataratas Nauyaca is a rewarding one, with a big pay off at the end – two dreamy cascading

Hiking to Cataratas Nauyaca

CAMPPHOTO/GETTY IMAGES ©

waterfall and a small cave on the opposite edge of the pool. Nonconfident swimmers shouldn't stray too far from the edges as the flow from the falls can be strong. There is usually a lifeguard at the side of the pool and there are changing facilities and toilets near the falls. Don't forget your sunscreen, towel and swimming gear.

Horseback Riding

One preferred option to get to Cataratas Nauyaca is via mule, carrying you 8km (round trip) through the protected reserve. Horse tours are only available at 8am. Tours include lunch and a snack. Book in advance.

Information

The Dominical Information Center (p163) runs guided tours from town to the waterfalls from US$70 per person, including lunch and departing daily at 8am. Those with wheels can drive up and pay at the office (entry US$9).

beauties clasped by jungle. The trail's first 2km section is a downhill dirt road (4WD drivers can skip this bit and cruise to a parking lot at the bottom of the hill), then it's a moderate 4km uphill leg-stretching trek to the falls. There are rest benches along the wide trail and a first toilet break around 2km from the falls, with resident peacocks and monkeys nearby. Wear sneakers or hiking shoes; the path is well marked but uneven and muddy in places, especially during or just after the rainy season.

Swimming

Cool off with a dip in the natural freshwater pool at Cataratas Nauyaca. The waterfall tumbles into the bowl-shaped deep plunge basin. It's possible to swim right up to the

Uvita

Just 17km south of Dominical, this growing village consists of some dirt roads lined with farms, guesthouses and shops, a cluster of strip malls by the main Costanera Sur (Ruta 34) entrance, and a scattering of hotels in the jungle-covered hills above. Uvita has retained its gentle pace of life during the low season, but otherwise has become quite a popular and buzzing travel destination thanks to its increasingly sought-after main attraction, Parque Nacional Marino Ballena. The marine reserve has become famous for its migrating pods of humpback whales and its virtually abandoned wilderness beaches, but there are also good waterfalls nearby.

Two of the country's most important tourist events happen yearly in Uvita: a popular **Whale and Dolphin Festival** (☑8729-3624; www.festivaldeballenasydelfines.com; ⊘Sep-Oct) celebrating the arrival of the humpbacks, and the country's biggest hippie gathering, the **Envision Festival** (www.envisionfestival.com; 4-day admission from US$389; ⊘late Feb), Costa Rica's answer to Burning Man at the beach.

◉ SIGHTS

Cascada Verde   Waterfall
(Calle Bejuco; US$2; ⊘8am-4pm; P) Around 2.5km inland and uphill (toward Cascada Verde hostel), this waterfall plunges into an inviting deep pool, perfect for a refreshing dip. Visitors may see daredevils lie down at the top and slide some 5m down the cascade. This isn't recommended; the official path to the top is in disrepair and fenced off (rule breakers use the obvious hole in the fence).

Farmers Market   Market
(☑8680-9752; ⊘8am-noon Sat) Held a short distance from the main entrance to Uvita, along the unpaved road, this sweet little farmers market on Saturdays is a good place to mingle with locals and longtime expats, and purchase psychedelic jewelry, locally grown fruit and vegetables, honey and home-cooked foods.

From left: Black-mandibled toucan; Mangroves (p153), Parque Nacional Marino Ballena; *Ceviche* and *patacones*

Rancho La Merced National Wildlife Refuge
Nature Reserve

(☑8861-5147, 2743-8032; www.rancholamerced. com; Ruta Nacional 34; horseback-riding tours US$50, sunset rides US$57, nature walks from US$40; ◷7am-4pm) Opposite the turnoff to Oro Verde, a few kilometers before Uvita, is this 506-hectare national wildlife refuge (and former cattle ranch), with primary and secondary forests and mangroves lining the Río Morete. Here you can go on guided nature hikes and birdwatching walks, horseback-ride to Punta Uvita or opt for the 'cowboy experience', which involves cattle roping, herding cows and riding around with real cowboys.

Reserva Biológica Oro Verde
Nature Reserve

(☑2743-8072, 8843-8833; www.uvita.info/en/ activity/230201; US$40; ◷tours 6:30am) A few kilometers before Uvita is a signed turnoff to the left. A rough dirt road (4WD only) leads 3.5km up the hill to this private reserve on the farm of the Duarte family, who have lived in the area for more than three decades. Two-thirds of the 155-hectare property is rainforest, where visitors can do a two- to three-hour guided birdwatching walk with a bilingual naturalist guide with birding equipment, followed by a Costa Rican breakfast. Reserve via the Uvita Information Center (p159).

✪ ACTIVITIES

Mad About Diving
Diving

(☑2743-8019; www.madaboutdivingcr.com; Calle Playa Bahía; 2-tank dives from US$130) Friendly, safe and professional diving operator, offering dives in the Parque Nacional Marino Ballena and full-day scuba excursions to Isla del Caño in Bahía Drake. The office operates irregular hours; book via the website or phone.

Rancho DiAndrew
Outdoors

(☑8475-1287; www.facebook.com/rancho. diandrew; Calle Río Morete; tours from US$69) Fun tour operator specializing in surf retreats and nature tours, the most popular

Eco Farmers Market

Self-caterers can stock up on local organic groceries and goodies at **Eco Feria Dominical** (Eco Farmers Market; ✆8935-3037; www.facebook.com/ecoferiadominical; Main St; ⏰8:30am-2:30pm Fri) Vendors range from chocolatiers, bakers and nut roasters to dairy producers and craft kombucha stalls. However, it's more than a food market. There's usually music, dancing and activities like yoga. The general ethos of the fair is to spread the message about living a more sustainable lifestyle. Next to the soccer pitch.

Fabrics for sale, Dominical
BLAKE BURTON/GETTY IMAGES ©

of which involves navigating a hidden gorge, plunging off a cliff and feasting on barbecue by the river. The *rancho* is perched in a patch of jungle near the town of San Josecito, and features tented cabins (summer only; single/double per night from US$75/85). Sweet views.

Uvita 360　　　　　　　Adventure
(✆8586-8745; surfing, kayaking & snorkeling from US$65, waterfalls & Manuel Antonio from US$95) Set up by friendly local Alvaro 'Tito' Azofeifa, this professional tour company will arrange all the fine details for exploring the major sights in the area. Visit Nauyaca Waterfalls and Parque Nacional Manuel Antonio, see the mangroves by kayak, snorkel the 'whale's tail' at Parque Nacional Marino Ballena or arrange surf lessons.

Bahía Aventuras　　　　　Adventure
(✆2743-8362, 8846-6576; www.bahiaaventuras.com; near Calle Bahía Ballena; adult/child snorkeling Marino Ballena from US$75/35, hiking Corcovado US$145/90, snorkeling Isla del Caño US$145/90; ⏰6:30am-5:30pm) Experienced tour operator in Uvita, running the gamut of tours, including a combo of snorkeling and whale-watching in Parque Nacional Marino Ballena, snorkeling around Isla del Caño in Bahía Drake, and hiking in Costa Ballena and Corcovado. The office is on the road parallel and north of Calle Bahía Ballena.

EATING

Sibu Cafe　　　　　　　　Cafe $
(✆2743-8674; Ruta Nacional 34; coffee US$2-5, mains from US$6; ⏰7am-9pm Mon-Sat, 9am-9pm Sun; ❄🛜🅿) Serving the best coffee for miles around, this little cafe hides in an Uvita strip mall. Latte art, eggs Benedict, chunky brownies and homemade lemon pie are all on the menu. Want something more substantial? The hardworking couple here also makes excellent salads, thin-and-crispy pizza, plus 10 hormone- and additive-free cuts of steak from a local farm in San Carlos. The red snapper in avocado sauce is also rather good. Wash it down with a house craft beer or smoothie.

Sabor Español　　　　　Spanish $$
(✆8367-7930, 8768-9160; Calle Esmo; tapas from US$7, mains US$13-35; ⏰6-9:30pm Tue-Sun; 🛜) After a successful run in Monteverde, charming Spanish couple Heri and Montse realized that they wanted to live by the ocean – to Uvita's good fortune. Thus, their sublime gazpacho, paella, *tortilla española* (Spanish omelet) and other Spanish specialties can now be savored with sangria and imported wine in a lovely *rancho* setting. Don't expect fast food; this is a leisurely experience.

Reservations advised. It's at the end of a dirt road near the beach in Playa Uvita.

El Ancla
Seafood $$

(☎2101-2489; https://el-ancla-seafood.business.
site; Ruta Nacional 34; ceviche from US$8, mains
from US$13; ⊙11am-9pm; Ⓟ🛜) Off the main
road into Uvita is this container-cum-sea-
food restaurant, with a simple deck out
front with tables and chairs. It serves
delectable *ceviche* made with high-quality
white marlin, and satisfying fishy mains
from tacos and mixed rice with shrimp to
pastas with mussels, shrimp and octopus.
Wash it down with a smoothie, cocktail or
craft beer.

Bar y Restaurante Los Laureles
Costa Rican $

(☎2743-8008; mains US$7-13; ⊙11am-8:30pm
Mon-Sat) Adorable casual family-run
restaurant serving mainly Costa Rican and
Tex-Mex cuisine, with innovative favorites
such as avocado hummus and nacho
patacones (fried green plantains cut in thin
pieces), and staples like chicken wings,
chili fries and quesadillas. The margaritas
are great, the service is top-notch and the
open-air setting, amid tropical foliage, is
super *tranquilo*.

🍷 DRINKING & NIGHTLIFE

Mosaic
Wine Bar

(☎2215-0068; www.mosaiccr.com; Calle Uvita;
⊙10am-10pm) A pleasant open-plan wine bar
serving a long list of imported wines from
South America and Europe. You can also
dabble in potent craft drinks like Malfy Gin
with pink grapefruit and blood orange, or
Cava sangria with brandy, triple sec, orange
juice and lemon. Tuck into good sushi and
Mediterranean-style tapas while you sip.
Live music takes place on Thursday nights.

ℹ️ INFORMATION

Uvita Information Center (☎2743-8072;
www.uvita.info; Ruta Nacional 34; ⊙9am-1pm &
2-6pm Mon-Sat) is a fine place to book tours and
transportation.

Overnight at the Waterfall

The bilingual, experienced guides of
Pacific Journeys (☎8325-9818, 2266-
1717; www.pacificjourneyscr.com; Las Tum-
bas; overnight waterfall tour per person from
US$159, with rappelling US$229, day trek per
person US$89) lead people to the top of
the 183m-high Diamante Falls – one of
the highest, most beautiful cascades
in the country – by scaling hundreds
of stairs up through a family-owned
private reserve amid lush primary forest
and past a botanical garden.

It takes about three hours and is
moderately difficult. Upon arrival at an
open-air cavern behind the waterfall,
the group unpacks and each selects
a mat to sleep on, with three massive
waterfalls visible from the campsite.

Candles and solar-powered lights
illuminate the paths and the kind and
knowledgeable guides prepare yummy
vegetarian meals in an open-air kitchen.
The place is decidedly rustic; still, it
features flush toilets and picnic benches
and is protected from the elements.
Rappelling excursions and hikes to
nearby swimming holes and cliff-jump-
ing sites get the adrenaline pumping
to the point few will mind the cold,
waterfall-fed showers.

Diamante Falls
PACIFIC JOURNEYS ©

ℹ️ GETTING THERE & AWAY

Most buses depart from the sheltered bus stops
on the Costanera in the main village. Private
shuttle companies – Grayline, Easy Ride and

Monkey Ride – offer pricier transfers from Uvita to Dominical, San José, Quepos, Jacó, Puerto Jiménez and other popular destinations. It's advantageous to have your own wheels around here.

Dominical

This was once a lazy little town that drew a motley crew of surfers, backpackers and affable do-nothings, a place where a traveler could wander the dusty roads, surfboard tucked under an arm, balancing the day's activities between wave riding and hammock hang time.

Those days aren't entirely gone, but in 2015 a bunch of paving stones laid along the beach became the town's first real road. An increasing population of expats and gringos have hunkered down here and some more sophisticated (though decidedly eco-friendly) businesses have begun to sprout. The place gets busiest in high season, particularly February, around Uvita's hippie festival Envision (p156). Rainier months remain as languidly 'old Costa Rica' as ever.

◉ SIGHTS

Alturas Wildlife Sanctuary
Nature Reserve

(☑2200-5440; www.alturaswildlifesanctuary.org; Calle San Martin, off Ruta 34; 1-1½hr tours min donation adult/child under 12yr US$25/15, tour & lunch combo adult/child US$35/22; ☺tours 9am, 11am, 1pm & 3pm Tue-Sun) Around 1.5km east and uphill from Dominical, this wildlife sanctuary takes in injured and orphaned animals as well as illegal pets. Its mission is to rehabilitate and reintroduce to the wild those that can be, and look after those that cannot. It has an 85% success rate. During the tour you meet its residents: a macaw missing an eye, three types of monkey, Bubba the famous coati, a toucan, sloths and more. Entertaining, educational and a terrific cause. Reserve a tour ahead of time.

Parque Reptilandia
Zoo

(☑8308-8855, 2787-0343; www.crreptiles.com; Ruta Nacional 243; adult/child US$12/6; ☺9am-4:30pm; 🅿🚻) Near the entrance to Nauyaca Waterfalls, this weathered reptile park sits on an acre of land and is a mini–Jurassic

Deadly fer-de-lance viper

DAVID HAVEL/SHUTTERSTOCK ©

Park. It's got everything from crocodiles to turtles and snakes to poison-dart frogs in glass-fronted terrariums. Our favorite is the viper section, where you can see Costa Rica's deadliest creatures, such as the fer-de-lance, pit viper and black-headed bushmaster. Friday is feeding day, when live mice are introduced into snake enclosures, which spectators may or may not love.

Don't miss Langka the Komodo dragon, Jumbo the enormous tortoise and Shakira the anaconda.

ACTIVITIES

Airborne Arts   Circus

(☑8302-4241, 8320-0929; 2hr group trapeze session per person from US$75, shared r incl meals from US$113) Ever felt like learning the flying trapeze in the middle of the Costa Rican countryside, with a view of a 100m waterfall? Do it with world-renowned acrobat couple Jonathon Conant and Christine Van Loo, who have constructed a circus-themed paradise south of the remote town of Las Tumbas. It's the perfect escape for those looking to learn how to fly. Bookings required.

Danyasa Yoga Arts School   Yoga

(☑2787-0229; www.danyasa.com; Main St; classes from US$10; ⊙shop 9:30am-8pm) This lovely Dominical yoga studio offers a variety of classes for all levels, including unique dance-yoga-flow hybrid styles and even ecstatic moon dance. The studio also serves as a center for retreats.

Alegria Soul Spa   Spa

(☑2787-0210; www.alegriasoulspa.com; Main St; massages from US$30; ⊙10am-6pm) Unwind after a surf session at this good-value day spa on the main street. Choose from relaxing Swedish-style, herbal, bamboo, reflexology, stone and lymphatic drainage massages.

Pineapple Tours   Kayaking

(☑8873-3283, 8362-7655; www.pineapple kayaktours.com; mangrove kayak tour US$75, Río Barú paddleboarding US$60, snorkeling US$80,

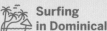 **Surfing in Dominical**

Dominical owes its fame to its seriously sick point and beach breaks, though surf conditions are variable. On smaller days at the right tide, it's possible to learn surfing here in the white-water, but beware of getting in too deep, as currents are strong and when swells are big you can really get trashed if you don't know what you're doing. Some beginners and surf schools head for nearby Playa Dominicalito, which is always tamer. Recommended surf schools:

Costa Rica Surf Camp (☑8812-3625, 2787-0393; www.crsurfschool.com; opposite Playa Dominical behind Hotel DiuWak; all-incl packages per week US$1717, group surf lessons from US$60, 2hr board hire US$6) Excellent school offering a two-to-one student-teacher ratio.

Sunset Surf (☑8917-3143; www.sunset-surfdominical.com; all-incl packages per week from US$1200; ⊙8am-4:30pm) Various packages including women-only groups (and all students get to use its organic sunblock).

Dominical Surf Adventures (☑2787-0431; www.dominicalsurfadventures.com; private surf lesson incl 2hr board rental US$70; ⊙8am-5pm Mon-Sat, 9am-3pm Sun) Super-friendly folks offering various surf lessons and packages.

Surfer, Dominical
JEN EDNEY/GETTY IMAGES ©

2hr surf rental US$5) With friendly guides, Pineapple Tours runs kayaking and stand-up paddleboarding (SUP) trips to local

Dining in Ojochal

This laid-back, spread-out village is the Costa Ballena's culinary epicenter, with several surprisingly good eateries and a multicultural expat population. Meals here are done with elegance and style, and foodies will be in their element trying the high standard of dishes. A car is advisable for restaurant-hopping.

Citrus (☏2786-5175; www.facebook.com/citrusojochal; Calle Tortuga Abajo; mains US$8-27; ☺8am-9pm Mon-Sat; 🅿❄🛜) Mediterranean bistro with gorgeous furnishings and unstuffy gourmet plates.

Exotica (☏2786-5050; Calle Tortuga Abajo; mains US$11-46; ☺5-9pm Mon-Sat) Has a sultry, jungle ambiance and nouveau-French dishes emphasizing a breadth of ingredients brought together in masterful combinations.

Azul (☏2786-5543; Calle Perezoso; mains US$10-28; ☺5-10pm; 🛜🚗) Chic restaurant inside El Castillo boutique hotel, with dreamy views of the Pacific and salivatingly prepared dishes like goat-cheese ravioli and expertly seared steak.

Pancito Cafe (☏8729-4115, 2786-5774; cnr Calles Tortuga Abajo & Soluna; pastries from US$3; ☺7am-5pm Mon-Sat) Passing through? Stop and grab a melt-in-the-mouth cocoa-dusted truffle and a divine spicy chicken empanada.

L'Epicerie Super & Deli (☏4702-7430; Calle Tortuga Abajo; ☺7am-7pm Mon-Sat, 8am-6pm Sun) Stop by for artisanal goods from the local area and abroad.

Chicken empanadas
BRENT HOFACKER/ALAMY STOCK PHOTO ©

caves, rivers and mangrove forests. It also does snorkeling tours to the 'whale's tail' in Parque Nacional Marino Ballena, and rents SUP gear, surfboards, kayaks, beach chairs and umbrellas. Find its office next to the police station in Dominical.

✖ EATING

Cafe Mono Congo
Cafe $

(www.cafemonocongo.com; mains US$4-9; ☺7am-5pm; 🛜🚗) Perch on a swing at the bar or at a riverside table to enjoy an espresso. This open-air cafe also dishes up tasty, simple breakfasts like *gallo pinto* (rice and beans) and *huevos rancheros* (Mexican eggs) and (largely veggie) lunches, using organic local produce. Find it at the junction of the road into town and the main drag.

Mama Toucan's
Health Food $

(☏8433-4235; www.mamatoucans.com; pizzas from US$6; ☺9:30am-6:30pm; 🚗) Selling gourmet, organic and vegan products and those free of 'artificial flavors, chemicals and bad vibes,' this super health-food store is ideal for self-catering. While groceries are a bit pricey, the 12in deli pizzas are a steal. Plus, grab a coconut for less than a dollar – and they'll cut it open and put a straw in it for you.

The delicatessen in-store also sells fresh salads and sourdough paninis. There's an ATM outside.

Phat Noodle
Thai $

(☏2787-0017; www.phatnoodlecostarica.com; mains US$9-11; ☺4:30-9pm Tue-Sun, 5-9pm Mon; 🚗) Set in a pretty garden, this Thai restaurant and bar serves up tasty piping-hot bowls of rice and noodles, along with spicy margaritas, all from inside a converted school bus.

Skilfully prepared menu items range from shrimp and crab rangoon to Thai coconut *ceviche* to green curry, and there are a great many vegan and gluten-free options as well.

Del Mar Taco Shop
Tacos $

(☑8428-9050; tacos US$4; ⊙11:30am-9pm)
On the approach to the beach this casual
surfer hangout serves some of the area's
best tacos (fresh fish, shrimp, beef, chicken
or veggie). The chips are mixed with
handmade nachos – pair them with the
superb guacamole. There's a variety of hot
sauces to slather over your order. On Taco
Tuesday (April to November) all tacos cost
just US$2.

Dominical Sushi
Sushi $$

(☑8826-7946; sushi rolls from US$7; ⊙1-10pm
Sun-Thu, 1-5pm Fri, 5-10pm Sat) Set back from
the main road through town, in an open-air
setting overlooking the Río Barú, this sushi
place takes advantage of the fresh tuna
and other fish caught daily in Dominical.
We're big fans of its ahi poke salad and tuna
sashimi, plus the *unagi* and rainbow rolls.
The menu is complemented by a selection
of Japanese beers and sake.

El Pescado Loco
Seafood $

(☑8303-9042; www.facebook.com/elpescad-
oloco.dominical; tacos US$7, fish & chips US$8;
⊙11:30am-8pm Mon-Sat) This little open-air
shack has only a handful of menu items,
but it knows what it's doing when it comes
to fish tacos with spicy mango salsa and
chunky guacamole. The onion rings and
fish and chips are tasty too. Only one
quibble: how about real cutlery instead of
disposable?

🍷 DRINKING & NIGHTLIFE

Fuego Brew Co   Craft Beer, Coffee
(☑8992-9559; www.fuegobrew.com; Main St;
⊙breakfast from 7am, bar 11:30am-10:30pm)

In the center of Dominical, with a doorway
decorated with two mini-flamethrowers,
this sleek establishment with a coffee shop,
glistening hardwood bar and restaurant is
the town's first craft brewery and coffee
roastery. Here you can sip *mango pale or
wina guanabana ale* all day long. Bartend-
ers are super nice and the meals (mains
US$11 to US$28) and java are tasty as!

Downstairs is the seven-barrel brewing
system and coffee roaster with take-out
service counter. Happy hour runs 4:30pm
to 5:30pm. There are plenty of cocktails
and a dozen imported wines to try too.

ⓘ INFORMATION

Dominical Information Center (☑2787-0454;
www.dominicalinformation.com; ⊙9:30am-5pm)
is on the main strip, near the entrance to Domin-
ical. This info center and tour provider has useful
maps of town and bus timetables for the entire
region. Bus-ticket, shuttle and tour booking
services available.

ⓘ GETTING THERE & AWAY

Gray Line, Easy Ride and Monkey Ride offer
private and shared shuttle services to popular
destinations such as Jacó, San José, Monteverde,
Tamarindo and Sierpe; Easy Ride has direct
services to Granada, Nicaragua.

Buses pick up and drop off passengers along
the main road in Dominical. Taxis to Uvita cost
US$10 to US$25, while the ride to Quepos costs
around US$60 and to Manuel Antonio it's around
US$70.

MANUEL ANTONIO

Manuel Antonio at a Glance...

The air in this small tropical outcrop of land, jutting into the Pacific, is heavy with humidity, scented with thick vegetation and filled with the calls of birds and monkeys. The reason to come here is Parque Nacional Manuel Antonio, one of the most picturesque bits of tropical coast in Costa Rica. If you get bored of cooing at the baby monkeys scurrying in the canopy and scanning for birds and sloths, the turquoise waves and perfect sand provide endless entertainment. Despite the area's overdevelopment, the rainforested hills and blissful beaches make the park a stunning destination worthy of the tourist hype.

One Day in Manuel Antonio

Head to **Parque Nacional Manuel Antonio** (p168) and hike the well-trodden trails and lounge on the picture-perfect beaches. Keep a lookout for monkeys, sloths and other **wildlife** (p172). At the end of the day, head to **Ronny's Place** (p183) for cocktails and splendid sunset views.

Two Days in Manuel Antonio

Spend your second day taking an adventure tour, whether that's a paddle-boarding outing with **Paddle 9** (p174), a guided coastal hike with **Unique Tours** (p174) or a canopy tour with **Amigos del Río** (p180). In the evening, head to Quepos for a scrumptious seafood dinner at **Gabriella's** (p178).

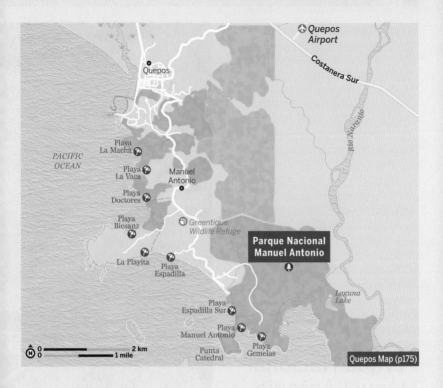

Quepos Airport

Costanera Sur

Quepos

Río Naranjo

PACIFIC OCEAN

Playa La Macha

Playa La Vaca

Manuel Antonio

Playa Doctores

Playa Biesanz

Greentique Wildlife Refuge

Parque Nacional Manuel Antonio

La Playita

Playa Espadilla

Laguna Lake

Playa Espadilla Sur

Playa Manuel Antonio

Punta Catedral

Playa Gemelas

0 — 2 km
0 — 1 mile

Quepos Map (p175)

Arriving in Manuel Antonio

The area is served by frequent flights and buses, and the roads are good (though the one leading from Quepos to Parque Nacional Manuel Antonio is winding, steep and narrow). Both Skyway (p179) and Sansa (p179) service Quepos, with prices varying according to season and availability. The airport is 5km out of town, and taxis make the trip for around US$10.

Where to Stay

The village of Manuel Antonio is the closest base for exploring the national park, though the selection of sleeping options is more varied in Quepos or on the Quepos–Manuel Antonio stretch of road. The Quepos–Manuel Antonio road is skewed toward high-end hotels, but plenty of noteworthy midrange and budget options are hidden along the way. Staying in Quepos offers a cheaper alternative to the sky-high prices at many lodges on the road to Manuel Antonio.

Squirrel monkey

Parque Nacional Manuel Antonio

A place of swaying palms and playful monkeys, sparkling blue water and a riot of tropical birds, Parque Nacional Manuel Antonio is the country's smallest (19.83 sq km) and most popular national parks.

Great For...

ⓘ Need to Know

☏2777-8551; US$16; ⊙7am-3:30pm Tue-Sun

★ **Top Tip**

Get here early (7am) and head for the park's furthest reaches to avoid the crowds.

Parque Nacional Manuel Antonio is a truly lovely place. The clearly marked trail system winds through rainforest-backed white-sand beaches and rocky headlands; the wildlife (iguanas, sloths, monkeys) is plentiful; and the views across the bay to the pristine outer islands are gorgeous.

The downside? The crowds. Visitors are confined to around 6.8 sq km of the park (the rest is set aside for ranger patrols battling poaching) and the place gets packed when mid-morning tour buses roll in.

Beaches

There are several beautiful beaches, two of which are just outside the park entrance: La Playita (p180) and the popular **Playa Espadilla**. Inside the park, **Playa Espadilla Sur** has gorgeous 'pinch-me' scenes of white sand, backed by lush tropical forest.

There are bathrooms, showers and drinking water at Playa Espadilla Sur but, as tempted as you are, swimming here can be dangerous – be aware of currents. A better option for swimming is **Playa Manuel Antonio**. With turquoise waters, this lovely forest-backed beach fronts a deep bay, and is sheltered by the Punta Catedral on the west side and a promontory on the east. Families love to watch the monkeys playing in the trees beyond the sand. Little **Playa Gemelas** is the beach to visit early in the morning: clasped by volcanic rock and jungle, it feels almost Jurassic, like it's been forgotten in time. Watch your footing as you wander, as iguanas like to bask in the sun here. Whichever beach you choose, they're all equally pristine and provide sunbathing opportunities.

Playa Espadilla

Rangers indefinitely closed Playa Puerto Escondido to visitors in 2017, but its beauty can still be admired from a lookout at the end of the short 350m **Puerto Escondido trail**.

Hiking

Parque Nacional Manuel Antonio has an official road, **Sendero El Perezoso**, which is paved and wheelchair-accessible and connects the entrance to the network of short trails. Most of them are easy; some of them are more strenuous with lots of steps along a secure boardwalk. All are well marked and heavily traversed, though there are some quiet corners near the ends of the trails. Off-trail hiking is not permitted.

Sendero Playa Gemelas is a short quarter-mile walk connecting to Sendero Los Congos and Sendero El Mirador, leading to a glorious less-trafficked and almost secret tiny beach. Come here early and you'll likely have the place to yourself.

For a moderate up-and-down trail, try **Sendero Punta Catedral**, which first goes over a natural bridge in between Playa Manuel Antonio and Playa Espadilla Sur, then into dense vegetation via concrete/gravel steps and low wooden walkways. There are a few stops at viewpoint platforms with glorious scenes of the Pacific and the offshore islands where frigate birds nest.

A primary forest and step-filled 1.3km trail that will get your heart racing is **Sendero El Mirador**. Heading inland and into the jungle from the east side of Playa Manuel Antonio, you take a moderate climb to a wooden lookout platform on a bluff overlooking Puerto Escondido and Punta Serrucho beyond. The vista is simply stunning. Humpback whales can occasionally be spotted in these waters. Punta Serrucho (or Saw Point), was so named due to its serrated edge, created due to the fact it sits right on a tectonic fault line.

Kayaking

Sea kayaking around the park's mangroves is a good way to glimpse the wildlife that this habitat supports. Long-standing operator Iguana Tours (p174) runs responsible kayaking trips.

> ☑ **Don't Miss**
>
> The pre-Columbian turtle trap, built out of rocks, at the western end of Playa Manuel Antonio.

SIMON DANNHAUER/SHUTTERSTOCK ©

> ✕ **Take a Break**
>
> Discuss animal sightings over fancy coffee drinks on the patio of Café Milagro (p181).

Brown pelican, Parque Nacional Manuel Antonio

Wildlife-Watching

Capuchin monkeys scurry across idyllic beaches, pelicans dive-bomb clear waters and sloths spy on trail hikers – the tiny Parque Nacional Manuel Antonio is packed with life.

Great For...

☑ Don't Miss

Howlers crossing the monkey bridges erected along the road between Quepos and Manuel Antonio.

Mammals

White-faced capuchins are very used to people, and normally troops feed and interact within a short distance of visitors; they can be encountered anywhere along the main access road and around Playa Manuel Antonio. The capuchins are the worst for snatching bags, so watch your stuff.

You'll probably also hear mantled howler monkeys soon after sunrise. Like capuchins, they can be seen anywhere inside the park and even along the road to Quepos – watch for them crossing the monkey bridges that were erected by local conservation groups.

Coatis can be seen darting across various paths and can get aggressive on the beach if you're eating. Three-toed and two-toed sloths are also common in the

CHRISTOPHER MILLIGAN/ALAMY STOCK PHOTO ©

ℹ Need to Know

A wildlife guide costs US$15 to US$25 per person for a two-hour tour. Ask to see the guide's ICT license before hiring.

✕ Take a Break

Grab lunch and enjoy the incredible ocean views at Agua Azul (p182).

★ Top Tip

Lenny Montenegro (☏8875-0437; 2hr group/private tour per person from US$25/40) is a recommended wildlife and bird guide.

as well as humpback whales passing by on their regular migration routes. Other possibilities include orcas (killer whales), false killers and rough-toothed dolphins.

Reptiles

Big lizards are also a feature at Manuel Antonio – it's hard to miss the large ctenosaurs and green iguanas that bask along the beach at Playa Manuel Antonio and in the vegetation behind Playa Espadilla Sur. To spot the well-camouflaged basilisk, listen for the rustle of leaves along the edges of trails, especially near the lagoon.

park. Guides are helpful for spotting sloths, as they tend not to move much.

The movements of the park's star and Central America's rarest primate, the Central American squirrel monkey, are less predictable. These adorable monkeys are more retiring than capuchins, and though they are occasionally seen near the park entrance in the early morning, they usually melt into the forest well before opening time. With luck, a troop could be encountered during a morning's walk, and they often reappear in beachside trees and on the fringes of Manuel Antonio village in the early evening.

Marine Animals

Offshore, keep your eyes peeled for pan-tropical spotted and bottlenose dolphins,

Birds

Manuel Antonio is not usually on the serious birdwatchers' trail of Costa Rica, though the list of birds here is respectable, and includes the blue-gray and palm tanager, great-tailed grackle, bananaquit, blue dacnis and at least 15 species of hummingbird. Regional endemics to look out for include the fiery-billed aracari, black-hooded antshrike, Baird's trogon, black-bellied whistling duck, yellow-crowned night heron, brown pelican, magnificent frigate bird, brown booby, spotted sandpiper, green heron and ringed kingfisher.

Quepos

Located just 7km from the entrance to Manuel Antonio, the small, busy town of Quepos serves as the gateway to the national park, as well as a convenient port of call for travelers in need of goods and services. Although the Manuel Antonio area was rapidly and irreversibly transformed following the ecotourism boom, Quepos has largely retained an authentic Tico feel.

 TOURS

Paddle 9   Water Sports

(☎2777-7436; www.paddle9sup.com; Ruta Nacional 618; 3hr tours from US$65, full-day tours from US$143; ⊗8:30am-4pm) This passionate, safety-conscious team has introduced SUP (stand-up paddleboarding) to Quepos and delights in showing visitors around the Pacific coast. Apart from the two-hour mangrove or ocean paddleboarding tours, the most popular outing is an eight-hour journey involving paddleboarding, lunch at a tilapia fish farm and swimming in various waterfalls.

Unique Tours   Adventure

(☎2777-1119; www.costaricauniquetours.com; rafting & waterfalls/ziplining/catamaran/horseback riding/kayaking from US$95/75/75/65/65) This established local operator organizes entertaining rafting tours on the Río Savegre, plus ocean and mangrove kayaking outings. It also does coastal hikes to Parque Nacional Manuel Antonio, ziplining, catamaran and horseback-riding tours plus much more. Prices vary depending on group size.

H2O Adventures   Adventure

(Ríos Tropicales; ☎2777-4092; www.h2ocr.com; Ruta Nacional 618; rafting with/without lunch US$95/85) The venerable Costa Rican rafting company Ríos Tropicales has a hugely popular franchise in Quepos called H2O Adventures, which organizes rafting outings on the Naranjo, El Chorro and Savegre rivers (the latter with a waterfall stop), as

well as kayaking and tubing outings. Rapids range from Class II to Class IV.

Oceans Unlimited   Diving

(☎2519-9544; www.scubadivingcostarica.com; Marina Pez Vela; 2-tank dive US$110; ⊗7am-5pm, dives 8am-noon) ✐ This shop takes its diving very seriously, and runs most of its excursions out to Isla Larga and Isla del Caño, which are south in Bahía Drake (connected via a two-hour bus trip). It also has a range of specialized PADI certifications, and regular environmental-awareness projects that make it stand out from the pack.

Manuel Antonio
Surf School   Surfing

(MASS; ☎2777-4842, 2777-1955; www.manuel antoniosurfschool.com; Ruta Nacional 618; 1hr lesson US$30, 3hr lesson group/private US$70/95, surf tour incl lunch & waterfall US$89) MASS offers friendly, safe and fun small-group surfing lessons daily, lasting for three hours and with a three-to-one student–instructor ratio. Find its stand about 500m up the Manuel Antonio road south of Quepos.

Iguana Tours   Adventure

(☎2777-2052; www.iguanatours.com; cnr Av 2 & Calle 5; horseback riding/catamaran/rafting/sea kayaking & snorkeling from US$80/70/70/65; ⊗6:30am-9pm) ✐ With tours that leave for destinations all over the central Pacific coast, this adventure-travel shop offers reputable river rafting, sea kayaking, horseback riding, mangrove tours and dolphin-watching excursions. It's no fly-by-night operation – it's been around since '89 – and has a proven commitment to ecotourism principles.

Titi Canopy Tours   Adventure

(☎2777-3130; www.titicanopytour.com; Costanera Sur at La Foresta Nature Resort; adult/child US$80/65; ⊗tours 7:30am, 11am & 2:30pm) This outfit has friendly, professional guides, who take adventure seekers on 12 ziplines (reaching up to 450m), 22 platforms, one rappel and a Tarzan swing. The lines are situated in the 15-hectare grounds of a private reserve filled with nature, and with

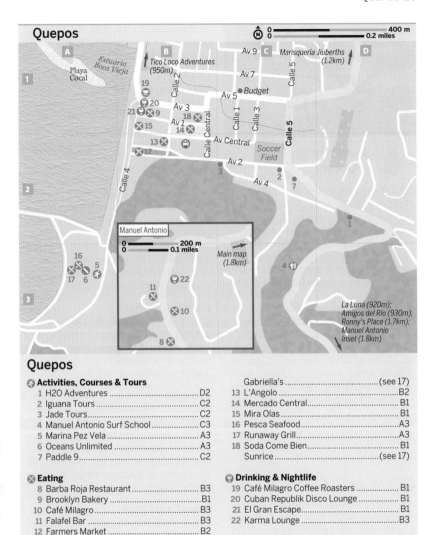

Quepos

lovely mountain and valley views. Rates include a Tico meal, fruit, drinks and local transportation.

Jade Tours
Adventure

(📞2777-0932; www.costaricajadetours.com; Av 2; nature tours from US$59; ⏱9am-8pm Sun-Tue, 7am-8pm Wed-Sat) Recommended agency for nature tours in Parque Nacional Manuel Antonio. Trips include transportation and a guide with a telescope (through which you can get pictures of sloths, monkeys and insects for your preferred social media profile). Also offers adventure day trips and private transportation. Prices listed online are more expensive than for walk-ins.

Sportfishing in Quepos

Sportfishing is big here, and offshore ventures are said to be best from December to April, when sailfish are being hooked. This is a high-dollar activity and you can expect to pay upwards of US$900 to hire a boat for the day. If you want to shop around a bit, visit the office of **Marina Pez Vela** (📞2774-9000; www.marinapezvela.com; Paseo del Mar, Calle 4), 500m south of the town center.

Outfitter **Quepos Sailfishing Charters** (📞8746-3970, in USA 800-388-9957; www.queposfishing.com; charters per day from US$1250) offers sportfishing charters on a fleet of variously sized boats, whether you're after sailfish, marlin, dorado or wahoo. Rates vary significantly depending on the season, number of people and size of boat.

Sailfish
KYLE HAASBROEK/GETTY IMAGES ©

⊗ EATING

One benefit of staying in Quepos proper is the accessibility of a wide range of dining opportunities, and there is also a couple of good markets.

Brooklyn Bakery
Bakery $

(📞8583-0541; www.facebook.com/thebrooklyn bakerycr; Av 1; bagels US$2, mains US$6-8; ⏰6am-3pm Mon-Sat; 📶🍴) Real New York–style bagels, lox salmon (a rarity in Costa Rica) and rye bread! This adorable little bakery bakes its fresh wares every morning, and light bites continue throughout the day, plus there's good iced coffee. Order

amazing salads and bagels, ciabatta or sourdough sandwiches with fillings from guacamole to tuna. Grab a delicious slice of lemon pie to go.

Marisquería Jiuberths
Seafood $

(📞2777-1292; off Ruta Nacional 235; mains US$6-21; ⏰11am-9:30pm) Run by a hardworking fisherman's family, this institution with brightly tiled floors serves the best seafood in town, yet is practically unknown to visitors because it's tucked away in the back streets of Quepos. Whether you have the catch of the day or the satisfying fish soup, *ceviche* or seafood mains, the portions are generous and the service attentive. Cash only.

Follow Ruta 235 out of town and it will be signposted on the left; it's a few minutes up an unpaved road. If in doubt, ask locals for directions as it's well known.

Farmers Market
Market $

(Calle 4; ⏰4-11pm Fri, 6am-noon Sat) Self-caterers should check out the farmers market near the waterfront, where you can buy directly from farmers, fisherfolk, bakers and other food producers.

L'Angolo
Deli $

(Restorante L'Angolo Gastronomia Italian Deli; 📞2777-7865; Calle 2; sandwiches US$6-7; ⏰11am-10pm Mon-Sat) This tiny deli with a couple of tables makes rather good pastas, salads and sandwiches with imported Italian meats and cheeses – the perfect picnic for the beach or a fishing trip.

Soda Come Bien
Cafeteria $

(📞2777-2550; Av 1, Mercado Central; mains US$3.50-6; ⏰6am-5pm Mon-Sat, to 11am Sun) The daily rotation of delicious cafeteria options here might include fish in tomato sauce, *olla de carne* (beef soup with rice) or chicken soup. Everything is fresh, the women behind the counter are friendly and the burly portions are a dream come true for hungry shoestringers. Or pick up a fresh *empanada* before or after a long bus ride.

Mercado Central · Market $

(Central Market; Av 1; meals from US$4; ⊙vendor hours vary) The Mercado Central is packed with produce vendors and good *sodas* (inexpensive eateries) too numerous to list, so follow your nose and the locals.

Mira Olas · Cafe $

(🖉2777-0811; Best Western Hotel Kamuk; breakfast from US$4; ⊙6am-9pm) Good-value, basic breakfasts and Tico meals are served at the open-air cafe inside Best Western Hotel Kamuk. The banana pancakes hit the spot. Those heading to Parque Nacional Manuel Antonio early will find that it's one of the only places open at the crack of dawn for breakfast.

Sunrice · Sushi $$

(🖉2519-9955; www.sunricerestaurant.com; Marina Pez Vela; poke bowls from US$12, dumplings US$9, sushi rolls from US$12; ⊙noon-9pm Tue-Sun) A Latin-influenced sushi and sake bar that fills its rolls with fresh tropical produce and local seafood bits. The spicy tuna over crispy rice cakes is a big hit, along with the salmon, avocado and mango poke bowl and the *omusubi* (Japanese rice balls). Dishes tend to be on the smaller side. Enjoy it on the outside tables.

Runaway Grill · American $$

(🖉2519-9095; www.runawaygrill.com; Marina Pez Vela; mains US$12-30; ⊙10am-10pm Mon-Fri, 8am-11pm Sat & Sun; P✳🖘) An all-round crowd pleaser, casual open-air Runaway Grill looks out on the yachts of the marina and its ceiling is covered in fishing hats. The menu spans fish, Mexican, Costa Rican, steaks, wraps, salads and more. Portions are sizeable and the service is friendly, but due to its upmarket location it's a little on the pricey side.

Pesca Seafood · Seafood $$

(🖉2519-9422; www.facebook.com/pesca seafood; Marina Pez Vela; mains US$11-26, sharing platters US$80; ⊙11:30am-10pm; P) This new kid on the block with fish shapes hanging from the ceiling is a good choice for seafood lovers. It serves up fresh morsels in various styles: the crowd-pleasing salmon *ceviche* arrives in a coconut, while the paella or seafood platter with tuna

Olla de carne (beef soup with rice)

X Marks the Spot

Locals have long believed that a treasure worth billions of dollars lies somewhere in the Quepos and Manuel Antonio area, waiting to be discovered. The legend was popularized by English pirate John Clipperton, who befriended the coastal Quepoa during his years of sailing to and from the South Pacific. Clipperton's belief stemmed from a rumor that in 1670 a number of Spanish ships laden with treasure escaped from Panama City moments before it was burned to the ground by Captain Henry Morgan. Since the ships were probably off-loaded quickly to avoid being raided at sea, a likely destination was the San Bernardino de Quepo Mission, which had strong loyalty to the Spanish crown.

Clipperton died in 1722 without ever discovering the legendary treasure, and the mission closed permanently in 1746, as most of the Quepoa had succumbed to European diseases. Although the ruins of the mission were discovered in 1974, they were virtually destroyed and had long since been looted. However, if the treasure was indeed as large as it's described in lore, it is possible that a few gold doubloons could still be lying somewhere in the area, waiting to be unearthed.

steak, shrimp, octopus, clams and a whole lobster are fun sharing options for bigger groups.

Gabriella's   Seafood $$$

(☏2519-9300; www.gabriellassteakhouse.com; Marina Pez Vela; mains US$23-53; ☺4-10pm; P❄🏠) A contender for the region's best restaurant, Gabriella's does many things well: the veranda catches the sunset and overlooks a gorgeous marina, and the service is attentive. But the food is the real star, with great emphasis on fresh fish and

mouthwatering steak. We're fans of the seared tuna with chipotle sauce and the spicy sausage and shrimp pasta. In a word: terrific.

Grab a happy-hour drink (two-for-one on selected cocktails, plus deals on wines and beers) from 5pm to 7pm and enjoy the sunset.

Claro Que Sí   Seafood $$$

(☏2777-0777; www.sicomono.com/dining; Hotel Sí Como No, Ruta Nacional 618; salads from US$8, mains US$18-39; ☺noon-10pm; 🏠🏃) ✔ A family-friendly restaurant that manages to tread the line between upscale and casual, Claro Que Sí proudly serves organic and locally sourced food items that are in line with the philosophy of its parent hotel, Sí Como No. Sustainably sourced meats and fish are expertly complemented with fresh produce, resulting in flavorful dishes typical of both the Pacific and Caribbean coasts.

Dishes range from the catch of the day to range-grown chicken and fresh homemade pasta. There's a separate kids' menu. Live music takes place between 6pm and 9pm on some evenings. Hotel nonguests must spend a minimum of US$10; after doing so ask your waiter for a free 'cine-pass' for the **cinema** (☺screenings 5pm & 8pm) next door.

🍷 DRINKING & NIGHTLIFE

Café Milagro Coffee Roasters   Cafe

(☏2777-1707; www.cafemilagro.com; Calle 4; ☺9am-5pm Mon-Sat) Café Milagro sources its coffee beans from all over Costa Rica and produces a variety of estate, single-origin and blended roasts to suit any coffee fiend's palate.

Cuban Republik Disco Lounge   Club

(☏8345-9922; www.facebook.com/cubanrepublik.quepos; cnr Ruta Nacional 235 & Av 3; cover charge Fri & Sat US$2-4; ☺10pm-2:30am Thu-Sat) Cuban Republik hosts the most reliable party in central Quepos, and has various drinks specials. The DJs get loud late into the night and women get in at discount on certain nights. It's a nice mixed Tico and gringo scene.

El Gran Escape   Bar

(☏2777-7850; www.elgranescapequepos.com; Av 3; ⏰11am-11pm; 🛜) This well-established pub offers a good happy hour (4:30pm to 6:30pm) with two-for-one cocktails, plus excellent fresh seafood, sports on the screen and delicious (though pricey) burgers. Prompt bar staff too. Bring your catch after your fishing trip and they will prepare it, cook it, and serve it back to you with two sides for US$14.

ℹ️ GETTING THERE & AWAY

Both **Skyway** (www.skywaycr.com) and **Sansa** (☏2290-4100, in USA 877-767-2672; www.flysansa.com) service Quepos. Prices vary according to season and availability, though you can pay a little less than US$85 for a flight from San José or Liberia. Flights are packed in the high season, so book (and pay) for your ticket well ahead of time and reconfirm often. The airport is 5km out of town, and taxis make the trip for around US$10.

All buses arrive at and depart from the busy, chaotic main terminal in the center of town. Scheduled private shuttles, operated by Gray Line, Easy Ride and Monkey Ride, run between Quepos/Manuel Antonio and popular destinations such as Jacó (US$39), Monteverde (US$59), Puerto Jiménez (US$79), San José (US$55) and Uvita (US$35).

ℹ️ GETTING AROUND

A number of international car-rental companies operate in Quepos, such as **Budget** (www.budget.co.cr), which has branches at the **airport** (Quepos La Managua Airport; ⏰8am-5pm Mon-Sat, to 4pm Sun) and in **Quepos town** (☏2774-0558; cnr Av 5 & Calle 1; ⏰8am-5pm Mon-Sat, to 4pm Sun); reserve ahead and reconfirm to guarantee availability.

Colectivo (shared) taxis run between Quepos and Manuel Antonio (around US$1 for short local distances). A private taxi will cost a few thousand

 Monkey Business

Your bag will be searched for snacks upon entering Parque Nacional Manuel Antonio – cigarettes, chips, junk food, alcohol, nuts, seeds and cans are prohibited. Water and soft drinks in reusable bottles, packed sandwiches and ready-cut fruit are allowed. There is now a **cafe** (www.sinac.go.cr; intersection of Playa Gemelas & Puerto Escondido; pastries from US$3, sandwiches US$8, ice cream US$6; ⏰7am-4pm) inside the park serving refreshments and hot foods. However, do not even think about feeding any food scraps to the monkeys, as this risks their health and negatively impacts the monkey population in the following ways:

● Monkeys are susceptible to bacteria transmitted from human hands.

● Irregular feeding will lead to aggressive behavior as well as create a dangerous dependency.

● Bananas are not their preferred food, and can cause serious digestive problems.

● Increased exposure to humans facilitates illegal poaching as well as attacks from dogs.

If you do happen to see someone feeding the monkeys, take the initiative and explain politely why it's detrimental.

White-headed capuchin
PESEK PHOTO/SHUTTERSTOCK ©

Saving the Squirrel Monkey

With its expressive eyes and luxuriant coat, the *mono tití* (Central American squirrel monkey) is a favorite among Costa Rica's four monkey species. It is also in danger of extinction, as there are only roughly 1500 of these animals left in Manuel Antonio, one of its last remaining native habitats.

Overdevelopment is one of the animal's greatest threats. To remedy this problem, a conservation project known as the Titi Conservation Alliance (www.monotiti.org) is taking bold measures to prevent further decline. This coalition of organizations is helping to create a sustainable wildlife corridor between Parque Nacional Manuel Antonio and the Zona Protectora Cerro Nara in the northeast.

To achieve this aim, it is reforesting the Río Naranjo, a key waterway linking the two locations. More than 65,000 trees have already been planted along 8km of the Naranjo. This not only has the effect of extending the monkeys' habitat but also provides a protected area for other wildlife to enjoy. Scientists at the Universidad Nacional de Costa Rica have mapped and selected sites for reforestation, and business owners in the area, as well as private donors, support the project financially.

Squirrel monkeys
ZORAN KOLUNDZIJA/GETTY IMAGES ©

colones. Catch one at the **taxi stand** (Av Central) south of the market. The trip between Quepos and the park should cost about US$15.

Manuel Antonio

◎ SIGHTS

Greentique Wildlife Refuge
Wildlife Reserve

(2777-0850; www.greentiquehotels.com; Ruta Nacional 618; adult/child 1hr tours US$25/15, 2hr tours US$35/25, 2hr night tours US$39/29 ⊙day tours 8am-4pm, night tours 5:30-7:30pm; ⊛) Biologist Jimmy Mata leads magical one- and two-hour sojourns through the Butterfly Atrium, Reptile & Amphibian Water Gardens and Crocodile Lagoon, as well as a night tour, in this 5-hectare haven of second-growth Pacific coast wet forest. Sloths, monkeys, baby crocodiles, armadillos and coatis are among the mammals you might see from the forest floor to the dripping canopy. Across from Sí Como No Resort.

La Playita
Beach

At the far western end of Playa Espadilla, beyond a rocky headland (wear sandals), this former nude beach remains one of Costa Rica's most famous gay beaches and a particular draw for young men. The beach is inaccessible around high tide, so time your walk, or access via the ultra-luxury Arenas del Mar hotel.

✪ ACTIVITIES

Amigos del Río
Adventure

(2777-0082; www.adradventurepark.com; Ruta Nacional 618; '10-in-One Adventure' US$139, rafting from US$70, kayaking from US$69) Pack all of your canopy-tour jungle fantasies into one day on Amigos del Río's '10-in-One Adventure,' featuring ziplining, a Tarzan swing, rappelling down a waterfall and more.

The seven-hour adventure tour includes a free transfer from the Quepos and Manuel Antonio area as well as breakfast and lunch. Amigos del Río is also a reliable outfit for kayaking and white-water-rafting trips.

El Avión (p182)

Cala Spa · Spa

(☎2777-0777; www.sicomono.com; Hotel Sí Como No; treatments US$40-147; ⏱10am-7pm) If you're sunburned and sore from exploring Manuel Antonio – even better if you're not – the Cala Spa offers aloe body wraps, citrus salt scrubs and various types of massage to restore body and spirit. Open daily by appointment only.

Tico Loco Adventures · Outdoors

(☎2777-0010; www.ticolocoadventures.com; Ruta Nacional 235; waterfall party tour min 4 people US$110, rafting from US$70) With a local office on the way into Quepos, this welcoming tour company offers rafting on the Naranjo river with Class III–IV rapids, and Savegre on Class II–III rapids, plus outdoor adventures that double as parties. The waterfall party tour involves a hike to majestic falls with a cooler of drinks.

⊗ EATING

The road to Manuel Antonio plays host to some of the best restaurants in the area, and many hotels along this road also have excellent restaurants open to the public. As with the area's sleeping venues, budget eating options are harder to find. Reservations are recommended on weekends and holidays, and during the busy dry season.

Falafel Bar · Mediterranean $

(☎2777-4135; Ruta Nacional 618; mains US$6.50-12.50; ⏱11am-8pm Tue-Sun; 🛜🖊) Adding to the diversity of cuisine to be found along the road, this falafel spot dishes up authentic Middle Eastern favorites. You'll also find plenty of vegetarian options, including couscous and fresh salads, stuffed grape leaves, fab fruit smoothies and even French fries for the picky ones. For the meat-eaters there are shawarmas and schnitzels. Yum.

Café Milagro · Fusion $$

(☎2777-2272; www.cafemilagro.com; Ruta Nacional 618; mains from US$7; ⏱7am-9pm;🖊) This is a fine stop for fancy coffee drinks and a satisfying full breakfast, lunch or dinner (eggs, quesadillas, sandwiches, salads and Tico plates), and there are plenty of vegan and veggie options on the menu. The patio has a lovely setting, surrounded by

 ### LGBT+ Manuel Antonio

For the jet-setting LGBT+ traveler the world over, Manuel Antonio has a reputation as a tolerant destination in comparison to its neighbors. Same-sex marriage became legal in Costa Rica in May 2020. But well before then, a rainbow community (predominantly gay men) blossomed in Manuel Antonio due to the settling of liberal-minded individuals and a burgeoning artist community.

With the recent Supreme Court ruling against the country's same-sex marriage ban, this area is set to become one of Costa Rica's premier destinations for same-sex weddings. Check out www. gaymanuelantonio.com for a full list of gay and gay-friendly accommodations, events, restaurants and bars. **Karma Lounge** (☑2777-7230; www.facebook. com/karmaloungema; off Ruta Nacional 618; ⊗8pm-2:30am Fri & Sat, until 1am Sun) is a very friendly spot with pop, disco and dance music.

During daylight hours, the epicenter of gay Manuel Antonio is the famous La Playita (p180), a beach with a long history of nude sunbathing for gay men. Alas, the days when you could sun in the buff are gone, but the end of La Playita is still widely regarded as a playful pickup spot.

La Playita
VIDERE STUDIOS/SHUTTERSTOCK ©

Agua Azul International $$

(☑2777-5280; www.cafeaguaazul.com; Ruta Nacional 618; breakfast from US$5, lunch mains US$9-24; ⊗11am-10pm Thu-Tue; ☻) Perched on the 2nd floor with uninterrupted ocean views, Agua Azul is a marvelous casual lunch spot on this stretch of road – perfect for early-morning park visitors who are heading back to their hotel. The breezy, unpretentious open-air restaurant, renowned for its 'big-ass burger,' also serves up the likes of fajitas, *panko*-crusted tuna and a tasty fish salad.

Barba Roja Restaurant Seafood $$

(☑2777-0331; www.barbarojarestaurante.com; Ruta Nacional 618; mains US$12-28; ⊗6:30am-10pm Tue-Sun) A Manuel Antonio area institution, the Barba Roja is both a lively pirate-themed bar and a seafood-and-steak spot with a respectable menu (try the coconut shrimp with mango or smoked meats). The terrace affords fantastic ocean views, best enjoyed with a local craft brew (from US$6), 'loco mojito' or sangria.

La Luna International $$$

(☑2777-9797; www.gaiahr.com; Gaia Hotel; mains US$13-39; ⊗6am-11pm; P☻♪) Unpretentious and friendly La Luna, inside the five-star Gaia Hotel, makes a lovely spot for a special-occasion dinner or sundowner, with fabulous martinis and a spectacular backdrop of jungle and ocean. An international menu offers everything from plantain and coconut-crusted mahi-mahi to grilled ginger chicken, and jumbo shrimp with tagliatelle. Separate vegetarian and vegan menu available.

🍸 DRINKING & NIGHTLIFE

Bars in several accommodations aside, there's no nightlife in Manuel Antonio village to speak of, though there are several clubs and bars along the road to Quepos.

El Avión Bar

(☑2183-7953, 2777-3378; www.elavion.net; Ruta Nacional 618; ⊗noon-10pm; ☻) Constructed around a 1954 Fairchild C-123 plane

tropical gardens, or order a sandwich for the park. Live music every night (7:30pm to 9:30pm).

(allegedly purchased by the US government in the '80s for the Nicaraguan Contras but never used), this striking bar-restaurant is a great spot for a beer, cocktail or wine and stellar sunset-watching. The Tico and international menu is overpriced, and the service could be improved, but you can't beat the setting.

In 2000 the enterprising owners of El Avión purchased the plane for the surprisingly reasonable sum of US$3000 (it never made it out of its hangar in San José because of the Iran–Contra scandal that embroiled Oliver North and his cohorts), and proceeded to cart it piece by piece to Manuel Antonio. It now sits on the side of the main road, where it looks as if it crash-landed into the side of the hill.

Ronny's Place   Bar

(📞2777-5120; www.ronnysplace.com; ⊗noon-10pm) The insane views of two pristine bays and jungle on all sides at Ronny's Place make it worth a detour for a drink and a tasty meal (mains US$14 to US$70). While plenty of places along this stretch of road boast similar views, the off-the-beaten-path location makes it feel like a secret find. Look for the well-marked dirt road off the main drag.

There's a long cocktail list of around two-dozen favorites, plus imported beers. Order special mains like coconut-breaded shrimp, whole red snapper or a seafood platter for two with lobster, tuna, mahi-mahi and calamari with garlic sauce. The

stone tables out front are the best for sunset viewing.

Z Poolside Bistro   Bar

(📞2777-6948; Ruta Nacional 618; ⊗7am-10pm) With one of the longest happy hours in town (noon to 6pm), Z Poolside Bistro is a mellow afternoon drinking spot. It's centered on a big pool, so you can catch some rays and take a dip while sipping on cocktails. On Sunday evenings (5pm to 9pm), it's more of a party scene: a DJs plays and deals mean drinks are flowing.

On Sundays get two-for-one margaritas, sangria and daiquiris, 40% off Champagne, and US$3 craft beers. There's also a full menu of poolside mains like burgers, grilled meats and snacks.

ℹ GETTING THERE & AWAY

Driving the winding 7km road between Quepos and Manuel Antonio village on any day but Monday means spending time in traffic jams and potentially exorbitant parking fees.

Note that the road to Manuel Antonio is very narrow and congested, so it's recommended to leave your car at your hotel and take an early-morning bus to the park entrance instead, then simply walk in. Alternatively, there are a few parking areas before the entrance that charge US$4 to US$20 per day, depending on the season and your negotiating skills. Arrive early if you intend to use these.

SOUTHERN NICOYA

Southern Nicoya at a Glance...

Word has spread about the hippie-chic outposts of Montezuma and dusty yet developing Santa Teresa. During the dry season, packs of international surfers and wanderers arrive, hungry for the wild beauty and soul-stirring waters on either side of the peninsula. It used to require hours of sweaty bus rides and sluggish ferries from the mainland to access this tropical land's end, but these days there are more roads and regular boat shuttles, making the southern peninsula altogether more accessible.

Two Days in Southern Nicoya

On your first day, relax into your vacay at **Playa Santa Teresa** (p192), one of Costa Rica's most stunning beaches, and throw in a surf or a yoga session if you're keen. Do lunch at **Earth Café** (p194) and a sushi dinner at **Koji's** (p195). Spend day two chillin' by the tide pools at **Playa Hermosa** (p192) or exploring the trails at **Reserva Natural Absoluta Cabo Blanco** (p188) and its gorgeous wilderness beach.

Four Days in Southern Nicoya

Base yourself for the next two days in Montezuma, and prioritize the trek to **Montezuma Waterfalls** (p190) for thrilling jumps and cooling dips. Have lunch at **Clandestina** (p199), then head to **Playa Montezuma** (p196) for an afternoon of swimming and sunbathing. Treat yourself to a delectable cliffside dinner at **Playa de los Artistas** (p198). On your last day, get an early start on the beach hike to **Playa Cocolito** (p196), where you can luxuriate in some of the most magnificent scenery around.

Golfo de Nicoya

20 km
10 miles

Carmona

Puntarenas

Jicaral   Lepanto   Playa Naranjo

Santa Marta

Cangrejal

Península de Nicoya

Isla San Lucas

Islita

Bejuco

La Javilla

San Francisco de Coyote

Paquera

Curú

Isla Tortuga

Pochote

Golfo de Nicoya

Playa Tambor

Tambor

Cóbano

Playa Cocolito
Playa Grande

Playa Manzanillo   Santa Teresa   Montezuma
Playa Hermosa
Playa Santa Teresa
Playa El Carmen
Mal País   Cabuya

Montezuma Waterfalls

PACIFIC OCEAN

Reserva Natural Absoluta Cabo Blanco

Montezuma Map (p197)

Arriving in Southern Nicoya

The road from Paquera to Cóbano is paved, but much of the southern peninsula is not, and it's quite a bumpy ride. Ferries carry cars and passengers across the Golfo de Nicoya (from Puntarenas to Paquera, p198), while boats bring passengers from Jacó to Montezuma. A quick flight from San José will deliver you to Tambor.

Where to Stay

Montezuma and Santa Teresa are the hubs of the southern peninsula, both with a great range of accommodation options catering to all budgets. But there are *cabinas* and other more interesting accommodations sprinkled all over this region. So if you prefer to nest in a quieter corner of the peninsula, you will surely find somewhere suitable to lay your head.

Reserva Natural Absoluta Cabo Blanco's beach

Reserva Natural Absoluta Cabo Blanco

At the tip of the Península de Nicoya, this unique park is covered by evergreen forests, bisected by a hiking trail and flanked by empty white-sand beaches and offshore islands.

Great For...

☑ **Don't Miss**

Picnicking and swimming at a deserted beach on the tip of the peninsula.

Just 11km south of Montezuma is Costa Rica's oldest protected wilderness area. Cabo Blanco comprises 12 sq km of land and 17 sq km of surrounding ocean, and includes the entire southern tip of the Península de Nicoya. The moist micro-climate on the tip of the peninsula fosters the growth of evergreen forests, which are unique when compared with the dry tropical forests typical of Nicoya. The park also encompasses a number of pristine white-sand beaches and offshore islands that are favored nesting areas for various bird species.

Hiking

From the ranger station, the **Sendero Sueco** (Swedish Trail) leads 4.5km down to a wilderness beach at the tip of the peninsula, while the **Sendero Danes** (Danish

Santa Teresa

Montezuma

Mal País

Cabuya

Reserva Natural Absoluta Cabo Blanco

❶ Need to Know

2642-0093; adult/child US$12/5; ⊙8am-4pm Wed-Sun

✕ Take a Break

Pack a picnic with burritos from Zwart Cafe (p193).

★ Top Tip

Cabo Blanco is called an 'absolute' nature reserve because, prior to the late 1980s, visitors were not permitted.

Trail) is a spur that branches from Sendero Sueco and reconnects 1km later. You can make this small 2km loop and stay in the woods, or take on the considerably more difficult (but much more rewarding) hike to the cape, heading down one way and taking the other path back up. Be advised that the trails can get muddy (especially in the rainy season) and are steep in certain parts – plan for about two hours in each direction. Monkeys, squirrels, sloths, deer, agoutis and raccoon abound at Cabo Blanco. Armadillos, *pizotes* (coatis), peccaries and anteaters are also occasionally sighted.

Brown Boobies

The coastal area is known as an important nesting site for the brown booby, mostly found 1.6km south of the mainland on **Isla Cabo Blanco** (White Cape Island). In

fact, the name 'Cabo Blanco' was coined by Spanish conquistadors when they noticed that the entire island consisted of guano-encrusted rocks.

Beaches

The wide, sandy pebble beach at the end of the trail is magnificent. It's backed by jungle and sheltered by two rugged headlands including one that stretches out into a rock reef with island views just offshore. The water is striped turquoise at low tide, but the cool currents still make for a refreshing dip. Visibility isn't always great for snorkeling but you may want to bring a mask anyway. Driftwood is smooth, weathered and piled haphazardly here and there. There are even picnic tables and a grill, if you care to get ambitious. Simply put, it is postcard perfect, and should be a required stop for visitors to the southern peninsula. Leave the beach by 2pm to get out before the park closes.

Take a dip along the waterfall trail

Montezuma Waterfalls

A river hike leads to a waterfall with a delicious swimming hole. Further along the trail, a second set of falls offers a thrilling 10m leap into deep water.

Head south past Hotel La Cascada, where you'll find a parking area. Then take the trail to the right just after the bridge. You'll want proper hiking footwear.

Waterfall Trail

The first waterfall has a lusciously inviting swimming hole, where you can cool off from the hike. Remember that it's shallow and rocky and not suitable for diving.

From here, if you continue on the well-marked trail that leads around and up, you will come to a second set of falls. This is where you'll find a good, clean 10m leap into the deep water below. To reach the jumping point, continue on the trail up the side of the hill until you reach the diving area. Do not attempt to scale the falls. The rocks are slippery and several travelers have met their deaths in this way.

Great For...

☑ Don't Miss

That agonizing, heart-thumping moment when you have to propel yourself off the rocks.

One of Montezuma's three waterfalls

ℹ Need to Know

parking US$2

✕ Take a Break

Recover from your adventure with gourmet tacos and craft beer at Clandestina (p199).

★ Top Tip

Hit the trail early and you may have the falls to yourself.

nine ziplines, you'll hike down – rather than up – to the waterfalls. Bring your swimwear, so you can jump from the rocks and cool off. Park at the canopy entrance for quick access to the falls via a suspension bridge (US$4 per person). This company has a spotless and relatively new lodge on the other side of the swinging bridge, Sun Trails Hotel, with the latest amenities.

From this point, the trail continues up the hill to the third and last set of falls. These are certainly magnificent to look at, but not suitable for jumping.

Playing It Safe

○ Don't attempt to jump into the lower pool, which is rocky and shallow.

○ Don't attempt to scale the waterfall.

○ Don't swim if the water level seems abnormally high.

Canopy Tour

Tour company **Sun Trails** (Montezuma Waterfall Canopy Tour; ☎2642-0808; www. montezumatraveladventures.com; tours from US$45; ☺9am, 1pm & 3pm) operates a 1½-hour canopy tour. After you've flown down

Butterfly Garden

South of town, you can tour the lush *mariposario* (butterfly garden) at Montezuma Gardens (p197), where the mysterious metamorphoses occur. You'll learn about the life cycles and benefits of a dozen local species, of which you'll see many colorful varieties. Note that it is a long and steep trek from town so you may want to consider a taxi. There's also a modern four-room B&B here that brews its own beer.

Santa Teresa & Mal País

Santa Teresa didn't even have electricity until the mid-1990s. Then one major landowner died and his property was subdivided, and the landscape north of the Playa El Carmen intersection changed forever. These days, ATVs are omnipresent, along with great restaurants and transformational ocean-view yoga dens. It's still a wonderful surfing town, though no longer a secret one, and there's a modicum of nightlife. The entire area unfurls along one bumpy coastal road that rambles south from Santa Teresa through Playa El Carmen and ends in the sleepy fishing hamlet of Mal País.

◉ SIGHTS

Playa Santa Teresa   Beach
Playa Santa Teresa is a long, stunning beach that's famous for its fast and powerful beach break. The waves are pretty consistent and can be surfed at virtually any time of day. At the north end of the beach, Roca Mar – aka Suck Rock – is an awesome point break and a local favorite.

The break La Lora is named for the nightclub that marks the turnoff from the main road, which is how you find it.

Playa Hermosa   Beach
Somewhere north of town, Playa Santa Teresa ends and Playa Hermosa starts. This gorgeous beach deserves its *hermosa* (beautiful) moniker and then some. It's wide and flat and spectacular at low tide. The beach nearly disappears at high tide. Somewhere between low and high is surf tide, when you can ride the wide beach break left or right from center. You can surf the point break (at the north end of the beach) at any time.

Playa El Carmen   Beach
Playa El Carmen, downhill from the main T-intersection coming into town, is a good beach break that can be surfed anytime. The beach is wide and sandy and curls into successive coves, so it makes good beach-combing and swimming terrain too.

Playa Manzanillo   Beach
About 8km north of the Playa El Carmen intersection (past Playa Hermosa), Playa

Playa Santa Teresa

FOTOS593/SHUTTERSTOCK ©

Manzanillo is a combination of sand and rock that's best surfed when the tide is rising and there's an offshore wind.

🟢 ACTIVITIES

Freedom Riding SUP Water Sports
(📞8737-8781, 2640-0939; www.sup-costarica. com; Mal País; rental half-/full day US$25/40, lessons US$50; ⊙9am-6pm) A stand-up paddle place with sharp management and excellent safety and instruction techniques. Andy offers lessons for first-timers and rentals for old pros, as well as tours that are entertaining for anyone. Located near the fishing pier in Mal País.

Canopy Mal País Adventure Sports
(📞2640-0360; www.canopymalpais.com; Justin's Rd; US$55; ⊙8am-5pm) You don't think of ziplining when you come to a surf town? You should. Just south of Mal País, Carlos and crew provide one of the most entertaining experiences around, joking so much you'll forget your fear of heights on the 11 cables, including one that stretches 500m across the jungle below. The last cable is a surfboard ride!

✂ EATING

If surfing and yoga are the top two activities in Santa Teresa and Mal País, then number three is surely eating. The dining is surprisingly sophisticated for a dusty little surf town. Indulge in gourmet burgers, sublime sushi, multicultural tapas or farm-to-table fusion goodness. Or, keep it real with a *casado* (set meal) from the local *soda*. It's all good.

Zwart Cafe Cafe $
(Zwart Art Cafe; 📞2640-0011; Santa Teresa; mains US$6-10; ⊙7am-5pm; 🛜🌱)
Zwart means 'black' in Dutch, but this shabby-chic, artist-owned gallery and cafe is all white (or mostly – damn dust!). You'll love the surf-inspired Technicolor canvases, the lively outdoor patio and the breakfasts, including chocolate-chip pancakes. At lunch it's all about the burritos and there

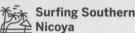

🌴 Surfing Southern Nicoya

The long, flat beach stretches for many kilometers along the southwestern coast of the peninsula. The area is saturated with surf shops – it's a good place to pick up an inexpensive board, which you can probably sell later. Most of the local shops also do rentals and repairs.

Kina Surf Shop (📞2640-0627; www. kinasurfcr.com; Santa Teresa; 2hr lessons US$60-80, board rentals per day US$15-20; ⊙9am-5pm) A terrific, efficient surf shop near the break in Santa Teresa. Kina claims to have the best selection of rental boards in the area, with 60-something quality boards available. The 90-minute lessons for beginner, intermediate and advanced surfers also come highly recommended.

Nalu Surf School (📞2649-0391, 8358-4436; www.nalusurfschool.com; Santa Teresa; board rental per day US$10-20, 1½hr group/private lessons US$55/75) Located 300m north of the Playa El Carmen intersection (next to Ronny's Supermarket), this surf school is recommended for its fun and professional approach to instruction. Lessons usually take place at Playa El Carmen.

Pura Vida Adventures (📞in USA 415-465-2162; www.puravidaadventures.com; Hotel Tropico Latino, Playa El Carmen; weekly rates incl meals from US$2995) Excellent women-only and co-ed retreats that combine surfing and yoga in weeklong.

Surfer, Playa Santa Teresa
GERHARD/ULLSTEIN BILD VIA GETTY IMAGES ©

Yoga
Classes

Many surfers know that yoga is the perfect antidote to their sore flippers. Several studios in the area offer drop-in classes.

Casa Zen (2640-0523; www.zencostarica.com; Santa Teresa; classes US$10) Two daily classes take place in a lovely open-air studio, surrounded by trees. Most of the classes are a hatha-inspired vinyasa flow, but there's also ashtanga and other styles. Yoga by candlelight is a sublime way to transition from day to night. Multi-class packages and lodgings are available. Located behind the Plaza Royal.

Yoga Studio at Nautilus (2640-0991; www.hotelnautiluscostarica.com; Santa Teresa; drop-in/private classes US$14/60; 9am & 6pm) What's not to love about rooftop yoga? Twice-daily classes are held on the deck at the Nautilus Boutique Hotel, offering lovely views of surrounding palm trees and the village. It offers vinyasa flow and kundalini, yin, hatha, ashtanga and power yoga. Multi-class packages available. Look for the Nautilus signs.

Horizon Yoga Hotel (2640-0524; www.horizon-yogahotel.com; Calle Buenos Aires, Santa Teresa; drop-in classes US$15) Offers two classes daily, in a serene environment overlooking the ocean. As with other schools, weekly and other passes are available. About 100m north of Supermarket Ronny, turn off the main road and drive 50m up the hill.

are plenty of vegan options. There's a dynamite used bookstore here too.

About 2km north of the T-intersection, on the right if you're heading north.

Earth Café Health Food $$
(8427-4928; www.facebook.com/earthcafe.st; Santa Teresa; mains US$11-13; 8am-5pm) For surfers and yogis, there is not a more perfect lunch spot. We're talking elaborate salads, savory toppings piled high on toast and big colorful bowls of tuna poke, vegetables and smoothie goodness that pop with spice and flavor. The green juices and coffee are also top-notch, and the service is super friendly.

Bajo El Arbol Tapas $$
(2640-0302; www.facebook.com/bajoelarbol-cr; Playa El Carmen; mains US$14-17; 6-10pm) If you can't afford a flight to Spain, just sit down 'Beneath the Tree.' Basque chef Julio's menu changes daily, but he whips up an extraordinary *escalivada* (eggplant and pepper dish), and the *pulpo a la gallega* (octopus), topped with crunchy sea salt, is so damned good it ought to be illegal. Add a half-bottle of Spanish wine, and you're set.

Burger Rancho Burgers $$
(www.facebook.com/burgerrancho; Santa Teresa; mains US$10-12; 11am-10pm;) Get your burger on at this open-air *rancho* that in 2019 found a new home just north of Kina Surf Shop. Check the blackboard for daily changing specials, including veggie choices like a portobello mushroom burger, fish options like a mahi-mahi with curry sauce, and other interesting burgers such as a chorizo one. Cocktails and craft beer also available.

Caracolas Seafood $$
(2640-0525; Mal País; mains US$7-23; 8am-9pm;) The lone *soda* at this end of the coast revamped its menu in 2019 and now emphasizes seafood and paellas. But you can still eat a classic *casado* off a timber table in a garden that rolls onto the rocky beach. It also does steak, chicken and vegetarian dishes, but the best reason to come here is to feel the ocean breeze.

Main shopping street, Mal País

El Carmen   Pizza $$

(☎2640-0110; Playa El Carmen; mains US$10-23; ⊙9am-10pm) The location right on the *playa* is hard to beat, and the list of *ceviche* and cooked fish shows it's more than just a pizzeria. It's a popular spot for sundowners, thanks to the happy-hour specials (two-for-one drinks) and the amazing show that takes place in the sky. Come hobnob with the locals and enjoy. Special events can be found on the Facebook page.

Koji's   Japanese $$

(☎2640-0815; www.kojisrestaurant.com; Playa Hermosa; sushi US$5-16, mains US$9-18; ⊙5:30-9:30pm Tue-Sun) Koji Hyodo's outdoor patio is a twinkling beacon of fresh, raw excellence. The atmosphere and service are superior, of course, but his food is a higher truth. The grilled octopus is barely fried and sprinkled with sea salt, and there's a per-

Koji Hyodo's outdoor patio is a twinkling beacon of fresh, raw excellence.

fectly sweet crunch to his softshell crab and lobster tempura. Uphill from the main road.

🍸 DRINKING & NIGHTLIFE

Banana Beach   Bar

(☎2640-0320; www.bananabeachcr.com; Santa Teresa) What began as a few tables and a hut in the sand has blossomed into Santa Teresa's liveliest sunset bar. Grab a fruity cocktail and plop down in an Adirondack chair, beach lounger or an old boat repurposed as a couch, and watch surfers dance across the waves at sunset.

Drift Bar   Bar

(☎8496-6056; www.driftbarcr.com; Santa Teresa; ⊙noon-11pm Mon-Thu, to midnight Fri & Sat, 3-10pm Sun) 🌱 Part cocktail bar, part vegetarian restaurant, part art gallery, Drift Bar is wholly satisfying. Drinks are made with cold-pressed juices and are best consumed in the chic lounge or while browsing the art. If you've got other obligations, you can always order a sealed cocktail in a glass bottle (along with a reusable bag of ice) to go. Don't forget to bring the bottle back!

Nativo Sports Bar
Sports Bar

(☑2640-0356; www.facebook.com/nativosports bar; Playa El Carmen; ⊗11am-midnight) Fans above (to cool the place), *fanaticos* below, watching every manner of sport on the four big screens. Baseball, hockey and, of course, *fútbol* (soccer) are all on the offing. There is a variety of food options besides the expected burger/nacho path: smoothies packed with fruits and vegetables, as well as fresh fish, hummus and salads.

⊕ ENTERTAINMENT

Kika
Live Music

(☑2640-0408; www.facebook.com/kika. santateresa; Santa Teresa; ⊗6-10pm) This Argentine-owned restaurant is a popular spot for dinner and drinks by candlelight (Grandma's pork gets rave reviews). But things really pick up after dark on Thursday, when live bands take the stage and attract a lively crowd for drinking and dancing. Cash only.

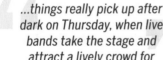

...things really pick up after dark on Thursday, when live bands take the stage and attract a lively crowd for drinking and dancing.

ⓘ GETTING THERE & AWAY

The southern Península de Nicoya roads leading to Santa Teresa and Mal País are improving. Nonetheless, whether you catch the bus/ferry, use a private shuttle or opt to drive yourself, be prepared for a bumpy ride for the last few miles.

ⓘ GETTING AROUND

Santa Teresa and Mal País are dirt-road types of towns: during the dry season, life gets extremely dusty. The preponderance of ATVs stirs up more grit (and the ire of locals); consider using a bicycle to get around town, so you're not contributing to the problem. If you must drive, please go slowly. Taxis between Mal País, Playa El Carmen and Santa Teresa range from US$5 to US$10.

Montezuma

Montezuma is a distinctly boho beach town that demands you abandon the car to stroll, swim and (if you can stroll a little further) surf. The warm and wild ocean and that remnant, ever-audible jungle have helped this rocky nook cultivate an inviting, mellow vibe. Typical tourist offerings such as canopy tours and waterfall hikes do a brisk trade here, but you'll also bump up against Montezuma's internationally in-flected, artsy-rootsy beach culture in yoga classes, volunteer corps, veggie-friendly dining rooms and neo-Rastas hawking handcrafted jewelry and uplifting herbs. No wonder locals lovingly call this town 'Montefuma.'

⊙ SIGHTS

Playa Cocolito
Beach

Here's your chance to see a waterfall crashing down a cliff, straight onto the rocks and into the ocean. El Chorro Waterfall is the pièce de résistance of Playa Cocolito, which is itself pretty irresistible.

It's a hot, two-hour, 12km hike from Montezuma: leave at sunrise to spot plenty of wildlife along the way. Alternatively, this is a popular destination for horseback riding, or you can grab a meal at **Tango Mar** (☑2683-0001; www.tangomar.com; Playa Quizales) then make the 20-minute hike at low tide from there. Otherwise, bring water and snacks as there are no facilities.

The waters here are a dreamy, iridescent azure, with pink rocky cliffs creating two inviting swimming areas. It's far enough from the action that you are likely to have the place to yourself.

Playa Montezuma
Beach

The best beach close to town is just to the north, where the sand is powdery and sheltered from big swells. This is your glorious sun-soaked crash pad. The water's shade of teal is immediately nourishing, the temperature is perfect and fish are abundant. At the north end of the beach, look for the trail that leads to a cove known

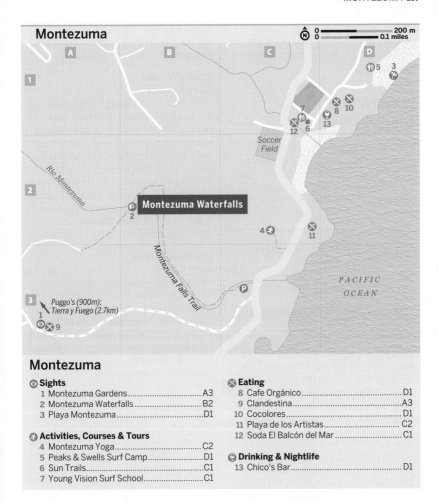

Montezuma

Montezuma

as **Piedra Colorada**. A small waterfall forms a freshwater pool, which is a perfect swimming spot.

Playa Grande
Beach

About 6km north of town, Playa Grande is the best surf beach in the area. It's a 3km-plus stretch of waves and sand, which never gets too crowded as it requires a 30-minute hike to get here. But what a hike it is, wandering along between the turquoise waters of the Pacific and the lush greenery of the Montezuma Biological Reserve.

Playa Grande is sometimes a destination for topless or nude sunbathers. This is not the cultural norm in Costa Rica, so please be discreet if you're trying to get rid of your tan lines.

Montezuma Gardens
Gardens

(Mariposario; ☎2642-1317; www.montezu-magardens.com; US$6; ⊗8am-5pm) About 1.5km south of town, alongside the waterfall trail (p191), you can tour this lush *mariposario* (butterfly garden) and nursery where the mysterious metamorphoses occur. You'll learn about the life cycles and benefits of a dozen local species, of which you'll see many colorful varieties. It's a long and steep trek from town so you may want to consider a taxi.

ACTIVITIES

Montezuma Yoga Yoga

(☎2642-0076; www.montezumayoga.com; classes US$15; ⏰8:30am & 6pm) Vinyasa and yin yoga classes are held in this gorgeous studio kissed by ocean breezes, sheltered by a peaked tin roof and serenaded by the sounds of nature. The Sunday-night candlelight flow class is a transformative experience. On the grounds of **Hotel Los Mangos** (www.hotellosmangos.com).

Young Vision Surf School Surfing

(☎8669-6835; www.youngvisionsurf.com; 2hr lessons US$50) Manny and Alvaro get rave reviews for their knowledge, enthusiasm and patience with new surfers of all ages. Daily lessons take place on Playa Grande, with no more than three people in the class. Surfboard, rash guard and fresh fruit are included. They also offer weeklong camps specifically for families, surfer chicks and yogis. Inquire at **Sano Banano** (☎2642-0638; www.elsanobanano.com) for details.

Peaks & Swells Surf Camp Surfing

(☎2642-0067; www.surfcamppeaksnswells.com; 7-day camp per person from US$2950) Weeklong camps geared to women, families and mountain bikers. If one of these is you, here's a chance to learn how to surf, following systematic methods of instruction. Located on the beach, just north of 'downtown' Montezuma.

Puntarenas–Paquera Ferry Trips

Car and passenger ferries bound for Paquera and Playa Naranjo depart several times a day from the **northwestern dock** (Av 3, btwn Calles 31 & 33) in Puntarenas. If you are driving and will be taking the car ferry, arrive at the dock early to get in line. The vehicle section tends to fill up quickly and you may not make it on. In addition, make sure that you have purchased your ticket from the walk-up ticket window before driving onto the ferry. You will not be admitted onto the boat if you don't already have a ticket.

Schedules change seasonally and can be affected by inclement weather. Check with the ferry office by the dock for any changes. Many of the hotels in town also post up-to-date schedules.

Coonatramar (☎2661-1069; www.coonatramar.com; Av 3; adult/child/bike/car US$2/1/4/35) has daily departures to Playa Naranjo (for transfer to Nicoya and points west) at 6:30am, 10am, 2:30pm and 7pm.

Naviera Tambor (☎2661-2084; www.navieratambor.com; Av 3; adult/child/bike/car US$1.50/1/4.50/23) has daily departures to Paquera (for transfer to Montezuma and Mal País) at 5am, 9am, 11am, 2pm, 5pm and 8:30pm.

EATING

Montezuma is experiencing the same food revolution that is taking place in other parts of the peninsula. Local ingredients are meeting international chefs, with magnificent results. Montezuma is also good for traditional Tico fare, often with ocean-side service.

Playa de los Artistas International $$

(☎2642-0920; mains US$9-18; ⏰4-9pm Mon-Fri, noon-4pm Sat) Most romantic dinner ever. If you're lucky, you'll snag one of the tree-trunk tables under the palms. The international menu with Mediterranean influences changes daily, though you can always count on fresh seafood roasted in the wood oven. The service is flawless, the cooking is innovative and the setting is downright dreamy. Cash only (back to reality) so bring lots.

Clandestina
Latin American $$

(☎8315-8003; www.facebook.com/clandes-tinamontezuma; mains US$9-15; ⊙11am-9pm Tue-Sat; 🛜🍴) The secret is out. The hottest restaurant in Montezuma is this awesome, artistic place in the trees at the butterfly gardens. Look for innovative takes on Central American standards, such as daily changing taco specials and delectable chicken mole enchiladas. Vegetarians are joyfully accommodated with yam and lentil cakes or *chilles rellenos* (stuffed peppers). Try the Butterfly Beer, brewed onsite.

Tierra y Fuego
Italian $$

(☎2642-1593; mains US$10-17; ⊙5-10pm Thu-Sun; 🅿🍴) Take a taxi up to this gem in the hills above Montezuma – fittingly in the Delicias neighborhood. This Italian outpost seems straight out of the Tuscan country-side, complete with brick ovens, and chickens roasting over the fire. The menu is mostly pizza and pasta, but the flavors are divine – not surprising given the ingredients are all imported or grown onsite.

Cocolores
International $$

(☎2642-0348; mains US$9-22; ⊙4-10pm Tue-Sun) Set on a beachside terrace lit by lanterns, Cocolores is one of Montezuma's top spots for an upscale dinner. The wide-ranging menu includes curries, pasta, fajitas and steaks, all prepared and served with careful attention to delicious details. Cash only.

Cafe Orgánico
Vegetarian $$

(☎2642-1322; www.organicocostarica.com; mains US$8-10; ⊙7am-10pm; 🍴) When they say 'pure food made with love,' they mean it – this healthy cafe turns out vegetarian and vegan dishes such as veggie burgers, smoothies named for local wildlife and

more (as well as meaty options too). Opposite the church square, on the road leading north to the beach.

The avocado ice cream is something everyone should try. There's live music almost nightly, including a popular open mic on Monday nights from 6:30pm to 9:30pm.

Soda El Balcón del Mar
Seafood $$

(☎8561-9870; mains US$8-12; ⊙7am-mid-night) Under new ownership, this rustic little restaurant has continued serving up lip-smacking whole fish, *casados* and grilled BBQ ribs. Grab a table on the 2nd-story balcony overlooking the beach and kiss the afternoon goodbye while watching flocks of pelicans dive bomb into the sea.

🍸 DRINKING & NIGHTLIFE

Chico's Bar
Bar

(⊙11am-2am) When it comes to nightlife, Chico's is the main game in town, which means that everybody – old, young, Ticos, tourists, rowdy, dowdy – ends up here eventually, especially on Thursday night, which is reggae night. Grab a table on the back patio for a lovely view of the beach and beyond. On the main road parallel to the beach.

ℹ GETTING THERE & AWAY

The easiest way to reach Montezuma is to abandon your own vehicle and hop on a boat shuttle from Jacó. It's also manageable by bus/ferry or car, and the road into town is now paved. Shuttle services offer a more convenient service between Montezuma and other peninsula towns, as far as to Liberia airport and beyond in some cases. Interbus (www.interbuscostarica.com) and **Tropical Tours** (☎2640-1900, WhatsApp 8890-9197; www.tropicaltoursshuttles.com; ⊙8am-9pm) are the most notable.

MONTEVERDE

Monteverde at a Glance...

Spread out on the slopes of the Cordillera de Tilarán, this area is a sprawling chain of villages, farms and nature reserves. The Reserva Biológica Bosque Nuboso Monteverde (Monteverde Cloud Forest Reserve) is the most famous one, but there are properties of all shapes and sizes – from tiny family farms to the vast Bosque Eterno de los Niños (Children's Eternal Rainforest) – that blanket the area in luscious green. As a result, there are trails to hike, birds to spot, waterfalls to swim and adventures to be had at every turn.

Two Days in Monteverde

For your first day, register in advance for a guided tour at the **Bosque Nuboso Monteverde** (p204), taking time afterwards to explore independently. Your second day is devoted to getting your adventure on, either flying through the treetops on a **canopy tour** (p210) or trekking and riding horseback through virgin jungle to **El Tigre Waterfalls** (p217). Don't miss dinner with a view at **Restaurante Celajes** (p225).

Four Days in Monteverde

On your third day, visit a local farm for an enlightening (and energizing) **coffee tour** (p208). When the sun sets, check out the area nightlife on a night tour at **Bosque Eterno de los Niños** (p217). Use your final day to learn about bugs at the **Butterfly Garden** (p214) followed by lunch at **Choco Café Don Juan** (p222).

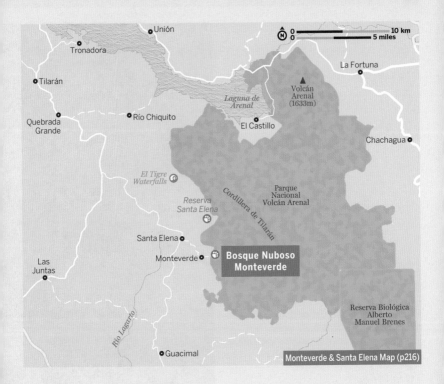

Monteverde & Santa Elena Map (p216)

Arriving in Monteverde

There is now an easy way to get to Monteverde and the surrounding environs – by bus or by car, on the newly paved main access road via Guacimal. There are two other access roads to Santa Elena – to the north via Tilarán and to the west via Las Juntas, but those are only partially paved and require at least an hour of winding and bumping up the mountain. If you're coming from Arenal, there's also a taxi-boat-taxi service that's pretty and scenic.

Where to Stay

Many lodgings are clustered in the villages of Santa Elena and Monteverde, but many more dot the landscape in the hills above Santa Elena and beyond. Before booking, consider carefully how remote you want to be (and whether or not you'll have your own vehicle). This area has a huge variety of accommodations at all price levels.

Strangler fig, Bosque Nuboso Monteverde

Bosque Nuboso Monteverde

Here is a virginal forest dripping with mist, dangling with mossy vines, gushing with creeks, blooming with life and nurturing rivulets of evolution.

Great For...

SANTA ELENA

MONTEVERDE

Bosque Nuboso Monteverde

ⓘ Need to Know

Reserva Biológica Bosque Nuboso Monteverde (Monteverde Cloud Forest Wildlife Biological Reserve; ☏2645-5122; www.cloudforestmonteverde.com; adult/student/child under 6yr US$25/12/free; ⊙7am-4pm)

★ **Top Tip**

The reserve's walking trails are almost always muddy, even during the dry season. Bring your boots!

History

This beautiful reserve came into being in 1972, when the Quaker community, spurred on by the threat of encroaching squatters, joined forces with environmental and wildlife organizations to purchase and protect an extra 328 hectares of land. This fragile environment relies almost entirely on public donations to survive. Today, the reserve totals 105 sq km.

Hiking

There are 10km of marked and maintained trails – take a photo of the map at the entrance. The most popular trails are to the east of the reserve entrance. **Sendero Bosque Nuboso** is a popular 1.9km interpretive walk through the cloud forest that begins at the ranger station (park entrance); it's paralleled by the more open, 2km **El Camino**, a favorite of birdwatchers. **Sendero Cuecha** begins at the reserve entrance and continues for 1km to a waterfall. You can take **Sendero Tosi** (800m) to return.

The gorgeous **Chomogo Trail** (1.8km) lifts hikers to 1680m, the park's highest point. The trail to the **Mirador La Ventana** (elevation 1550m) is moderately steep and leads further afield to a wooden deck overlooking the continental divide.

Wildlife-Watching

Monteverde is a birdwatching paradise, with the list of recorded species topping out at more than 400. The resplendent quetzal is most often spotted during the March and April nesting season, though you may get lucky any time of year. Keep

Three-wattled bellbird

your ears open for the three-wattled bellbird, a kind of cotinga that is famous for its distinctive call. If you're keen on birds, a specialized bird tour is highly recommended.

For those interested in spotting mammals, the cloud forest's limited visibility and abundance of higher primates (human beings) can make wildlife-watching quite difficult. That said, there are some commonly sighted species including coatis, howler monkeys, capuchins, sloths, agoutis and squirrels (as in 'real' squirrel, not the squirrel monkey). Most animals avoid the main trails, so get off the beaten track.

☑ Don't Miss

The magical, misty view from the Continental Divide.

CHRISTOPHER BECERRA/SHUTTERSTOCK ©

Tours

Although you can (and should) hike around the reserve on your own, a guide will provide an informative overview and enhance your experience. Make reservations at least a day in advance for park-run tours. The English-speaking guides are trained naturalists; proceeds benefit environmental education programs in local schools. The reserve can also recommend excellent guides for private tours.

Birdwatching (☑2645-5122; tours incl entry fee US$85; ⊙tours depart 6am) These early-morning walks usually last four to five hours (for three to six people), checking off as many as 40 species of birds (out of a possible 400).

Natural History (☑2645-5122; adult/student incl entry fee US$45/32; ⊙tours depart 7:30am, 11:30am & 1:30pm) Take a 2½- to three-hour guided walk in the woods. You'll learn all about the characteristics of a cloud forest and identify some of its unique flora. Your ticket is valid for the entire day, so you can continue to explore on your own when the tour is over.

Night Tours (☑2645-5122; www.cloudforest-monteverde.com; with/without transportation US$29/23; ⊙tours depart 6pm) Observe the 70% of regional wildlife that has nocturnal habits. Frogs, bats and other night critters are increasingly active as the sun sets. Tours are by flashlight (bring your own for the best visibility).

Plan Ahead

Due to its fragile environment, the reserve allows a maximum of 160 people at any given time (usually reached by 10am in the dry season). Make reservations or arrive early.

✗ Take a Break

Stop at Cafe Colibrí (p224) for a post-hike snack and to snap some hummingbird photos.

Don Juan coffee tour

ATLANTIDE PHOTOTRAVEL/GETTY IMAGES ©

Coffee Tours

If you're curious about the magical brew that for many makes life worth living, tour one of the coffee plantations and learn all about how Costa Rica's golden bean goes from plant to cup.

Great For...

☑ Don't Miss

Taking a bumpy ride in a traditional ox cart.

Tour Operators

Café de Monteverde

Stop by the **shop** (☎2645-7546, 2645-7550; www.cafedemonteverde.com; Monteverde; tours adult/child US$30/15; ☉coffee tasting 7am-6pm, tours 8:30am, 1:30pm & 3pm) ☛ in Monteverde to take a crash course in coffee and sample the delicious blends. Or, sign on for the three-hour tour on sustainable agriculture, which visits organic *fincas* (farms) implementing techniques like composting and solar energy. Learn how coffee growing has helped to shape this community and how it can improve the local environment.

Kind of makes you want to pour yourself another cup!

Coffee ready for export

STIG STOCKHOLM PEDERSEN/GETTY IMAGES ©

Don Juan Coffee Tour

Three-in-one tours by **Don Juan** (☎2645-6858, 2645-7100; www.donjuancr.com/monteverde; Santa Elena; adult/child US$33/14, night tour US$37/19; ☉tours 8am, 10am, 1pm, 3pm & 5:30pm) cover all your favorite vices (OK, maybe not *all* your favorites, but three of the good ones). It's a pretty cursory overview of how sugarcane is harvested and processed; how cacao beans are transformed into dark, decadent chocolate; and how coffee happens, from plant to bean to cup.

El Trapiche

Visit the picturesque family *finca* **El Trapiche** (☎2645-7650; www.eltrapichetour.com; Santa Elena; adult/child US$35/13; ☉tours 10am & 3pm Mon-Sat, 3pm Sun) in Santa Elena, where they grow not only coffee but also sugarcane, bananas and plantains. See the coffee process firsthand, take a ride in a traditional ox cart, and try your hand at making sugar. Bonus: lots of samples along the way, including sugarcane liquor, sugarcane toffee and – of course – delicious coffee. Kids love this one.

Chocolate, Too!

And if you're not a coffee drinker, try the **Caburé Chocolate Tour** (☎2645-5020; www.cabure.net; Monteverde; US$15; ☉tours 1pm & 4pm Mon-Sat). Bob, the owner of the Caburé chocolate shop in Monteverde, shares his secrets about the magical cacao pod and how to transform it into the food of the gods. There are plenty of opportunities for taste testing along the way, and you'll try your hand at making truffles.

Ziplining in Monteverde

Canopy Tours

The wild-eyed faces and whoop-de-whoop soundtrack are all the proof you need: clipping into a high-speed cable and soaring across the treetops is pure joy.

Great For...

☑ **Don't Miss**

Howling like Tarzan as you sail through the jungle on the aptly named swing.

Wonder where the whole canopy tour craze was born? Santa Elena is the site of Costa Rica's first ziplines, today eclipsed in adrenaline by dozens of imitators who have followed, some of which are right here in town. You won't be spotting any quetzals or coatis as you whoosh your way over the canopy, but if you came to Costa Rica to fly, this is the absolute best place to do it. If you want to explore the treetops at your own pace, several outfits also have systems of hanging bridges and tree-climbing adventures. Transportation from your lodging is usually included.

Original Canopy Tour

The storied zipline **tour** (☎2645-5243; www.theoriginalcanopy.com; adult/student/child US$45/35/25; ☺tours 7:30am, 10:30am & 2:30pm) that started the trend. With 10 cables, a Tarzan swing, a climb up the center of an old fig tree and a thrilling rappel, it's a lot of fun. Your adrenaline rush may not be as big as at some of the other canopy tours, but you'll enjoy smaller groups and more emphasis on the natural surroundings.

Original Canopy is located way uphill near the Cloud Forest Lodge, 2km off the main Santa Elena–Monteverde Rd.

Selvatura

One of the bigger games in town, **Selvatura** (☎4001-7899, in USA 800-771-1803; www.selvatura.com; canopy tour US$55, walkways US$39, animal exhibits US$6-17; ☺tours 8:30am, 11am, 1pm & 2:30pm) has 13 cables, 15 platforms and a Tarzan swing over a stretch of incredibly beautiful primary cloud forest. In addition to the cables, it features eight

Hanging bridge in the treetops

hanging bridges on its 'Treetop Walkways' and extras including a hummingbird garden, a butterfly garden and an amphibian and reptile exhibition.

Selvatura is 6km north of Santa Elena, near the reserve. There's a booking office in town near the church.

SkyTrek

This seriously fast canopy tour, zooming over swatches of primary forest, consists of eight platforms attached to steel towers spread out along a road. Speeds reach up to 64km/h, which is probably why **SkyTrek** (Sky Adventures; ☏2479-4100, USA 844-468-6759; www.skyadventures.travel; Santa Elena; adult/student/child SkyWalk US$41/33/28, SkyTrek US$84/70/58; ☺8am-3pm, SkyWalk to 2pm) was the first canopy tour with a real brake system.

SkyWalk, also within the Sky Adventures park, is a 2km-long guided tour over six suspended bridges.

The newest attraction is an arboreal tree-climbing adventure (adult/student/child US$42/34/29). It involves scaling four trees (the tallest is 20m) that are outfitted with handholds and straps. As you climb, you are belayed in harnesses that ensure safety and allow for an easy rappel back to the ground.

The Longest Zipline in Latin America

Aventura (☏2645-6388; www.aventura canopytour.com; Ruta 619, Santa Elena; adult/child canopy tours from US$57/46, bridges from US$40/34; ☺tours 8am, 11am, 1pm & 3pm) boasts the longest zipline (nearly 1600m!) in Latin America. The nine cables are supplemented with a Tarzan swing, a 15m rappel and two Superman ziplines that make you feel as if you're flying. It also has a network of suspension bridges, laced through secondary forest.

JOSH MILLER PHOTOGRAPHY/GETTY IMAGES ©

Monteverde & Santa Elena

Strung between two lovingly preserved cloud forests, this slim corridor of civilization consists of the Tico village of Santa Elena and the Quaker settlement of Monteverde, each with an eponymous cloud forest reserve. The cloud forests are premier destinations for everyone from budget backpackers to families and well-heeled retirees.

On a good day, the Monteverde area is a place where you can be inspired about the possibility of a world in which organic farming and alternative energy sources are the norm; on a bad day, it can feel like Disneyland in Birkenstocks. Take heart in the fact that the local community continues to fight the good fight to maintain the fragile balance between nature and commerce.

◎ SIGHTS

The sights in Monteverde and Santa Elena are mostly geared to bringing the wildlife a little closer, whether it's bats, butterflies, frogs, snakes or flowers. These stops can be entertaining and educational – especially for children – but it's even more rewarding when you see these creatures in the wild. And you're in the wild now, so go out there and see it.

Butterfly Garden   Zoo

(Jardín de Mariposas; ☑2645-5512; www.monteverdebutterflygarden.com; Cerro Plano; adult/student/child US$17.50/13.50/5.50; ⊘8:30am-4pm) Head here for everything you ever wanted to know about butterflies. There are four gardens representing different habitats; they're home to more than 40 species. Up-close observation

> *Kids love this place, and knowledgeable naturalist guides truly enhance the experience.*

cases allow you to witness the butterflies as they emerge from the chrysalis (if your timing is right).

Other exhibits feature the industrious leafcutter ant and a tarantula hawk specimen (the wasp that eats tarantulas!) and lots of scorpions. Kids love this place, and knowledgeable naturalist guides truly enhance the experience with an enlightening hour-long tour (complimentary with admission).

Ranario   Zoo

(Monteverde Frog Pond; ☑2645-6320; Santa Elena; per attraction US$15.50, package ticket for frogs & insects US$20; ⊘9am-8:30pm) Returning to its former glory as the Ranario (Frog Pond; it's changed name a few times), this place also features an insect house. The frogs are still the highlight – 28 species reside in transparent enclosures lining the winding indoor jungle paths. Sharp-eyed guides point out frogs, eggs and tadpoles with flashlights. Your ticket entitles you to two visits, so come back in the evening to see the nocturnal species.

Jardín de Orquídeas   Gardens

(Orchid Garden; ☑2645-5308; www.monteverdeorchidgarden.net; Santa Elena; adult/child over 6yr/under 6yr US$13/7/free; ⊘9am-5pm) This sweet-smelling garden in Santa Elena has shady trails winding past more than 500 types of orchids. On your guided tour, you'll see such rarities as *Platystele jungermannioides,* the world's smallest orchid. If you have orchids at home, here's your chance to get expert tips on how to keep them beautiful and blooming. If you're expecting massive sprays of colorful blooms, though, think again – most specimens require the magnifying glass given to you at the entrance to be seen.

Bat Jungle   Zoo

(☑2645-9999; www.batjungle.com; Monteverde; adult/child US$17/14; ⊘9am-6pm) The Bat Jungle in Monteverde is a small but informative exhibit, with good bilingual educational displays and a habitat housing almost

100 free-flying bats. Make a reservation for your 45-minute tour to learn about echolocation, bat wing aerodynamics and other amazing flying-mammal facts. The bats are on a reversed day/night schedule so they are most active from 9am to 5pm. Located beneath Café Caburé (p224).

El Arbol Hueco
Natural Feature

FREE There's no sign, no website, and last we checked, nobody was collecting any money for this delightful roadside attraction. It's simply a hollowed-out fig tree (or, rather, a few interlocking ones) that happens to have 'branches' creating an easy-to-use ladder. You can shimmy up the center of the tree and then your friend can take a sweet photo of you from the bottom, for the 'gram.

Do wait your turn and climb carefully, as there's no safety equipment. To get there, take the road heading north of Santa Elena for about 600m, and you'll see a small, unmarked trail heading west. The tree is only 25m from the road.

Friends Meeting House
Church

(www.monteverdequakers.org; Monteverde; ⏱meetings 10:30am Sun, 9am Wed) This simple meeting house in Monteverde is the 'church' of the American Society of Friends, or the Quakers, who first settled this area and committed to protect a portion of the cloud forest.

In 1949 four Quakers in Alabama were jailed for their refusal to be drafted to fight in the Korean War. In response, a group of 44 Quakers from 11 families left the US and headed for (much) greener pastures, literally. The Quakers settled in Monteverde (Green Mountain) for two reasons – the absence of a military, and the cool mountain climate. Ensconced in their isolated refuge, they adopted a simple, trouble-free life of dairy farming and cheese production.

Years later, in an effort to protect the watershed above its 15-sq-km plot in Monteverde, the Quaker community agreed

Santa Elena Reserve

Though Monteverde's cloud forest reserve (p204) gets all the attention, the misty **Reserva Santa Elena** (Reserva Bosque Nuboso Santa Elena; ☎2645-7107, 2645-5390; www.reservasantaelena.org; entrance adult/student US$16/9, guided hike US$33; ⏱7am-4pm) has plenty to recommend it. You can practically hear the epiphyte-draped canopy breathing in as water drops onto the leaf litter and mud underfoot. The odd call of the three-wattled bellbird and the low crescendo of a howler monkey punctuate the higher-pitched bird chatter. While Monteverde entertains more than 200,000 visitors annually, Santa Elena sees closer to 20,000 tourists each year, meaning its dewy trails are usually far quieter.

This cloud forest is slightly higher in elevation than Monteverde's; as some of the forest is secondary growth, there are sunnier places for spotting birds and other animals. There's a stable population of monkeys and sloths, many of which can be seen on the road to the reserve. Unless you're a trained ecologist, the old-growth forest in Santa Elena will appear fairly similar to that found in Monteverde.

Wild plant, Reserva Santa Elena
YASEMIN OLGUNOZ BERBER/SHUTTERSTOCK ©

to preserve the mountaintop cloud forest, eventually leading to the establishment of the reserve (p204).

Monteverde & Santa Elena

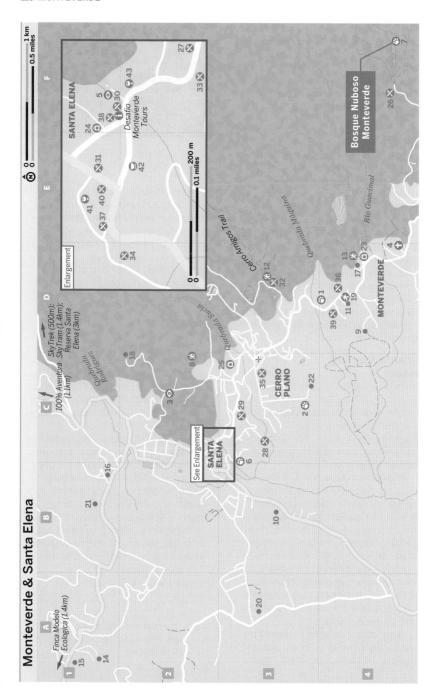

SkyTrek (500m);
SkyTram (1.4km);
Reserva Santa
Elena (3km)

100% Aventura
(1.1km)

Finca Modelo
Ecologica (1.4km)

Quebrada
Rodriguez

Quebrada Sucia

Cerro Amigos Trail

Quebrada Maxina

Rio Guacimal

SANTA ELENA

CERRO
PLANO

MONTEVERDE

Bosque Nuboso
Monteverde

Enlargement

SANTA ELENA

Desafio
Monteverde
Tours

See Enlargement

SANTA
ELENA

Monteverde & Santa Elena

ACTIVITIES

In addition to the two biggies anchoring this area at the north and south, Monteverde and Santa Elena are home to dozens of smaller private reserves. The Monteverde and Santa Elena reserves are special – very special – because they are essentially the only cloud forest reserves in the area. But if you want to immerse yourself in nature, get some exercise, spot some monkeys, admire a scenic vista or cool off in a waterfall, there are countless places to do so (most of which will be significantly less crowded than the Monteverde reserve).

El Tigre Waterfalls   Outdoors

(☑8391-9625; www.eltigrewaterfalls.com; US$79; ⊙tour begins 7:30am) For the able-bodied and adventure-minded, this is Monteverde's best new jungle trek. The 4½-hour journey into 60 hectares of forestland involves a little of everything: some hiking here, a hanging-bridge crossing

there, some horseback riding here, a river plunge there. The rough and mostly virgin territory brims with wildlife, and is often remembered by travelers as the vacation's highlight. A knowledgeable guide and transport are included. Lunch can be purchased at the end of the tour.

Bosque Eterno de los Niños   Hiking

(Children's Eternal Rainforest, BEN; ☑4001-4866; https://acmcr.org; adult/child US$15/10, guided night hike US$24/20, transportation per person US$5; ⊙8am-5pm, night hike 5:30pm; ⓜ) ✐ What became of the 1980s efforts of a group of Swedish schoolchildren to save the rainforest? Only this enormous 2300-sq-km reserve – the largest private reserve in the country. It's mostly inaccessible to tourists, with the exception of the well-marked 4.5km **Sendero Bajo del Tigre**, which is actually a series of shorter trails. Make reservations in advance for the popular two-hour night hikes.

At the entrance there's an education center for children and a fabulous vista over the reserve. The Estación Biológica San Gerardo, reachable by a rather gnarly 2½-hour trail from Reserva Santa Elena (p215), is managed by BEN and has dorm bunk beds for researchers and students, but you may be able to stay overnight with prior arrangements. In 2020, a new tax will raise rates for hiking and stays by 4%.

Aguti Reserve
Hiking

(☑4000-3385; www.agutimonteverde.com; US$15; ☺7am-3:30pm) Open since 2018, this is Monteverde's newest private reserve. Its 4km network of trails make figure eights up and down a mountainside, looping through *matapalo* trees (strangler figs) over hillside lookouts and, if you're lucky, past the reserve's curious spokescreature – the agouti. It sort of looks like a giant rabbit got busy with a hamster. The other solid find here is the three-wattled bellbird, a migratory species with a piercing call and a ridiculous mustache.

Tours of the reserve are also on offer, including guided walks (from US$35), night hikes (from US$25) and birdwatching excursions (from US$65).

Curi-Cancha Reserve
Hiking, Birdwatching

(☑8448-8283, 2645-6915; www.reservacuri cancha.com; entrance US$15, night tour US$20, natural history tour US$20, bird tour US$70; ☺7am-3pm, guided hike 5:30-7:30pm) Bordering Monteverde but without the crowds, this lovely private reserve on the banks of the Río Cuecha is popular among birders. There is about 8km of well-marked trails, a hummingbird garden and a view of the continental divide and the Golfo de Nicoya. Make reservations for the guided hikes, including the early-morning bird walks and specialized three-hour natural history walks.

Cerro Amigos
Hiking

Take a hike up to the highest peak (1842m) in the area for good views of the surrounding rainforest and, on a clear day, Volcán Arenal, 20km away to the northeast. Behind **Hotel Belmar** (☑2645-5201; www.hotelbelmar.net) in Cerro Plano, take the dirt road going downhill, then the next left. The trail ascends roughly 300m in 3km.

Note that this trail does not connect to the trails in the Monteverde reserve (p204).

Revive Healing Arts
Massage

(☑8372-2002; www.revivehealingarts.com; Monteverde; treatments from US$55; ☺by appointment) Owner Karen Gordon's signature offering, the Mountain Massage, is custom designed to soothe your aching muscles, no matter what adventures you've been on. She also offers Reiki, craniosacral therapy and personalized retreat programs.

☉ TOURS

There's not a lot of diversity when it comes to tours in the Monteverde/Santa Elena region. Aside from the canopy and coffee tours, most reserves offer guided hikes, morning bird walks and spooky night hikes. Horseback-riding tours are especially good in Monteverde, though. You don't have to be an expert rider; most companies (and horses) are used to beginners. There are normally several options for routes and duration, ranging from two hours to full days.

Sabine's Smiling Horses
Horseback Riding

(☑8385-2424; www.horseback-riding-tour.com; rides per hour US$25; ☺tours 9am, 11am & 3pm) Conversant in four languages (in addition to equine), Sabine will make sure you're comfortable on your horse, whether you're a novice rider or an experienced cowboy. Her long-standing operation offers a variety of treks including a popular waterfall tour (three hours) and a magical full-moon tour (monthly), and she keeps Arabian horses for endurance riding. Multiday rides must be booked well in advance.

Finca Modelo
Ecologica
Adventure

(📞2645-5581; www.familiabrenestours.com; La Cruz; treetop/canyoning/combo US$45/79/113; ⏲tours 8am, 11am, 2pm & 5:30pm) The Brenes family *finca* offers a number of unique and thrilling diversions. The masterpiece is the two-hour canyoning tour, which descends six glorious waterfalls, the highest of which is 40m. No experience necessary, just an adventurous spirit. The treetop tour involves climbing a 40m ficus tree, using ropes and rappels to go up and down.

The *finca* is located 2km north of Santa Elena in the village of La Cruz; transportation from your hotel is included in the price.

Horse Trek
Monteverde
Horse Riding

(📞English 8359-3485, Spanish 8379-9827; www.horsetrekmonteverde.com; Ruta 606, Santa Elena; 2/5hr tour US$49/85; ⏲7am-7pm Mon-Fri, 10am-6pm Sat-Sun) Owner and guide Marvin Anchia is a Santa Elena native, a professional horse trainer and an amateur naturalist who offers an excellent, intimate horseback-riding experience. Choose between scenic two-hour and all-day rides on the outskirts of town where few other tourists venture, and multiday cowboy experiences. The horses are well cared for, well trained and a joy to ride.

SkyTram
Cable Car

(📞2479-4100, in USA 844-468-6759; www.skyadventures.travel; Santa Elena; adult/student/child US$48/40/33; ⏲8am-3pm) Owned by SkyTrek (p213), SkyTram is a wheelchair-accessible gondola that floats gently over the cloud forest. On a clear day you can see from the volcanoes in the east to the Pacific in the west. Packages are available if you're also interested in the SkyTrek (canopy tour) and SkyWalk (hanging bridges).

Caballeriza
El Rodeo
Horseback Riding

(📞2645-5764; elrodeo02@gmail.com; Santa Elena; from US$45; ⏲8am-4:30pm) Based at a local *finca*, this outfit offers tours on private trails through rainforest, coffee plantations and grasslands, with plenty of pauses to spot wildlife and admire the fantastic landscapes. The specialty is a sunset tour to a spot overlooking the Golfo de Nicoya. *¡Que hermoso!* (How beautiful!)

Monteverde Extremo
Adventure

(📞8305-0126, 4001-8295; www.monteverdeextremo.com; Santa Elena; canopy tour US$50, bungee US$80, Tarzan swing US$44; ⏲8am-4pm) This place has a canopy ride that allows you to fly Superman-style through the air; the highest and most adrenaline-addled Tarzan swing in the area; and a bungee jump from 150m. One way or another, you will scream. Located in secondary forest, the views are marvelous but they herd some pretty big groups through here, so it's not exactly a nature experience.

Valle Escondido
Hiking

(Hidden Valley; 📞2645-5156; www.valleescondidopreserve.com; Cerro Plano; day entry US$16, night tour adult/child US$26/16; ⏲6am-4:30pm, night tour 5:30pm) Reserve in advance for the popular two-hour guided night tour, then come back the next day to explore the reserve on your own. Located behind Monteverde Inn in Cerro Plano, the well-marked trail winds through a deep canyon into a 17-hectare reserve, passing wonderful vistas and luscious waterfalls.

💬 **Spanish & Other Courses**

The nonprofit **Monteverde Institute** (📞2645-5053; www.monteverde-institute.org; Monteverde; weeklong courses US$390, homestay per day incl meals US$25.50) offers interdisciplinary courses in Spanish, as well as more specialized programs in tropical ecology, conservation and ecotourism, among other topics. Courses are occasionally open to the public, as are volunteer opportunities in education and reforestation.

From left: Blue morpho butterfly (p214); *Horchata* drink; Ziplining on a canopy tour (p210)

It's recommended for birding and wild-life-watching during the day, when it's quiet with few tourists.

Santa Maria Night Walk   Hiking

(☎2645-6548; www.nightwalksantamarias. com; Santa Elena; US$25; ☺tour 5:45pm) Night walks are popular around these parts, mainly because 80% of the cloud forest creatures are nocturnal. This one takes place on a private Santa Elena *finca* with a 10-hectare swath of primary and secondary forest. Expert guides point out active nocturnal wildlife, ranging from snakes and spiders to sloths and kinkajous. Flashlights provided.

🛍 SHOPPING

Luna Azul   Jewelry

(☎2645-6638; www.facebook.com/lunaazul monteverde; Santa Elena; ☺10am-7pm) In a new home next to Pensión Santa Elena, this cute gallery and gift shop is packed to the gills with locally made jewelry, clothing, soaps, sculpture and macramé, among other things. The jewelry in particular is

stylish and stunning, crafted from silver, shell, crystals and turquoise.

Monteverde
Art House   Arts & Crafts

(Casa de Arte; ☎2645-5275; www.facebook.com/ monteverde.arthouse; Cerro Plano; ☺9am-6pm Mon-Sat, 10am-6pm Sun) You'll find several rooms stuffed with colorful Costa Rican artistry here. The goods include jewelry, ceramic work, Boruca textiles and traditional handicrafts. There's a big variety of offerings, including some paintings and more contemporary work, but it's mostly at the crafts end of the arty-crafty spectrum. Great for souvenirs.

Heladería Monteverde   Food & Drink

(☎2645-6889; Monteverde; ☺8am-5pm) Formerly the Monteverde Cheese Factory, this business was started in 1953 by Monteverde's original Quaker settlers. It produced everything from a creamy Gouda to a very nice sharp white cheddar, as well as other dairy products such as yogurt and, more importantly, ice cream and milk shakes. Now owned by the Mexican giant Sigma

THEPALMER/GETTY IMAGES ©

Alimentos, the shop still sells products made with the original recipes.

Don't miss the chance to sample Monte Rico cheese, a Monteverde original. Sadly, tours of the facility are no longer offered.

 EATING

The kitchens of Santa Elena and Monteverde offer high quality but poor value. You'll be delighted by the organic ingredients, local flavors and international zest, but not by the high price tags. Even the local *sodas* (places serving counter lunches) and bakeries are more expensive than they ought to be. Santa Elena has the most budget options.

 Santa Elena

Orchid Coffee Cafe $

(✆2645-6850; www.orchidcoffeecr.com; mains US$8-12; ⏰7am-8pm; 🛜🖊) Feeling peckish? Go straight to this lovely Santa Elena cafe, filled with art and light. Grab a seat on the front porch and take a bite of heaven. It calls itself a coffee shop, but there's a full menu of traditional and nontraditional breakfast items, sweet and savory crepes, interesting and unusual salads, and thoroughly satisfying sandwiches.

Taco Taco Mexican $

(✆2645-7900; www.tacotaco.net; mains US$5-8; ⏰11am-10pm; 🛜) A wildly popular terrace restaurant offering tasty Tex-Mex tacos, plus burritos and quesadillas filled with shredded meats like chicken and *carnitas* (pork). There's also slow-roasted short rib, roasted veggies and battered mahi-mahi. The only difficulty is deciding what to eat (though you really can't go wrong). When the place is slammed, service can be painfully slow.

Raulito's Pollo Asado Chicken $

(✆8308-0810; mains US$4-5; ⏰8am-11pm) Scrappy street dogs and chatty *taxistas* (taxi drivers) vie for attention at this porcelain-countered wonder. Golden, crispy chicken morsels are transferred from the spit to your plate with a heap of rice, fries, salad or *gallo pinto* (rice and beans). Wash it down with an icy *horchata* (rice milk and cinnamon drink) and still walk away with some beer money.

Sabor Tico
Soda $

(☑2645-5827; www.restaurantesabortico.com; Centro Comercial, mains US$7-11; ☼7am-10pm) Ticos and travelers alike rave about this local joint. Look for tasty twists on the standard fare, such as *olla de carne* (beef soup), *chorreadas Ticas* (fried corn cakes with sour cream) and tamales (holiday fare, typically). The *gallos* (soft tortillas with delicious fillings of your choice) are a perfect alternative to the more filling *casados* (set meals) for lunch.

> *The* gallos *are a perfect alternative to the more filling* casados *(set meals) for lunch.*

Soda La Amistad
Soda $

(☑2645-6108; mains US$6-9; ☼11am-9:30pm; 🖉) Friendly and family run, this is a well-loved *soda* that's convenient if you're staying along this side road. You'll find typical, tasty *casados*, burgers, pasta and a list of handy translations on the menu. Herbivores will appreciate the veggie options, which include one burger and a *casado*. These folks know their stuff (and it's cheap).

Choco Café Don Juan
Cafe $$

(☑2645-7444; www.facebook.com/chococafed-onjuan; mains US$7-15; ☼8am-8pm; 🖥🖉) This little cafe roasts beans from its coffee farm (p209) and uses fancy machinery (La Marzocco!) to serve up the best cup of joe in Monteverde. The food is also excellent, with healthy salads and heaping plates of pasta,

fish, chicken and steak, plus delicious baked goods for dessert. There's great porch seating, but the indoor environs are downright dainty.

Toro Tinto
Steak $$

(☑2645-6252; www.facebook.com/torotinto.cr; mains US$15-25; ☼6-10pm) This Argentine steakhouse will warm your cloud-soaked soul with its cozy atmosphere and open kitchen. Then it'll sate your hunger with steaks that are perfectly cut and grilled to order, plus unexpected specials and delicious desserts. The wine selection is good – mostly Chilean and Argentine – but pricey.

Morpho's Restaurant
International $$

(☑2645-7373; www.morphosrestaurant.com; mains US$8-20; ☼11am-9:15pm; 🖉) In new digs with a killer sunset view, this double-decker restaurant is a favorite in Santa Elena for its varied menu combining local ingredients with gourmet flair. There is a good number of vegetarian options (salads, soups, pastas, etc), but do take note that the 'veggie burger' is really just an egg sandwich. Arrive early for a prime table on the terrace.

Happy-hour two-for-one drinks last from 3:30pm to 5pm.

Tree House Restaurant & Café
Cafe $$$

(☑2645-5751; www.treehouse.cr; mains US$15-22; ☼11am-10pm; 🖥) It's a fine line between hokey and happy. But this restaurant – built around a hundred-year-old *higuerón* (fig) tree – definitely raises a smile. There's a menu of well-prepared if overpriced standards, from carpaccio to burgers to *comida típica* (regional specialities). The service is spot-on. It's a lively space to have a bite, linger over wine and occasionally catch live music.

Cold? Try the Chocolate Tree House, a devilish dash of coffee with chocolate-flavored liqueurs.

★ Top Five for Foodies

Restaurante Celajes (p225)

Choco Café Don Juan

Sofia (p225)

Morpho's Restaurant

Tree House Restaurant & Café

Chimichanga

The Tale of the Golden Toad

Once upon a time in the cloud forests of Monteverde, there lived the *Bufo periglenes* (golden toad), also known as the *sapo dorado*. Because this bright burnt-yellow, exotic little toad was sporadically seen scrambling amid the Monteverde leaf litter – the only place in the world where it appeared – it became something of a Monteverde mascot. Sadly, the golden toad has not been seen since 1989 and is now believed to be extinct.

Ultimately, scientists decided the main culprit was the worldwide spread of chytridiomycosis disease (caused by the fungus *Batrachochytrium dendro-batidis,* in case you were wondering), which some scientists believe climate change has been fueling. Then there's always the global issue of habitat loss, an equally bleak story.

According to the Global Amphibian Assessment, 42% of the world's 7993 known amphibians are currently threatened with extinction. In response to this dire statistic, an international coalition of zoos and wildlife conservation organizations have jointly established Amphibian Ark (www.amphibianark.org), an attempt to 'bank' as many species as possible in the event of further die-offs. As for the golden toad, some folks are still looking.

Golden toad

El Jardín International $$$

(☏2645-5057; www.monteverdelodge.com; Monteverde Lodge, Santa Elena; mains US$12-24; ☺7am-10pm; ☏) The menu at this fine-dining establishment is wide ranging, always highlighting the local flavors. But these are not your typical *tipica* (traditional plates). A case in point: the beef tenderloin marinated for five hours in a coffee liquor and served with cashew butter and mashed casava. The setting – with windows to the trees – is lovely and the service is superb. Romantics can opt for a private table in the garden.

🍴 Cerro Plano & Monteverde

Cafe Colibrí Cafe $

(☏2645-7768; Monteverde; sandwiches US$5-7; ☺7am-4:30pm) Just outside the reserve gates, the 'Hummingbird Cafe' is a top-notch spot to refuel after a hike in the woods. The drinks will warm your body, but the sound of dozens of hummingbirds in the garden will delight your heart. Many say the sandwiches are just OK; come for the coffee (US$2) and hummingbirds. Great photo ops.

An identification board shows the nine species that you're likely to see.

Stella's Bakery Bakery $$

(☏2645-5560; Monteverde; mains US$8-15; ☺6:30am-6pm; ☏) A bakery for birders. Come in the morning for strong coffee and sweet pastries, or later for rich, warming soup, and sandwiches on homemade bread. Plates such as the *huevos rancheros* (Mexican eggs) satisfy, especially with a heap of passion-fruit cheesecake for dessert. Whenever you come, keep on eye on the bird feeder, which attracts tanagers, motmots and an emerald-green toucanet.

A steakhouse opened here in 2018 and serves guests after the cafe closes, from 6pm to 10pm.

Café Caburé Cafe $$

(☏2645-5020; www.cabure.net; Monteverde; lunch US$6-12, dinner US$14-18; ☺9am-9pm Mon-Sat; ☏) This Argentine cafe above the Bat Jungle (p214) specializes in creative and delicious everything, from sandwiches on homemade bread and fresh salads, to more elaborate fare such as sea bass in almond sauce or filet mignon with chimichurri. Save room for dessert: the chocolate treats are high art. There's hot chocolate, an Argentine brownie and (yes!) the cafe's Chocolate Tour (p209).

Tramonti   Italian $$

(☎2645-6120; www.tramonticr.com; Monteverde; mains US$10-16; ☺11:30am-9:30pm; 🍴) Tramonti offers authentic Italian fare, specializing in fresh seafood, hearty pastas and wood-fired pizzas. With a greenery-filled dining room twinkling with lights, the ambiance is relaxed yet romantic. If you're up in Monteverde and don't feel like venturing into town, this is a real crowd-pleaser. Several pizzas and pastas are suitable for vegetarians. There's a decent selection of wines from Italy and Argentina.

Sofia   Fusion $$

(☎2645-7017; Cerro Plano; mains US$14-18; ☺11:30am-9:30pm; 🍴) With its Nuevo Latino cuisine – a modern fusion of traditional Latin American cooking styles – Sofia has established itself as one of the best places in town. Our faves include plantain-crusted sea bass, seafood chimichanga, and beef tenderloin with roasted red pepper and cashew sauce. The ambiance is enhanced by groovy music, picture windows, romantic candle lighting and potent cocktails.

Restaurante
Celajes   International $$$

(☎2645-5201; www.hotelbelmar.net/restaurant-monteverde-celajes; mains US$15-22; ☺6:15-10am & noon-9pm; P🍴) 🍴 Ease into a studded leather armchair in the lounge and indulge with a dazzling cocktail designed by the country's finest mixologist. Then around sunset, go for a table on the veranda, with views across the cloud forest all the way to the Golfo de Nicoya. Proceed with the farm-to-table feast composed mainly of ingredients from the restaurant's organic farm.

The inventive soups and salads, croquettes, and grilled meat plates are all beautifully presented, and the service is excellent.

Huevos rancheros (Mexican eggs)

KONSTANTIN KOPACHINSKY/SHUTTERSTOCK ©

Paving the Way

A 1983 feature article in *National Geographic* billed the Monteverde and Santa Elena area as the place to view one of Central America's most famous birds – the resplendent quetzal. Suddenly, hordes of tourists armed with tripods and telephoto lenses started braving Monteverde's notoriously awful access roads, which came as a huge shock to its Quaker community.

In an effort to stem the tourist flow, local communities lobbied to stop developers from paving the roads. It worked for a while, but eventually, the lobby to spur development bested the lobby to limit development. After several years of delays and broken contract agreements since the project first began in 2017, the paving of the main access road was finally completed in early 2020.

The better road will inevitably mean more visitors, and this precious experiment in sustainable ecotourism will undergo a whole new set of trials.

Resplendent quetzal
MALLARDG500/GETTY IMAGES ©

 DRINKING & NIGHTLIFE

Nightlife in these parts generally involves a guided hike and nocturnal critters, but since these misty green mountains draw artists and dreamers, there's a smattering of regular cultural offerings. When there's anything going on, you'll see it heavily advertised around town. You'll also see some action at the bars in Santa Elena, especially during the dry season.

Bar Amigos Bar
(☏2645-5071; www.baramigos.com; Santa Elena; ⊙11:40am-2am) With picture windows overlooking the mountainside, this Santa Elena mainstay evokes the atmosphere of a ski lodge. But there are DJs, karaoke and pool tables plus sports on the screens. This is the one consistent place in the area to let loose, so there's usually a good, rowdy mix of Ticos and tourists.

The food, such as the *chifrijo* (rice and pinto beans with fried pork and capped with fresh tomato salsa and corn chips), is surprisingly good.

Monteverde Beer House Beer Garden
(☏2645-7675; www.facebook.com/monteverde beerhouse; Santa Elena; ⊙10am-10pm; 🛜) It's not a brewery – contrary to the sign – but it does offer a selection of local craft beers. There's a shady deck out back and smiling servers on hand; it's a perfect atmosphere for kicking back after a day of adventures.

The Middle Eastern food (mains US$6 to US$10) is hit or miss, but if you're hungry, go for the *shakshuka* (baked eggs in a tomato and pepper sauce).

ℹ GETTING THERE & AWAY

While most Costa Rican communities regularly request paved roads in their region, preservationists in Monteverde have done the opposite, and most roads around here are shockingly rough. Even if you arrive on the newly paved road via Guacimal, you'll still want a 4WD to get to the more remote lodges and reserves.

There are three roads from the Interamericana. Coming from the south, the first well-signed turnoff is at Rancho Grande (18km north of the Puntarenas exit). The first stretch of this route (from Sardinal to Guacimal) was paved in 2011. The remaining 17km (from Guacimal to Santa Elena) was finished in early 2020. The

MILOSZ MASLANKA/SHUTTERSTOCK ©

Santa Elena

drive now takes about 2½ hours if there's no traffic.

A second, shorter road goes via Juntas, but it's not paved except for the first few kilometers.

Finally, if coming from the north, drivers can take the paved road from Cañas via Tilarán and then take the rough road from Tilarán to Santa Elena.

If you're coming from Arenal, consider taking the lakeside route through Tronadora and Río Chiquito, instead of going through Tilarán. The roads are rougher, but the panoramas of the lake, volcano and surrounding countryside are magnificent.

There are two gas stations open for business in the area, one of which is in Cerro Plano.

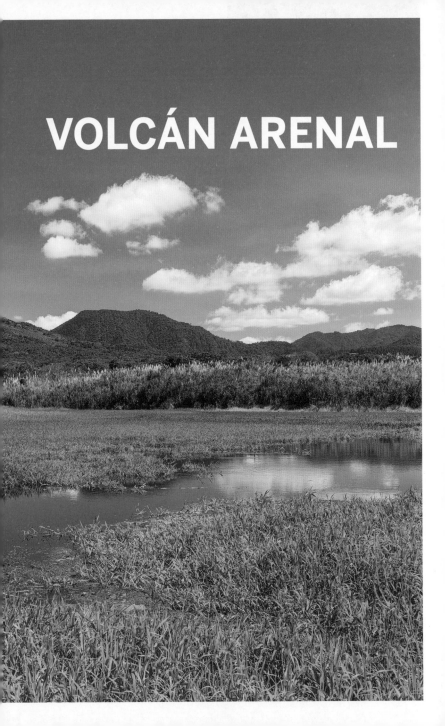

VOLCÁN ARENAL

In this Chapter

Volcán Arenal at a Glance...

You know about the region's main attraction: that volcano, surrounded by old lava fields, bubbling hot springs and a stunning lake. Even though the regular eruptions have ceased, there's still plenty of adventure here. There are trails to hike, waterfalls to rappel down, and sloths to spot. No matter your preferred method of exploring – hiking, biking, horseback riding, ziplining – you can do it here. And when your body's had enough, you can ease into a volcano-heated pool to soak away your aches and pains.

Two Days in Volcán Arenal

On your first day, set out on the well-marked trail system within **Parque Nacional Volcán Arenal** (p232), venturing to waterfalls, lava flows or crater lakes. Afterwards, head to the **hot springs** (p236) for a well-deserved soak. On your second day, take a detour to El Castillo to visit the **Butterfly Conservatory** (p246) and have lunch at **La Ventanita** (p247).

Four Days in Volcán Arenal

If you have the luxury of a third day, return to the park to hike along old lava flows and spy on sloths. Travel on horseback or by mountain bike if you prefer. Your fourth day is free for a hike and swim at **Catarata Río Fortuna** (p238). Alternatively, take a day trip to **Proyecto Asis** (p240) to support the animal sanctuary.

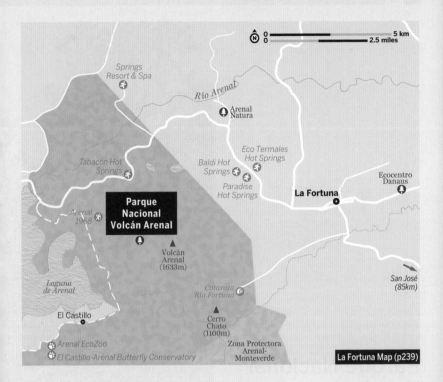

Springs
Resort & Spa

Río Arenal

Arenal
Natura

Eco Termales
Hot Springs

Tabacón Hot
Springs

Baldi Hot
Springs

Paradise
Hot Springs

La Fortuna

Ecocentro
Danaus

**Parque
Nacional
Volcán Arenal**

*Arenal
1968*

Volcán
Arenal
(1633m)

*Laguna
de Arenal*

Catarata
Río Fortuna

San José
(85km)

El Castillo

Cerro
Chato
(1100m)

Arenal EcoZoo

El Castillo-Arenal Butterfly Conservatory

Zona Protectora
Arenal-
Monteverde

La Fortuna Map (p239)

Arriving in Volcán Arenal

The roads in the region are mostly in fine condition, with good highways branching out from La Fortuna: heading west, past the park entrance and around the lake; heading south through Chachagua and beyond; or heading east toward Muelle and Ciudad Quesada (San Carlos). Buses ply all of these routes. Tour operators and shuttle buses supplement the public transportation, making it one of the easiest regions to navigate without your own vehicle.

Where to Stay

While there are some decent lodgings in La Fortuna itself (especially budget options), you might want to base yourself uphill – nearer to the hiking, hanging bridges and hot springs – or a bit south of town where you'll hardly hear a peep at night. Even the lakefront properties around El Castillo and the Laguna de Arenal are close enough to use as a base for exploring the region.

Sendero Las Coladas (p234)

Parque Nacional Volcán Arenal

Volcán Arenal no longer lights up the night sky with molten lava, but it still provides a rugged terrain for hiking and a rich habitat for wildlife. There are volcanic vistas to the massive lake below (which teems with fish, if that's your sport), birdlife in the canopy for the binocular crowd, and waterfalls and hot springs to soak in.

Great For...

ℹ Need to Know

Parque Nacional Volcán Arenal
(☏2461-8499; adult/child US$15/5; ⊗8am-4pm, last entrance 2:30pm)

★ **Top Tip**

The ranger station has trail maps available.

For most of modern history, Volcán Arenal was just another dormant volcano surrounded by fertile farmland. But for about 42 years – from its destructive explosion in 1968 until its sudden subsiding in 2010 – the volcano was an awe-striking natural wonder, producing menacing ash columns, massive explosions and streams of glowing molten rock almost daily.

The fiery views are gone for now, but Arenal is still a worthy destination, thanks to the dense forest covering its lower slopes and foothills, and the picture-perfect conical shape up top (often shrouded in clouds, but still). The Parque Nacional Volcán Arenal is part of the Area de Conservación Arenal, which protects most of the Cordillera de Tilarán. This area is rugged and varied, rich with wildlife and laced with trails.

Hiking

Although it's no longer erupting (or perhaps because it is not), Volcán Arenal is the big hiking draw here. There is a well-marked trail system within the park, and several private reserves on its outskirts. Waterfalls, lava flows and crater lakes are all worthy destinations, which you can reach without a guide.

From the **ranger station** (☑2461-8499; adult/child US$15/5; ☺8am-4pm), you can hike the **Sendero Los Heliconias**, a 1km circular track that passes by the site of the 1968 lava flow. A 1.5km-long path branches off this trail and leads to an overlook. The **Sendero Las Coladas** also branches off the Heliconias trail and wraps around the volcano for 2km past the 1993 lava flow before connecting with the **Sendero Los Tucanes**, which extends for another 3km

Volcán Arenal

through the tropical rainforest at the base of the volcano. To return to the parking area, you'll have to turn back – you'll get good views of the summit on the way.

From the park headquarters (not the ranger station) is the 1.3km **Sendero Los Miradores**, which leads down to the shores of the volcanic lake and provides a good angle for volcano viewing. Also from the park headquarters, the **Old Lava Flow Trail** is an interesting and strenuous lower elevation trail following the flow of the massive 1992 eruption. The 4km round trip takes two hours to complete. If you want to keep hiking, combine it with the **Sendero**

El Ceibo, a scenic 1.8km trail through secondary forest.

In 2017, a new 'sector peninsula' set of trails opened, comprising 1.2km of trails, an observation tower and a scenic lake overlook. Although last entry to the national park is at 2:30pm, you may be allowed to enter and stay at the new sector later.

There are also trails departing from **Arenal Observatory Lodge** (✆2479-1070, reservations 2290-7011; www.arenalobservatory lodge.com; d/tr/q without bathroom US$100/115/130, with bathroom from US$140/155/185; P❄@🖢🕿🏊) and on a nearby private reserve, **Arenal 1968**. This network of trails along the original 1968 lava flow is right next to the park entrance. There's a *mirador* (lookout) that on a clear day offers a picture-perfect volcano view. It's located 1.2km from the highway turnoff to the park, just before the ranger station.

Tours

In addition to hiking, it's also possible to explore the park on horseback, mountain bike or ATV.

Two-hour tours on horseback depart from **Arenal Wilberth Stables** (✆2479-7522; www.arenalwilberthstable.com; 1/2hr US$40/65; ⊙7:30am, 11am & 2:30pm) at the foot of Arenal. The ride takes in forest and farmland, as well as lake and volcano views. The stables are opposite the entrance to the national park, but there's an office in La Fortuna, next to Arenal Hostel Resort.

Desafío Adventure Company (p242) is a tour agency with the widest range of tours in La Fortuna, including horseback-riding treks and mountain-bike expeditions to Volcán Arenal.

ERIN DONALSON/SHUTTERSTOCK ©

Natural thermal pools, Río Tabacón

BOWIN NICOLAS/SHUTTERSTOCK ©

Hot Springs

Beneath La Fortuna the lava is still curdling and heating countless bubbling springs. Soak your bones in one of the many spas, and let your mind unravel with a poolside daiquiri.

Great For...

☑ Don't Miss

Sitting in a hot tub with a cool cocktail and a marvelous volcano view.

Eco Termales Hot Springs

Everything from the natural circulation systems in the pools to the soft lighting is understated, luxurious and romantic at this gated, reservations-only **complex** (☑2479-8787; www.ecotermalesfortuna.cr; Via 142; with/without meal US$72/44; ☉10am-4pm & 5-10pm; 🐾) 🍸 about 4.5km northwest of town. Lush greenery surrounds the walking paths that cut through these gorgeous grounds. A limited number of visitors are admitted at a time, to maintain the ambiance of serenity and seclusion.

Paradise Hot Springs

This low-key **place** (www.paradisehotspringscr.com; Via 142; adult/child US$28/16, incl meal US$45/27; ☉11am-9pm) has one lovely, large pool with a waterfall and several smaller, secluded pools, surrounded by lush

MICHAEL ZYSMAN/SHUTTERSTOCK ©

Tabacón Hot Springs

Some say it's cheesy and some say it's fun. (We say it's both.) At **Tabacón Hot Springs** (📞2519-1999; www.tabacon.com; day pass incl lunch & dinner adult/child US$115/40; ⏱10am-10pm) 🍴, broad-leaf palms, rare orchids and other florid tropical blooms part to reveal a 40°C (104°F) waterfall pouring over a fake cliff, concealing constructed caves complete with camouflaged cup holders. Lounged across each well-placed stonelike structure are overheated tourists of various shapes and sizes, relaxing.

Baldi Hot Springs

Big enough so that there's something for everyone, **Baldi** (📞2479-9917; www.baldihotsprings.cr; with/without buffet US$63/41; ⏱9am-10pm; 🅿), about 4.5km northwest of town, has 25 thermal pools ranging in temperature from 32°C (90°F) to a scalding 67°C (153°F). There are waterfalls and soaking pools for chill-seekers and 'Xtreme' slides for thrill-seekers, plus a good-size children's play area. At night, the thumping music and swim-up bars attract a young party crowd, but drinks are pricey!

vegetation and tropical blooms. The pools vary in temperature (up to 40°C/104°F), some with hydromassage. Paradise is much simpler than the other larger spring settings, but there are fewer people, and your experience is bound to be more relaxing and romantic.

Springs Resort & Spa

If you're looking for a luxurious hot-spring experience, **Springs** (📞2401-3313, in USA 954-727-8333; www.thespringscostarica.com; 2-day admission US$65; ⏱8am-10pm; 🅿) features 28 free-form pools with varying temperatures, volcano views, landscaped gardens, waterfalls and swim-up bars, including a jungle bar with a waterslide. The whole scene is human-made, yet lovely.

La Fortuna

Careful crossing the bustling streets, but don't forget to look up and beyond the crowds: whether the majestic volcano is cloud-shrouded or sunshine-soaked, it's always something to behold. The town remains the top destination in Costa Rica, even though the great mountain stopped spewing its molten discharge in 2010 – there's just so much to do.

⊙ SIGHTS

Viento Fresco   Waterfall

(☑2695-3434; Ruta 145, Campos del Oro; adult/child US$16/12, horseback tour US$55/45; ☉7:30am-5pm) If you're traveling between Monteverde and Arenal, there's no good excuse for skipping this stop. Viento Fresco is a series of five cascades, including the spectacular Arco Iris (Rainbow Falls), which drops 75m into a refreshing shallow pool that's perfect for swimming. There are no crowds or commercialism to mar the natural beauty of this place. You'll probably have the falls to yourself, especially if you go early in the day.

Ecocentro Danaus   Nature Reserve

(☑2479-7019; www.ecocentrodanaus.com; with/without guide US$18/12, guided night tour US$38; ☉7:30am-5pm, night tour 5:30pm; ⛟) ✑ This center, 4km east of town, has a well-developed trail system that's excellent for birding, as well as for spotting mammals such as coatis and agoutis (racoons and rodents of unusual size). The admission fee includes a visit to a butterfly garden, a ranarium featuring poison-dart frogs, and a small lake containing caiman and turtles. Reserve in advance for any guided tour (recommended), the morning birding tour, or the excellent night tour. Bilingual guides are knowledgeable and good spotters.

Catarata Río Fortuna   Waterfall

(La Fortuna Waterfall; www.cataratalafortuna.com; Diagonal 301; US$15; ☉8am-5pm; ⓟ) You can glimpse the sparkling 70m ribbon of clear water that pours through a sheer canyon of dark volcanic rock arrayed in bromeliads and ferns with minimal sweat equity. But it's worth the climb down to see it from the jungle floor. Though it's dangerous to dive beneath the thundering falls, a series of perfect swimming holes with spectacular views tile the canyon in aquamarine. Early arrival recommended: the parking lot fills quickly. Don't leave any valuables in your car.

Arenal Natura   Park

(☑2479-1616; www.arenalnatura.com; day/night/bird tour US$36/45/50; ☉8am-5:30pm; ⛟) Located 6km west of La Fortuna, this is a well-manicured nature experience that includes frogs, turtles, snakes and crocs, all in their appointed places. The birdlife is also prodigious here. Excellent naturalist guides ensure that you don't miss anything hiding in the trees, and there's a photography tour to help you capture it all. Discounted rates for children and students.

⟳ TOURS

Don Olivo Chocolate Tour   Tours

(☑6110-3556, 2469-1371; http://chocolate-donolivo.wixsite.com/chocolatedonolivo; Via 142; tour US$25; ☉8am, 10am, 1pm & 3pm; ⛟) Let don Olivo's heirs, Otto and Maynor, show you around their *finca,* showing off various fruits, herbs and – of course – cacao plants. The process of turning this funny fruit into the decadent treat that we all know and love is truly fascinating. Bonus: lots of taste-testing along the way. Finish with a piping hot coffee and scrumptious hot chocolate.

Bogarin Trail   Wildlife Watching

(☑8420-3661; www.lafortunasancarlos.com/bogarin-trail-2; unguided/guided US$10/35; ☉6am-4pm) Giovanni Bogarin spent years developing this wonderful, flat, 2km trail system just outside of La Fortuna proper, and it's a gem of a little stroll, perfect for early-morning birders (see the rare

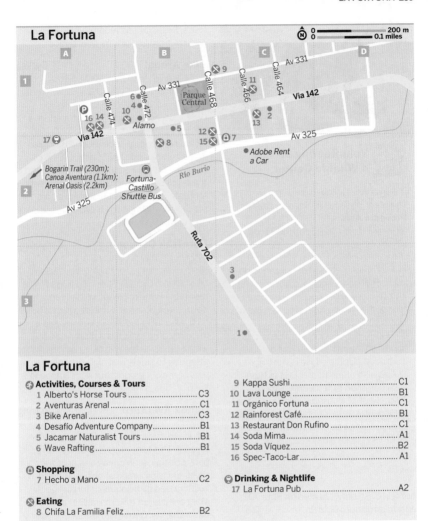

La Fortuna

white-throated crake) or later-rising sloth seekers. Guides will help you to spot animals better. Look for the orange arrow as you walk up from town.

The owners of the property have unfortunately leased part of this space to another company, who 'guarantee' sloth sightings in their Jurassic-Sloth-like, super-slick operation on the main road. Don't be fooled – Giovanni is the real deal.

Alberto's Horse Tours
Horseback Riding

(📞2479-7711, 2479-9043; www.facebook.com/albertoshorses; Ruta 702; US$85; ⏰8:30am-1:30pm) Alberto and his son lead popular horseback-riding trips to the Catarata Río Fortuna. It's a three- or four-hour trip, but you'll spend about an hour off your horse, when you hike down to the falls for a swim or a photo op. Beautiful setting, beautiful

Volunteering at a Wildlife Center

It's an animal rescue center. It's a volunteer project. It's Spanish classes. **Proyecto Asis** (☑2475-9121; www. institutoasis.com; adult/child US$35/20, incl volunteering half-day US$58/35, full-day US$93/55; ☺tours 8:30am & 1pm Mon-Fri) ✿ is a community-based organization doing a lot of good, and you can help. The introductory experience is a 1½-hour tour of the wildlife rescue center, but it's worth springing for the three-hour 'volunteering' experience, which includes hands-on interaction with the animals. It's pricey, but the cause is worthy.

Asis also offers homestays in the local community. It's located about 20km west of Quesada, past the village of Florencia. Buses between La Fortuna and Quesada can drop you at the gate. Reserve at least a day in advance.

Coati
TANGUY DE SAINT-CYR/SHUTTERSTOCK ©

horses. Cash only. Located on Ruta 702, about 2km south of town.

Arenal Oasis   Wildlife
(☑2479-9526; www.arenaloasis.com; night/ bird walks US$40/65, child under 12yr half price; ☺bird walk 6:45am & 2pm, night tour 5:45pm) This wild frog sanctuary, created by the Rojas Bonilla family, is home to some 35 species of croaking critters. The frogs are just the beginning of this night walk, which continues into the rainforest to see other nocturnal animals. If you're more of a morning person, it also does birdwatching

tours. Reservations recommended. Located 3km from La Fortuna's center.

Bike Arenal   Cycling
(☑2479-9020, WhatsApp 8854-9020; www. bikearenal.com; cnr Ruta 702 & Av 319A; rental per day/week US$15/150, half-/full-day tour US$75/110; ☺7am-6pm) This outfit offers a variety of bike tours for all levels of rider, including a popular ride around the lake and a half-day ride to El Castillo. E-bikes are good for the torturous inclines around these parts. Make advance arrangements for rental and an English-speaking bike mechanic will bring the bicycle to you. Bike-hike combos available.

PureTrek Canyoning   Canyoning
(☑2479-1313, in USA 866-569-5723; www. puretrekcanyoning.com; 4hr tour incl transportation & lunch US$105; ☺7am-10pm; ⊞) ✿ The reputable PureTrek leads guided rappels down three waterfalls, one of which is 50m high. Also included: rock climbing and a 'monkey drop,' which is actually a zipline with a rappel at the end of it. High marks for attention to safety and high-quality gear. It gets some big groups, but does a good job keeping things moving.

Canoa Aventura   Canoeing
(☑2479-8200; www.canoa-aventura.com; Via 142; canoe or kayak trip from US$59; ☺6:30am-10pm) ✿ This long-standing family-run company specializes in canoe and float trips (leisurely trips aimed at observation and relaxation) led by bilingual naturalist guides. Most are geared toward wildlife- and birdwatching. Canoa is the sister company of the **Maquenque Lodge** (☑2479-7785; www.maquenqueecolodge.com; incl breakfast s/d/tr from US$111/138/164, tree houses s/d/tr US$167/207/246; ⓟ🛜🐾) ✿ in Boca Tapada and can arrange an overnight stay there.

Jacamar Naturalist Tours   Hiking
(☑2479-9767; www.arenaltours.com; Via 142, Parque Central; river safari/birdwatching US$59/68; ☺7am-9pm) Recommended for its variety of naturalist hikes, including Volcán Arenal, waterfall and hanging bridges. The guides are knowledgeable.

Canopy Tours Canopy Tour

(☎2479-1100; www.arenalparaisoresort.com; Arenal Paraíso Resort, Via 142; tours US$50; ⏰8am-5pm; 👪) A dozen cables zip across the canyon of the Río Arenal, giving a unique perspective on two waterfalls, as well as the rainforest canopy. Also includes admission to the resort's swimming pool and 13 thermal pools, which are hidden among the rocks and greenery on the hillside.

Arenal Mundo Aventura Adventure

(☎2479-9762; www.arenalmundoaventura. com; adult/child canopy tours US$70/53, hiking US$55/39, Maleku cultural experience US$36/20; ⏰8am-1:30pm; 👪) An all-in-one adventure park, this place offers various guided hikes, rappelling and horseback riding, as well as a canopy tour. It also hosts performances of indigenous Maleku dance and song. It's 2km south of La Fortuna, on the road to Chachagua.

Aventuras Arenal Tours

(☎2479-9133; www.aventurasarenal.com; Via 142; kayaking, safari float or volcano hike US$63, horse riding from US$89; ⏰7am-8pm) Around for more than 25 years, this outfit organizes a variety of local day tours on bike, boat and horseback. It also does trips further afield, including to Caño Negro and Río Celeste.

Canopy Los Cañones Canopy Tour

(☎2479-1047, WhatsApp 8986-1000; www. hotelloslagos.com; US$55) 🍴 Located at the Hotel Los Lagos, the Canopy Los Cañones has 12 cables over the rainforest, ranging from 50m to 500m long. The price includes admission to a frog farm, crocodile farm, butterfly farm, hot springs, natural pools and waterslides, all on the hotel grounds. Located about 6km west of La Fortuna, just off Via 142.

Ecoglide Canopy Tour

(☎2479-7120; www.arenalecoglide.com; US$75; ⏰canopy tours at 8am, 10am, 1pm & 3pm; 👪) Ecoglide features 11 cables, 13 platforms and a 'Tarzan' swing. You can combine with other tours, such as birdwatching, a night

🔭 Represa Arenal

Forget for a moment that there are always ecological issues associated with dams and revel in the fact that this one created a rather magnificent lake (it took a village, or two, in the exchange). In the absence of wind, the glassy surface of Represa Arenal (Arenal Dam) reflects the volcano and the surrounding mountains teeming with cloud forest. Formerly, crowds congregated to admire the view and snap photos. Safety reasons have compelled the authorities to clear this area to avoid traffic snarls, so it's not easy to stop for the obligatory selfie any longer.

Unlike the fly-by view you'll get on a zipline canopy tour, a walk along **Mistico Hanging Bridges** (Puentes Colgantes de Arenal; ☎2479-8282; www.misticopark. com; adult/child US$24/free, tours US$36-47; ⏰7:30am-4:30pm, tours 6am, 9am & 2pm) allows you to explore the rainforest and canopy from six suspended bridges and 10 traditional bridges at a more natural and peaceful pace. All are accessible from a single 3km trail that winds through a tunnel and skirts a waterfall.

Hanging bridge, Mistico Park

walk, and rafting. Located about 5km west (uphill) from La Fortuna.

Wave Rafting Rafting

(☎2479-7262; www.waveexpeditions.com; cnr Calle 472 & Av 331; river trips US$65-100; ⏰6am-9pm) Wave Expeditions runs the wild Ríos Toro and Sarapiquí, as well as the mellower

★ **Top Five for Wildlife**

Arenal Oasis (p240)

Aventuras Arenal (p241)

Canoa Aventura (p240)

Jacamar Naturalist Tours (p240)

Ecocentro Danaus (p238)

From left: Agouti; Heliconia plant; Collared araçari

Balsa, in both rafts and tubes. There's also hiking, horseback riding, canopy, canyoning and chocolate tours on offer, through second-party tour companies.

Desafío Adventure Company
Adventure

(✆2479-0020; www.desafiocostarica.com; Calle 472; tours from US$65; ◷6:30am-9pm) This tour agency has the widest range of tours in La Fortuna – everything from paddling trips on the Río Balsa, horse-riding treks to Volcán Arenal, adventure tours rappelling down waterfalls, safari floats on the Sarapiquí, and mountain-bike expeditions. It can also arrange your transfer to Monteverde and Guanacaste.

🔒 SHOPPING

Hecho a Mano
Arts & Crafts

(Handmade Art Shop; ✆8611-0018; www.facebook.com/handmadeartshop; Calle 468; ◷9am-9pm Mon-Fri, from 10am Sat & Sun) There's no shortage of souvenirs for sale in La Fortuna, but this shop is something special, carrying an excellent selection of

arts and crafts by local and national artists. You'll find representative pieces from Costa Rica's many subcultures, including Boruca masks, Rasta handicrafts, lots of macrame and some lovely handmade jewelry.

Neptune's House of Hammocks
Homewares

(Neptuno Casa de Hamaca; ✆2479-8269; Diagonal 301; ◷8am-6pm) On the road to La Fortuna Waterfall, Rastaman Daniel has been watching the tourist traffic come and go for more than a decade while he and Yesenia weave magic hammocks (US$40 to US$50) and swinging chairs. Take a breather and test one out.

EATING

Unless you're eating exclusively at *sodas*, you'll find the restaurants in La Fortuna to be more expensive than in other parts of the country. But there are some excellent, innovative kitchens, including a few that are part of the farm-to-table movement. The restaurants are mostly clustered in town,

JOSIANNE TOUBEAX/GETTY IMAGES ©

but there are also places to eat on the road heading west.

Soda Mima
Soda $

(Off Via 142; mains US$5; ⊙6am-8pm Mon-Sat, to noon Sun) Though nothing fancy from afar, the love radiates outward from Mari and Alvaro's kitchen to warm your belly and your heart. Cheap, delicious *casados* (set meals) and *gallo pinto* (rice and beans) are standard fare; add some eye-watering *chilera* (peppers distilled in vinegar) from the big jar if you dare.

Rainforest Café
Cafe $

(☑2479-7239; Calle 468; mains US$7-10; ⊙7am-10pm; 🛜🍴) We know it's bad form to start with dessert, but the irresistible sweets at this popular spot are beautiful to behold and delicious to devour. There's also a full menu of coffees, including some tempting specialty drinks (such as Mono Loco: coffee, banana, milk, chocolate and cinnamon).

Spec-Taco-Lar
Tex-Mex $

(tacos & burritos US$6-10; ⊙6am-10pm) Best place in town, hands down. Cesar cranks

up weepy *ranchera* music while you drink in the atmosphere: a troika of sombreros and painted skulls complete the faux-Tex-Mex motif. But the food is why you're here, and it's showstopping: from incredible street corn with chipotle-and-cheese toppings, to standard tacos and burritos with five homemade salsas, you can't miss.

If you're looking to get your drink on, stick around after dinner.

Kappa Sushi
Sushi $

(Calle 468, btwn Av 331 & Av 333; sushi & rolls US$7-11; ⊙noon-10pm; 🍴) When you're surrounded by mountains and cattle farms, who's thinking of sushi? Well, you should. The fish is fresh (you're not *that* far from the ocean) and the preparations innovative. The dragon roll (shrimp tempura, avocado, and eel sauce) is a favorite. Enjoy the view of Arenal while you feast on raw fish – or go for the veg options.

Soda Víquez
Soda $

(☑2479-8772; cnr Calle 468 & Av 325; mains US$6-10; ⊙8am-10pm; 🍴) Travelers adore the local flavor that's served up at Soda Víquez (in all senses of the expression). It's a super-friendly spot, offering tasty *típico* (traditional dishes), especially *casados,* rice dishes and fresh fruit *batidos* (shakes). Prices are reasonable and portions ample. 'Friendship is born from our service' is their motto – need we say more?

Gecko's
Waterfall Grill   International $

(☏2479-1569; www.facebook.com/geckogourmet; mains US$6-10; ⊙11am-5pm) What began as a snack counter on the last pass before La Fortuna Waterfall has turned into a full-blown fusion excursion by Scott, famous for his love of food and dogs. The new menu has received rave reviews – why not stop by after a dunk in the river?

Brisas Del Lago   Soda $

(☏2695-3363; San Luis; mains US$6-11; ⊙11am-10pm Tue-Sat, from 1pm Sun; P⚡) If you don't mind a little detour, here is your lunch stop between Monteverde and Arenal. Simple Tico fare is done with panache at this dressed-up *soda*. It marinates chicken breasts in its own BBQ sauce, skewers Thai-style shrimp and slathers up teriyaki

chicken. The garlic fish is sensational. Just past the Catholic church in the community of San Luis.

Orgánico Fortuna   Vegetarian $$

(☏8572-2115; www.organicofortuna.com; Calle 466; mains US$9-15; ⊙9am-7pm Mon-Sat) A lovely little family operation that preaches better living through better eating, and the proof is in the pudding (or maybe the falafel). Delicious, locally sourced ingredients are used and offerings are prepared with care: smoothies, a tasty organic roast coffee (Cerro del Fuego) with almond milk, and even gluten-free bread and other options.

Lava Lounge   International $$

(☏2479-7365; www.facebook.com/lavalounge-costarica; Via 142; mains US$10-15, specials US$23-25; ⊙7am-10:30pm; P⚡♪) This open-air restaurant has become a go-to spot for post-activities lunch or dinner. There is pizza and pasta, wraps and salads, and loads of vegetarian options. The reggae throbs nonstop under a *palapa* (thatched) roof. Add colorful cocktails, hip service and

Gallo pinto (rice and beans)

occasional DJ/live music, and the place is pretty irresistible.

Owner-chef Scott also runs Gecko's Waterfall Grill and **Costa Rica Dog Rescue** (🖉2479-1569; www.crdogrescue.com; donation US$30-60).

Chifa La Familia Feliz   Fusion $$

(🖉8469-6327; Calle 472; mains US$8-15; ⊙11am-10pm; 🛜🖉🎵) If you're looking for a change of taste – a *real* change from *casados* and pizza – check this out. *Chifa* is Peruvian Chinese fried rice, and chef Martin Gonzalez also whips up *causas* (yellow-potato dishes), *ceviches*, and *anticuchos* (skewers) with equal enthusiasm and skill. He goes out of his way to welcome and satisfy all comers.

Restaurant
Don Rufino   International $$$

(🖉2479-9997; www.donrufino.com; cnr Via 142 & Calle 466; mains US$16-40; ⊙11:30am-9:30pm) The vibe is trendy at this indoor-outdoor grill. The highlight is the perfectly prepared grilled meats: the New York Steak with mushrooms is to die for. If you're cutting back, go for Grandma's BBQ chicken (wrapped in a banana leaf) or a house favorite, the *kabocha* squash risotto with grilled chicken breast and chimichurri-glazed shrimp.

🍷 DRINKING & NIGHTLIFE
La Fortuna Pub   Pub

(www.facebook.com/lafortunapub; Via 142; ⊙2pm-midnight Sun-Thu, to 1am Fri-Sat) Just uphill from the town center, this place is all about Tico artisanal beers, offering a dozen different home-country bottled *cervezas*. It also brews in small batches that disappear quickly, so watch its Facebook page for the next arrival. A standard pub-food menu satisfies, while Friday's open mic often devolves into a boozy karaoke session.

ℹ️ GETTING THERE & AWAY

The fastest public transit route between Monteverde and La Fortuna is the taxi-boat-taxi combo (formerly known as jeep-boat-jeep, which sounds sexier but it was the same thing).

It is actually a minivan with the requisite yellow '*turismo*' tattoo, which takes you to Laguna de Arenal, meeting a boat that crosses the lake, where a 4WD van on the other side continues to Monteverde. It's a terrific transportation option that can be arranged through almost any hotel or tour operator in La Fortuna or Monteverde (US$25, four hours).

This is now the first transportation choice for many traveling between La Fortuna and Monteverde as it's incredibly scenic and reasonably priced.

ℹ️ GETTING AROUND

La Fortuna is easy to access by public transportation, but nearby attractions such as the hot springs, Parque Nacional Volcán Arenal and Laguna de Arenal demand internal combustion (or a tour operator). A day trip to Río Celeste, Caño Negro or Venado Caves might also merit renting a car for the day.

Adobe Rent a Car (🖉2479-7202; www.adobecar.com; Av 325; ⊙8am-5pm)

Alamo (🖉2479-9090; www.alamocostarica.com; cnr Via 142 & Calle 472; ⊙7:30am-5:30pm)

El Castillo

Just an hour around the bend from La Fortuna, the tiny mountain village of El Castillo is a beautiful, bucolic alternative. This picturesque locale, created as a relocation zone after the great eruption of 1968, has easy access to Parque Nacional Volcán Arenal and amazing, up-close views of the looming mountain – with less of the tourist madness of its bigger neighbor. A recently paved road makes getting here a lot smoother than in the past.

There is a tight-knit expat community here, some of whom have opened appealing lodges and top-notch restaurants. There are hiking trails and swimming holes. There are also a few worthy attractions, including a butterfly house and an eco-zoo. The only thing El Castillo doesn't have is a sidewalk. And maybe that's a good thing.

◉ SIGHTS

Arenal EcoZoo   Zoo

(El Serpentario; ☏2479-1059; El Castillo-La Fortuna road; adult/child US$15/12, with guide US$23/16; ☺8am-7pm) This snake house offers a hands-on animal experience, as in, handling and milking a venomous snake. It's home to a red-tailed boa (one of the largest snakes in the world), as well as frogs, amphibious lizards, iguanas, turtles, scorpions, tarantulas and butterflies. Good photo ops! Ask about feeding time if you want to see snakes devouring bugs, frogs and even other snakes. Located on the main road uphill from the lake, which connects to La Fortuna.

El Castillo-Arenal Butterfly Conservatory   Wildlife Reserve

(☏2479-1149; www.butterflyconservatory.org; El Castillo-La Fortuna road; adult/student US$17/12; ☺8am-4pm) More than just a butterfly conservatory (although it has one of the largest butterfly exhibitions in Costa Rica). Altogether there are six domed habitats (re-creating the butterflies' natural Costa Rican ambiance), a ranarium, an insect museum, a medicinal herb garden, and an hour's worth of trails through a botanic garden and along the river. The birding is also excellent here, and there are wonderful volcano views. The conservatory is located on the main road uphill from the lake.

Wheelchair accessible. Multilingual docents.

⊙ TOURS

La Gavilana   Tours

(☏2479-1747, 8433-7902; www.gavilana.com; El Castillo-La Fortuna road; 1hr/half-day Food Forest hike from US$30/75; ☺by appointment) The culinary adventurers here offer a Food Forest trail hike to their farm near the Río Caño Negro. Additional adventures on offer include a fermentation workshop, while artistic types can join Hannah in the mural painting class. All classes by appointment only. The office is on the main road uphill from the lake.

From left: Tiger longwing butterfly, El Castillo-Arenal Butterfly Conservatory; Palm tree, Rancho Margot; Red-tailed boa

Sky Adventures

Canopy Tour

(☑2479-4100; www.skyadventures.travel; adult/
child Sky Walk US$39/27, Sky Tram US$48/33,
Sky River Drift US$81/64, Sky Limit US$84/n/a,
Sky Trek US$84/58; ☺7:30am-4pm) El Castil-
lo's entry in the canopy-tour category has
ziplines (Sky Trek), a floating gondola (Sky
Tram) and a series of hanging bridges (Sky
Walk). It's safe and well run; visitors tend to
leave smiling. A unique combo, Sky River
Drift combines a zipline with tree-climbing
and river tubing, while Sky Limit combines
ziplining with rappel and other high-altitude
challenges.

Rancho Adventure Tours

Adventure

(☑8302-7318; www.ranchomargot.com; Rancho
Margot; farm tour US$35, other tours US$55)
Part resort lodge, part organic farm,
Rancho Margot offers a good selection of
guided tours, including horseback riding
on the southern side of Laguna de Arenal,
lake kayaking, and touring the ranch itself
to learn about the workings of a sustainable farm. A half-day tour of the ranch, with
lunch, costs US$50.

Located where the El Castillo–La Fortuna
road intersects with Rancho Margot Rd.
The farm tour is free to guests of the ranch.

✖ EATING

La Ventanita

Cafe $

(☑2479-1735; El Castillo-La Fortuna road; mains
US$4-6; ☺11am-9pm; 🖊) *La Ventanita* is the
'little window' where you place your order.
Soon, you'll be devouring the best *chifrijo*
(rice-and-pinto beans bowl with fried
pork, fresh salsa and corn chips) in the
province, along with a nutritious, delicious
batido (fruit shake). It's typical food with a
twist – pulled pork and bacon burritos, for
example. Desserts include flan and carrot
cake.

Pizza John

Pizza $$

(pizzas US$11-19, calzones US$6-10; ☺noon-
8pm) Old John has gone to the pie-in-the-
sky, but his recipes and legacy live on with
his widow Myra, who still whips up delicious
pizzas, calzones and homemade ice cream
to beat the band, including wonders such

Ziplining, El Castillo (p245)

as chocolate-ginger and Costa Rican coffee. The garden setting – orchids, fragrant rosemary – is a plus, too.

Fusion Grill   Fusion $$

(2479-1949; www.fusiongrillrestaurant.com; El Castillo-La Fortuna road; mains US$12-20; 7am-10pm) Set in an open-air dining room with incredible volcano views, Fusion Grill shows off a little swank (at least, more than other restaurants in El Castillo). Chef Adrian Ramirez whips up a mean *parrillada mixta* (mixed grill), but your favorite part of the meal might be the specialty desserts such as pineapple or banana flambé. Located uphill from the lake.

DRINKING & NIGHTLIFE

There's only a couple of drinking spots in El Castillo. You have more options in La Fortuna, but it's tricky business getting back here after dark, especially after a few cold ones.

Balazos   Bar

(8317-0537; noon-midnight) In a town crying out for a little nightlife, Balazos ('shots' in Spanish) offers some – as well as locally loved seafood and *ceviche*, and

handy showers and bathrooms for the campers across the road. It's the only late-night option in El Castillo. Draws a mixed and younger crowd. Located 1km west of the soccer field.

GETTING THERE & AWAY

El Castillo is located 8km past the entrance to Parque Nacional Volcán Arenal. The newly paved road has made driving here much easier.

There is one public bus coming and going to La Fortuna: it departs La Fortuna at 7am, and returns to La Fortuna at 5pm.

A private **shuttle bus** (8887-9141; Calle 472; US$10) runs from the Super Christian #1 in La Fortuna (45 minutes, US$10) at 9am, 1:30pm and 6:30pm. The shuttle runs from El Castillo to Fortuna at 8am, 10am and 4pm. Although this is a frequent service for workers, contact the father and son drivers Arturo and Luis in advance; their van will be either white, grey or green. This shuttle bus can also drop you at the entrance to the national park for US$4.

A new bridge (approved in 2019) crossing the Rancho Margot property is destined to cut the journey to Monteverde nearly in half, with vehicles able to avoid circling Laguna de Arenal.

SARAPIQUÍ VALLEY

Sarapiquí Valley at a Glance...

This flat, steaming stretch of finca-dotted lowlands was once part of the United Fruit Company's vast banana holdings. More recently, the river again shot to prominence as one of the premier destinations in the country for kayakers and rafters. With the Parque Nacional Braulio Carrillo as its backyard, this is also one of the best regions for wildlife-watching, especially considering how easy it is to get here.

One Day in Sarapiquí Valley

If you only have one day in the Valle de Sarapiquí, you ought to spend it on the river, kayaking or **rafting** (p254) over the thrilling white water. Refuel at **Rancho Magallanes** (p258) before retiring to your ecolodge to watch the birds.

Two Days in Sarapiquí Valley

Slow things down on day two, with a wildlife-watching **boat tour** (p260) on the Río Sarapiquí or a farm tour (with degustation!) at **Costa Rica Best Chocolate** (p258) or **Organic Paradise** (p258).

Don't leave town without traversing the magical hanging bridge and trails of **Tirimbina Rainforest Center** (p259).

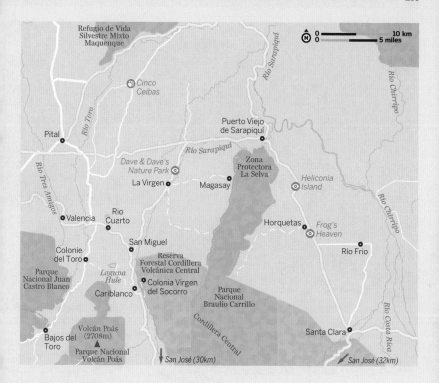

Arriving in Sarapiquí Valley

Rte 4 connects the region's towns and villages. In the east, the highway hooks up with Rte 32, which continues on to Siquirres. In the west, it joins with Rte 32, continuing south toward San José. The Vuelta Kooper Chilamate highway opened in 2017, cutting travel time to La Fortuna by half. Buses ply all of these routes.

Where to Stay

In addition to raging rapids and prowling animals, there are a slew of stellar lodges in the region, featuring rainforest trails, suspension bridges and chocolate tours. Even budget travelers have a few interesting and atmospheric options in and around Chilamate, although the cheapest places to stay are in town (Puerto Viejo or La Virgen).

Rafting on the Río Sarapiquí

WOLFGANG KAEHLER/LIGHTROCKET VIA GETTY IMAGES ©

White-Water Rafting

The Río Sarapiquí offers a pretty special package: high-adrenaline kayaking and rafting in the midst of wildlife-rich rainforest. A 'river float' is a milder option, and better suited for animal-spotting. Hold on tight as you surf those rapids – but keep your eyes open!

The Río Sarapiquí isn't as wild as the white water on the Río Pacuare near Turrialba, but it will get your heart racing. Even better, the dense jungle that hugs the river-bank is lush and primitive, with chances to glimpse wildlife from your raft. All of the outfitters ride the same rapids, offering roughly the same Class II–IV options at similar prices.

Great For...

☑ **Don't Miss**

Spotting birds, monkeys and iguanas as you cruise down the river.

Tour Operators

Aventuras del Sarapiquí (☎2766-6768; www.sarapiqui.com; river trips US$60-95) This highly recommended outfitter offers land, air and water adventures. In addition to white-water rafting (both Class II and III/IV trips), you can also fly through the air on a 12-cable canopy tour. Or, stay down to earth with horseback riding, mountain

Zipline canopy tour, Aventuras del Sarapiquí

KEVIN SCHAFER/GETTY IMAGES ©

biking or good old-fashioned hiking. Situated just off the highway.

Sarapiquí Outdoor Center (SOC; ☎2761-1123; www.costaricaraft.com; 2/4hr rafting trip US$65/90, guided kayak trips from US$90) David Duarte is the local paddling authority. In addition to its own rafting excursions, SOC offers kayak rental, lessons and clinics. Indie paddlers should check in for up-to-date river information. If you need somewhere to sleep before you hit the water, you can crash in the simple rooms or camp in one of the available, all-inclusive tents – no equipment necessary. Located about 18km southwest of Sarapiquí, off Hwy 126.

Green Rivers (☎2766-5274; www.sarapiquigreenrivers.com; tours US$60-85; 👪) Operating out of Posada Andrea Cristina B&B, the ever-amiable Kevín and Evelyn

Martínez offer a wide variety of rafting and kayaking tours, from family-friendly floats to adrenaline-pumping, rapid-surfing rides. They also know their nature, so they do natural history and bird tours too.

Tropical Duckies (☎2761-0095, 8760-3787; www.tropicalduckies.com; off Hwy 126; US$65; ⊙departs 9am & 1pm; 👪) Highly recommended for beginners and families, this outfit does tours and instruction in inflatable kayaks, which allow for a fun paddle even when the river is low. Paddle on flat moving water or Class III rapids (or somewhere in between). Reserve ahead.

Aguas Bravas (☎2292-2072, 2761-1645; www.aguasbravascr.com; rafting trips US$65-80, safari float US$65; ⊙9am-5:30pm) This well-established rafting outfit has set up shop along the Río Sarapiquí (complete with onsite hostel). Aguas Bravas has two tours on offer: take a gentle safari float to spot birds, iguanas, caimans and other wildlife, or sign up to splash through 14km of 'extreme rapids' on the San Miguel section of the river. Both include a spot of lunch.

La Virgen

Tucked into the densely jungled shores of the wild and scenic Río Sarapiquí, La Virgen was one of the small towns that prospered during the heyday of the banana trade. Although United Fruit has long since shipped out, the town remains dependent on its nearby pineapple fields. And it still lives by that river.

For more than a decade, La Virgen was the premier kayaking and rafting destination in Costa Rica. But a tremendous 2009 earthquake and landslide altered the course of the river and flattened the town's tourist economy. Some businesses folded, others relocated to La Fortuna, and a few held on. Now independent kayakers are starting to come back and there are a couple of river outfitters offering exhilarating trips on the Class II–IV waters of the Río Sarapiquí.

◎ SIGHTS

Cinco Ceibas   Wildlife Reserve
(☑2476-0606; www.cincoceibas.com; full-day tour incl lunch US$70-125) Finca Pangola

(11 sq km) contains a swathe of dense, green primary rainforest, home to some of the country's oldest and largest trees. Including, yes, five glorious ceiba trees that you'll see as you walk 1.2km along the raised wooden jungle boardwalk. The stroll is paired with horseback riding, kayaking or an ox-cart ride for a carefully choreographed adventure.

Frog's Heaven   Gardens
(Cielo de Ranas; ☑8891-8589, 2764-2724; www.frogsheaven.org; Horquetas; adult/child US$25/12; ☺8am-8pm; ⊕) ✐ The frogs hop free in this lovely tropical garden, a perfect habitat for more than 28 species. On bilingual guided tours you're likely to see old favorites such as the red-eyed tree frog and poison-dart frogs, as well as some lesser-known exotic amphibians, such as the translucent glass frog and the wrinkly Mexican tree frog. Come for the twilight tour (5pm) to see a whole different frog world. Find it diagonal from the church.

From left: Scarlet-rumped tanager; Heliconia rostrata; Horseback riding, Hacienda Pozo Azul Adventures

ONDREJ PROSICKY/SHUTTERSTOCK ©

WOLFGANG KAEHLER/LIGHTROCKET VIA GETTY IMAGES ©

Dave & Dave's
Nature Park   Birdwatching

(☑2761-0801; www.sarapiquieco-observatory.
com; US$40; ☺by guided tour only) Father and
son Dave and Dave greet all-comers to this
4.5-hectare reserve on the Río Sarapiquí,
200m north of the cemetery. You don't
have to be a birder to get great glimpses
or photos from the two viewing platforms,
with feeders attracting toucans, trogans,
tanagers and 10 species of hummingbird.
Follow one of the Daves on a trail system
that winds through secondary forest all the
way down to the river. A welcome bonus is
the free coffee.

There are no scheduled tour hours, but
one of the Daves should be able to help you
upon arrival.

🕝 TOURS

Hacienda Pozo
Azul Adventures   Adventure

(☑2438-2616, in USA & Canada 877-810-6903;
www.pozoazul.com; tours US$48-88) Spe-
cializes in adventure activities, including
horseback-riding tours, a canopy tour over
the lush jungle and river, rappelling, mountain biking, and assorted river trips. It's the
best-funded tour concession in the area,
catering largely to groups and day-trippers
from San José. Located about 18km southwest of Sarapiquí, off Hwy 126.

EATING

La Virgen has a few favorite restaurants
along the highway serving tried and true
Tico favorites. It's nothing extraordinary,
but you won't go hungry.

Rusti Tico's   Fusion $

(☑8877-8928; Chilamate; mains US$7-10;
☺6am-10pm Fri-Wed) Here's a spot for the
frugal gourmet. Chef Horacio prepares
everything from spaghetti in white sauce,
with *patacones* (plantain fritters) on the
side, to steamed fish with vegetables, in a
savory white mushroom gravy. Carnivores
and vegans are given the same attentive
service at this clean and friendly roadside
eatery on the main highway, about 9km
west of Sarapiquí.

Taking a Farm Tour

While agriculture remains the primary money-maker in the region, tourism also has a role to play in the local economy. Entrepreneurial local farmers supplement their agricultural activities with farm tours, allowing visitors a view into Tico rural lifestyles, sustainable farming practices, and the ins and outs of producing delicious food.

Costa Rica Best Chocolate (☑8816-3729, 8501-7951; adult/child US$34/23; ⊘tours 8am, 10am, 1pm & 3pm) Where does chocolate come from? This local Chilamate family can answer that question for you, starting with the cacao plants growing on their farm. The two-hour demonstration covers the whole chocolate-making process, with plenty of tasting along the way. Buy one of their four artisanal bars at tour's end. About 5km west of downtown Puerto Viejo, on the main highway.

Organic Paradise Tour (☑2761-0706; www.organicparadisetour.com; adult/child US$35/14; ⊘tours 8am, 10am, 1pm & 3pm) Take a bumpy ride on a tractor-drawn carriage and learn everything you ever wanted to know about pineapples (and peppers). The two-hour tour focuses on the production process and what it means to be organic; it also offers real insight into Costa Rican farm culture, as well as practical tips such as how to choose your pineapple at the supermarket.

Raw cacao beans

JEROEN MIKKERS/SHUTTERSTOCK ©

Rancho Magallanes   Costa Rican $
(☑2766-5606; chicken US$5-12; ⊘10am-10pm) Rancho Magallanes is a sweet roadside restaurant with a wood-burning brick oven where it roasts whole chickens and serves them quite simply with tortillas and banana salsa. You can dine with the truckers by the roadside or in the more upscale riverside dining area, painted with colorful jungle scenes.

🍷 DRINKING & NIGHTLIFE

Bar & Cabinas El Río   Bar
(☑2761-0138; ⊘noon-10pm) At the southern end of town, turn off the main road and make your way down to this atmospheric riverside hangout, set on rough-hewn stilts high above the river. Locals congregate on the upper deck to sip cold beers and nosh on filling Tico fare (mains US$6 to US$9).

ℹ️ GETTING THERE & AWAY

La Virgen lies on Hwy 126, about 8km north of San Miguel and 17km west of Puerto Viejo de Sarapiquí. It's a paved but curvy route (especially heading south, where the road starts to climb into the mountains). Buses ply this route from San José via San Miguel to Puerto Viejo, stopping in La Virgen along the way. Local buses run hourly between La Virgen and Puerto Viejo de Sarapiquí (US$1, 30 minutes) from 6am to 8pm.

Puerto Viejo de Sarapiquí

At the scenic confluence of the Ríos Puerto Viejo and Sarapiquí, this was once the most important port in Costa Rica. Boats laden with fruit, coffee and other commercial exports plied the Sarapiquí as far as the Nicaraguan border, then turned east on the Río San Juan to the sea.

Today it is simply a gritty but pleasant palm-shaded market town. The town has made concessions to the new economy, with the local polytechnic high school offering students advanced tourism, ecology and agriculture degrees. The school even has its own reserve, laced with trails.

Visitors, meanwhile, can choose from any number of activities in the surrounding area, such as birdwatching, rafting, kayaking, boating and hiking.

SIGHTS

Heliconia Island — Gardens

(☑2764-5220; www.heliconiaisland.com; self-guided/guided tours US$10/18; ☺8am-5pm; P👪) ✎ Down a rugged road and across the hanging bridge is home to more than 80 varieties of heliconias, tropical flowers, plants and trees. The 2-hectare island overlooking the Río Puerto Viejo is also a refuge for 228 bird species, including the sought-after dusky-faced tanager. Since the original owners sold, the gardens are not as spectacular, though still great for birding.

⊙ TOURS

The boat traffic at the dock in Puerto Viejo is no longer transporting commuters who have somewhere to go. Nowadays it's used primarily for tourist boats cruising the Ríos Sarapiquí and Puerto Viejo looking for birds and monkeys. On a good day, passengers might spot an incredible variety of water birds, not to mention crocodiles, sloths, two kinds of monkeys and countless iguanas sunning themselves on the muddy riverbanks or gathering in the trees.

Las Arrieras Nature Reserve — Birdwatching

(☑8510-4236; arrierasreserve@gmail.com; Horquetas; entrance US$5, full-day tour US$40) University of Costa Rica biologist David Segura offers informative birding and naturalist tours on his property, Las Arrieras ('the army ants') Nature Reserve. He's just downhill from **Yatama Ecolodge** (☑7015-1121; www.yatamaecolodge.com; per person incl 3 meals US$80) ✎, and you can camp here, too (US$10). Check out his Instagram.

Tirimbina Rainforest Center & Lodge — Wildlife

(☑2761-0055, 2761-0333; www.tirimbina. org; day pass US$18) Situated 2km from La Virgen, this is a working environmental

Pineapples picked and ready for export

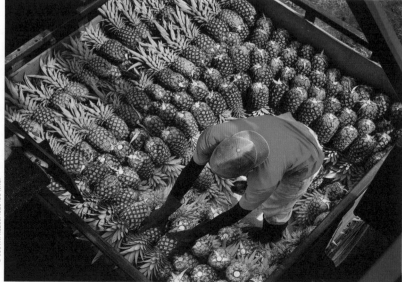

Estación Biológica La Selva

Not to be confused with Selva Verde Lodge in Chilamate, Estación Biológica La Selva is a working biological research station equipped with laboratories, experimental plots, a herbarium and an extensive library. The station is usually teeming with scientists and students researching the nearby private reserve.

The area protected by La Selva is 16 sq km of premontane wet tropical rainforest, much of which is undisturbed. It's bordered to the south by the 476-sq-km Parque Nacional Braulio Carrillo, creating a protected area large enough to support a great diversity of life. More than 886 bird species have been recorded here, as well as 120 mammal species (including five species of big cat), 1850 species of vascular plants (especially from the orchid, philodendron, coffee and legume families) and thousands of insect species – with 500 types of ant alone.

Reservations are required for three-hour **guided hikes** (☎ext 1340 2524-0607, in USA 919-684-5774; www.tropicalstudies.org; guided hike US$40, birdwatching hike US$50; ⏲guided hike 8am & 1:30pm, birdwatching hike 5:45am) with a bilingual naturalist guide. You'll head across the hanging bridge and into 57km of jungle trails, some of which are wheelchair accessible. Unguided hiking is forbidden, but you're allowed to wander a bit after your guided tour. Make reservations for the popular guided birdwatching hikes.

Leafcutter ant

KEVIN WELLS PHOTOGRAPHY/SHUTTERSTOCK ©

research and education center. Tirimbina reserve has over 9km of trails; tours include birdwatching, an educational (irregular) bat program, night walks and a recommended chocolate tour.

The 345-hectare private reserve is connected to the nearby Sarapiquís Rainforest Lodge by two long suspension bridges. The island between is not open to the public. Esteemed international bat researcher Bernal Rodriguez Herrera of the University of Costa Rica does much of his work here.

Oasis Nature Tours Boating
(☎2766-6108, 2766-6260, 8816-6462; www.oasisnaturetours.com; full-day tour incl transportation from San José US$85-100, 2hr safari boat tour US$35) This is one of several guides running boat tours on the local rivers. Also offers ziplining, rafting and other guided adventures. Make a right out of the bus terminal, look for the sign marking an alley, then go down the alley and into the blue house.

Anhinga Tours Boating
(☎2766-5858, 8346-1220; www.anhinga.jimdo.com; Av 7; tours per person US$25) This local guide takes travelers out to explore the Río Sarapiquí and its tributaries. Located in one of the last houses on the left as you walk toward the river – it is a blue house with an awning, and is not always attended.

EATING

Many of the lodgings in and around Puerto Viejo have onsite restaurants or provide meals. Otherwise, there are several *sodas* in Puerto Viejo de Sarapiquí and a supermarket at the western end of town. A couple of interesting restaurants are along the highway between Puerto Viejo and La Virgen (not your typical *sodas*).

Restaurante y Pizzeria La Casona Pizza $$
(☎2766-7101; www.hotelaraambigua.com; meals US$8-16; ⏲8am-10pm; 📶👪) The restaurant at Hotel Ara Ambigua is particularly recommended for its oven-baked pizza and

JOSE MICHAEL MURILLO ROJAS/GETTY IMAGES ©

Red-eyed tree frog (p256)

traditional homemade cuisine served in an open-air *rancho* (small house). If you're looking for something beyond the pizza/*casado* routine, try the tangy Frida Kahlo chicken.

Restaurante El Bambú
Costa Rican $$

(Hotel El Bambú, Calle Central; mains US$8-12; ⊘8am-10pm; 🖉) Heaping helpings of Costa Rican food and other items dominate the menu: three different vegetarian pastas are on offer, as well as steaks, rice-and-beans with Caribbean chicken, sandwiches and a giant burger. The open-air *palapa* encourages you to linger and enjoy.

❶ GETTING THERE & AWAY

Puerto Viejo de Sarapiquí has been a transportation center longer than Costa Rica has been a country, and it's easily accessed via paved major roads from San José, the Caribbean coast and other population centers. There's a taxi stop across from the bus terminal, and drivers will take you to the nearby lodges for US$5 to US$10.

Brown booby (p189), Isla Cabo Blanco

In Focus

Coffee beans (p269)

History

Costa Rica's history remains a loose sketch during the reign of its pre-Columbian tribes, and Europe's 'discovery' of the place was followed by the subjugation of its indigenous peoples. But in the mid-20th century, it radically departed from the script by abolishing its army, diversifying its economy and brokering peace in the region, creating today's stable, environmentally friendly nation.

11,000 BCE
Humans occupy Costa Rica and flourish due to rich land and marine resources along both coastlines.

1000 BCE
The Huetar power base in the Central Valley is solidified following the construction and habitation of the ancient city of Guayabo.

100 BCE
Costa Rica joins a trade network that moves gold and goods from Mexico to the Andean empires.

FRANKAZOID/GETTY IMAGES ©

Stone spheres, Diquís Valley (p266)

INSPIRED BY MAPS/SHUTTERSTOCK ©

Lost Worlds of Ancient Rica

The coastlines and rainforests of Central America have been inhabited by humans for at least 10,000 years, but ancient civilizations in Costa Rica are largely the subject of speculation. It is thought that the area was something of a backwater straddling the two great civilizations of the Andes and Mesoamerica, with the exception of the Diquís Valley along the Pacific coast, where archaeological finds suggest that a great deal of trading took place between early inhabitants of Costa Rica and their more powerful neighbors. On the eve of European discovery some 500 years ago, an estimated 400,000 people were living in today's Costa Rica.

Unlike the massive pyramid complexes found throughout other parts of Latin America, the ancient towns and cities of Costa Rica (with the exception of Guayabo) were loosely organized and had no centralized government or ceremonial centers. The settlements fought among each other, but for the purpose of getting slaves rather than to extend their territory. Not known for building edifices that would stand the test of time, Costa Rica's

1502	1522	1562
Christopher Columbus docks off the coast and, due to all the gold he sees, dubs it *costa rica* ('rich coast').	Spanish settlement develops in Costa Rica, though it's decades before the colonists can get a sturdy foothold.	The first permanent Spanish colonial settlement in Costa Rica is established in Cartago by Juan Vásquez de Coronado.

★ Pre-Columbian Sites

Monumento Nacional Arqueológico
Guayabo, Turrialba

Hacienda Barú, Dominical

Sitio Arqueológico Finca 6 (p147),
Sierpe

Finca Cántaros, San Vito

Monumento Nacional Arqueológico Guayabo, Turrialba

MARCO LISSONI/SHUTTERSTOCK ©

early inhabitants did, however, leave behind mysterious relics: enormous stone spheres, liberally scattered around the Diquís Valley.

Heirs of Columbus

On his fourth and final voyage to the Americas in 1502, Christopher Columbus was forced to drop anchor near present-day Puerto Limón after a hurricane damaged his ship. While waiting for repairs, Columbus ventured into the verdant terrain and exchanged gifts with hospitable and welcoming chieftains. He returned from this encounter claiming to have seen 'more gold in two days than in four years in Española.' Columbus dubbed the stretch of shoreline from Honduras to Panama 'Veraguas,' but it was his excited descriptions of *costa rica* (the 'rich coast') that gave the region its lasting name. At least that's how the popular story goes.

Anxious to claim the country's bounty, Columbus petitioned the Spanish Crown to have himself appointed governor. But by the time he returned to Seville, his royal patron Queen Isabella was on her deathbed, which prompted King Ferdinand to award the prize to Columbus' rival, Diego de Nicuesa. Although Columbus became a very wealthy man, he never returned to the Americas. He died of heart failure in 1506 after being worn down by ill health and court politics.

To the disappointment of his conquistador heirs, Columbus' tales of gold were mostly lies and the locals were considerably less than affable. Nicuesa's first colony in present-day Panama was abruptly abandoned when tropical disease and warring tribes decimated its ranks. Successive expeditions launched from the Caribbean coast also failed as pestilent swamps, oppressive jungles and volcanoes made Columbus' paradise seem more like a tropical hell.

A bright moment in Spanish exploration came in 1513 when Vasco Núñez de Balboa heard rumors about a large sea and a wealthy, gold-producing civilization across the mountains of the isthmus – these almost certainly referred to the Inca empire of present-day Peru. Driven by equal parts ambition and greed, Balboa scaled the continental

1737	1808	1821
The future capital of San José is established, sparking a rivalry with neighboring Cartago that culminates in a civil war.	Coffee, set to become the nation's main agricultural crop, arrives from Cuba.	Following a declaration by Mexico on behalf of Central America, Costa Rica gains its independence from Spain.

divide, and on September 26, 1513, he became the first European to set eyes upon the Pacific Ocean. Keeping up with the European fashion of the day, Balboa immediately proceeded to claim the ocean and all the lands it touched for the king of Spain.

The thrill of discovery aside, the conquistadors now controlled a strategic western beachhead from which to launch their conquest of Costa Rica. In the name of God and king, aristocratic adventurers plundered indigenous villages, executed resisters and enslaved survivors throughout the Península de Nicoya. However, none of these bloodstained campaigns led to a permanent presence, as intercontinental germ warfare caused outbreaks of feverish death on both sides. The indigenous people mounted a fierce resistance to the invaders, which included guerrilla warfare, destroying their own villages and killing their own children rather than letting them fall into Spanish hands.

New World Order

It was not until the 1560s that a Spanish colony was firmly established in Costa Rica. Hoping to cultivate the rich volcanic soil of the Central Valley, the Spanish founded the village of Cartago on the banks of the Río Reventazón. Although the fledgling colony was extremely isolated, it miraculously survived under the leadership of its first governor, Juan Vásquez de Coronado. Some of Costa Rica's demilitarized present was presaged in its early colonial government: preferring diplomacy over firearms to counter the indigenous threat, Coronado used Cartago as a base to survey the lands south to Panama and west to the Pacific, and secured deed and title over the colony.

Though Coronado was later lost in a shipwreck, his legacy endured. Costa Rica was an officially recognized province of the Virreinato de Nueva España (Viceroyalty of New Spain), which was the name given to the viceroy-ruled territories of the Spanish empire in North America, Central America, the Caribbean and Asia.

For roughly three centuries, the Captaincy General of Guatemala (also known as the Kingdom of Guatemala), which included Costa Rica, Nicaragua, Honduras, El Salvador, Guatemala and the Mexican state of Chiapas, was a loosely administered colony in the vast Spanish empire. Since the political and military headquarters of the kingdom were in Guatemala, Costa Rica became a minor provincial outpost that had little if any strategic significance or exploitable riches.

As a result of its status as a swampy, largely useless backwater, Costa Rica's colonial path diverged from the typical pattern in that a powerful landholding elite and slave-based economy never gained prominence. Instead of large estates, mining operations and coastal cities, modest-sized villages of smallholders developed in the interior Central Valley. According to national lore, the stoic, self-sufficient farmer provided the backbone for 'rural democracy' as Costa Rica emerged as one of the only egalitarian corners of the Spanish empire.

Equal rights and opportunities were not extended to the indigenous groups and, as Spanish settlement expanded, the local population decreased dramatically. From 400,000

1838	**1856**	**1889**
Costa Rica becomes entirely independent.	Costa Rica quashes the expansionist aims of hawks in the US by defeating William Walker and his invading army.	Costa Rica's first democratic elections are held.

Bahía Drake's Plundered Treasure

British explorer, government-sponsored pirate and slaver Sir Francis Drake is believed to have anchored in Bahía Drake in 1579. Rumor has it that he buried some of his plundered treasure here, but the only solid memorial to the man is a monument that looks out to his namesake bay.

at the time Columbus first sailed, the population was reduced to 20,000 a century later, and to 8000 a century after that. While disease was the main cause of death, the Spanish were relentless in their effort to exploit the natives as an economic resource by establishing the *encomienda* system that applied to indigenous males and gave the Spaniards the right to demand free labor. Many were worked to death. Central Valley groups were the first to fall, though outside the valley several tribes managed to survive a bit longer under forest cover, staging occasional raids. However, as in the rest of Latin America, repeated military campaigns eventually forced them into submission and slavery, though throughout that period many clergymen protested the brutal treatment of indigenous subjects and implored the Spanish Crown to protect them.

Fall of an Empire

Spain's costly Peninsular War with France from 1808 to 1814 – and the political turmoil, unrest and power vacuums that it caused – led Spain to lose all its colonial possessions in the first third of the 19th century.

In 1821 the Americas wriggled free of Spain's imperial grip following Mexico's declaration of independence for itself as well as the whole of Central America. Of course, the Central American provinces weren't too keen on having another foreign power reign over them and subsequently declared independence from Mexico. These events hardly disturbed Costa Rica, which learned of its liberation a month after the fact.

The newly liberated colonies pondered their fate: stay together in a United States of Central America or go their separate national ways. At first they came up with something in between, namely the Central American Federation (CAF), though it could neither field an army nor collect taxes. Accustomed to being at the center of things, Guatemala also attempted to dominate the CAF, alienating smaller colonies and hastening the CAF's demise. Future attempts to unite the region would likewise fail.

Meanwhile, an independent Costa Rica was taking shape under Juan Mora Fernández, the first head of state (1824–33). He tended toward nation building, and organized new towns, built roads, published a newspaper and coined a currency. His wife even partook in the effort by designing the country's flag.

Life returned to normal, unlike in the rest of the region, where post-independence civil wars raged on. In 1824 the Nicoya-Guanacaste region seceded from Nicaragua and joined its more easygoing southern neighbor, defining the territorial borders. In 1852 Costa Rica

1919
Federico Tinoco Granados is ousted as the dictator of Costa Rica in one of the few violent episodes in an otherwise peaceful history.

1940s
José Figueres Ferrer champions social-democratic policies and opposes the ruling conservatives.

1949
Hoping to heal old wounds and look forward, the temporary government enacts a new constitution that abolishes the army.

received its first diplomatic emissaries from the US and Great Britain.

Coffee Rica

In the 19th century, the riches that Costa Rica had long promised were uncovered when farmers realized that the soil and climate of the Central Valley highlands were ideal for coffee cultivation. Costa Rica led Central America in introducing the caffeinated bean, which transformed the impoverished country into the wealthiest in the region.

An export market was discovered, and the Costa Rican coffee boom was on. The drink's quick fix made it popular among working-class consumers in the industrializing north. The aroma of riches lured a wave of enterprising German immigrants, enhancing technical and financial skills in the business sector. By century's end, more than one-third of the Central Valley was dedicated to coffee cultivation, and coffee accounted for more than 90% of all exports and 80% of foreign-currency earnings.

The coffee industry in Costa Rica developed differently from those in the rest of Central America. As elsewhere, there arose a group of coffee barons – elites who reaped the rewards of the export bonanza – but Costa Rican coffee barons lacked the land and labor to cultivate the crop. Coffee production is labor-intensive, with a long and painstaking harvest season. Costa Rica's small farmers became the principal planters, and the coffee barons monopolized processing, marketing and financing. The coffee economy in Costa Rica created a wide network of high-end traders and small-scale growers, whereas in the rest of Central America a narrow elite controlled large estates worked by tenant laborers.

Coffee wealth became a power resource in politics. Costa Rica's traditional aristocratic families were at the forefront of the enterprise. At mid-century, three-quarters of the coffee barons were descended from just two colonial families. The country's leading coffee exporter at this time was President Juan Rafael Mora Porras (1849–59), whose lineage

The Little Drummer Boy

During your travels through the countryside, you may notice statues of Juan Santamaría, a drummer boy from Alajuela. He is one of Costa Rica's most beloved national heroes.

In April 1856 the North American mercenary William Walker and his ragtag army attempted to invade Costa Rica during an ultimately unsuccessful campaign to conquer all of Central America. Walker had already managed to seize control of Nicaragua, taking advantage of the civil war that was raging there. It didn't take him long after that to decide to march on Costa Rica, though Costa Rican president Juan Rafael Mora Porras guessed Walker's intentions and recruited a volunteer army of 9000 civilians. They surrounded Walker's army in an old *hacienda* (estate) in present-day Parque Nacional Santa Rosa. The Costa Ricans won the battle and Walker was forever expelled from Costa Rican soil, but Santamaría was ostensibly killed while daringly setting fire to Walker's defenses.

1963	1987	1994
Reserva Natural Absoluta Cabo Blanco becomes Costa Rica's first federally protected conservation area.	President Óscar Arias Sánchez wins the Nobel Peace Prize for his work on the Central American peace accords.	The indigenous people of Costa Rica are finally granted the right to vote.

went back to the colony's founder, Juan Vásquez de Coronado. Mora was overthrown by his brother-in-law after the president proposed to form a national bank independent of the coffee barons. The economic interests of the coffee elite would thereafter become a priority in Costa Rican politics.

Banana Empire

The coffee trade unintentionally gave rise to Costa Rica's next export boom: bananas. Getting coffee out to world markets necessitated a rail link from the central highlands to the coast, and Limón's deep harbor made an ideal port. Inland was dense jungle and insect-infested swamps, which prompted the government to contract the task to Minor Keith, the nephew of an American railroad tycoon.

The project was a disaster. Malaria and accidents churned through workers. To entice Keith to continue, the government turned over 3200 sq km of land along the route and provided a 99-year lease to run the railroad. In 1890 the line was finally completed and running at a loss.

Keith had begun to grow banana plants along the tracks as a cheap food source for the workers. Desperate to recoup his investment, he shipped some bananas to New Orleans in the hope of starting a side venture. He struck gold, or rather yellow. Consumers went crazy for the elongated finger fruit. By the early 20th century, bananas surpassed coffee as Costa Rica's most lucrative export and the country became the world's leading banana exporter. Unlike in the coffee industry, the profits were exported along with the bananas.

United Fruit owned huge swaths of lush lowlands, much of the transportation and communication infrastructure, and bunches of bureaucrats. The company drew a wave of migrant laborers from Jamaica, changing the country's ethnic complexion and provoking racial tensions. In its various incarnations as the United Brands Company (known as Yunai, *el pulpo* and, later, Chiquita), the company was virulently anti-union and maintained control over its workforces by paying them in redeemable scrip rather than cash for many years. Amazingly, the marks that *el pulpo* left on Costa Rica are still present, including the rusting train tracks.

Birth of a Nation

The inequality of the early 20th century led to the rise of José Figueres Ferrer, a self-described farmer-philosopher. The son of Catalan immigrant coffee planters, Figueres excelled in school and went to Boston's MIT to study engineering. Upon returning to Costa Rica to set up his own coffee plantation, he organized the hundreds of laborers on his farm into a utopian socialist community and appropriately named the property La Luz Sin Fin (The Struggle Without End).

In the 1940s Figueres became involved in national politics as an outspoken critic of President Calderón. In the midst of a radio interview in which he bad-mouthed the

2000	2010	2010
The population of Costa Rica tops four million.	Costa Rica elects its first female president, National Liberation Party candidate Laura Chinchilla.	Volcán Arenal, the country's most active volcano for over four decades, stops spitting lava and enters a resting phase.

president, police broke into the studio and arrested Figueres. He was accused of having fascist sympathies and was banished to Mexico. While in exile he formed the Caribbean League, a collection of students and democratic agitators from all over Central America who pledged to bring down the region's military dictators. When he returned to Costa Rica, the Caribbean League, now 700 men strong, went with him and helped protest against those in power.

> ### Bitter Fruit
>
> For details on the role of Minor Keith and the United Fruit Company in lobbying for a CIA-led coup in Guatemala, pick up a copy of the highly readable *Bitter Fruit* by Stephen Schlesinger and Stephen Kinzer.

When government troops descended on the farm with the intention of arresting Figueres and disarming the Caribbean League, it sparked a civil war. The moment had arrived: the diminutive farmer-philosopher now played the man on horseback. Figueres emerged victorious from the brief conflict and seized the opportunity to put into place his vision of Costa Rican social democracy. After dissolving the country's military, Figueres quoted HG Wells: 'The future of mankind cannot include the armed forces.'

As head of a temporary junta government, Figueres enacted nearly a thousand decrees. He taxed the wealthy, nationalized the banks and built a modern welfare state. His 1949 constitution granted full citizenship and voting rights to women, African Americans, indigenous groups and Chinese minorities. Today Figueres' revolutionary regime is regarded as the foundation of Costa Rica's unarmed democracy.

The American Empire

Throughout the 1970s and '80s, the sovereignty of the small nations of Central America was limited by their northern neighbor, the US. Big sticks, gunboats and dollar diplomacy were instruments of a Yankee policy to curtail socialist politics, especially the military oligarchies of Guatemala, El Salvador and Nicaragua.

In 1979 the rebellious Sandinistas toppled the American-backed Somoza dictatorship in Nicaragua. Alarmed by the Sandinistas' Soviet and Cuban ties, fervently anticommunist president Ronald Reagan decided it was time to intervene. Just like that, the Cold War arrived in the hot tropics.

The organizational details of the counterrevolution were delegated to Oliver North, an eager-to-please junior officer working out of the White House basement. North's can-do creativity helped to prop up the famed Contra rebels to incite civil war in Nicaragua. While both sides invoked the rhetoric of freedom and democracy, the war was really a turf battle between left-wing and right-wing forces.

Under intense US pressure, Costa Rica was dragged in. The Contras set up camp in northern Costa Rica, from where they staged guerrilla raids. Not-so-clandestine CIA operatives and US military advisors were dispatched to assist the effort. A secret jungle airstrip

2013	2014	2015
The murder of environmentalist Jairo Mora Sandoval brings attention to the dangers conservationists face in Costa Rica.	Luis Guillermo Solís is elected president by default when his opponent withdraws from the race.	A Costa Rican judge grants a common-law marriage to a same-sex couple, a first in Costa Rica and in Central America.

was built near the border to fly in weapons and supplies. To raise cash for the rebels, North allegedly used this covert supply network to traffic illegal narcotics through the region.

The war polarized Costa Rica. From conservative quarters came a loud call to re-establish the military and join the anticommunist crusade, which was largely underwritten by the US Pentagon. In May 1984 more than 20,000 demonstrators marched through San José to give peace a chance, though the debate didn't climax until the 1986 presidential election. The victor was 44-year-old Óscar Arias Sánchez, who, despite being born into coffee wealth, was an intellectual reformer in the mold of José Figueres Ferrer, his political patron.

Once in office, Arias affirmed his commitment to a negotiated resolution and reasserted Costa Rican national independence. He vowed to uphold his country's pledge of neutrality and to vanquish the Contras from the territory. The sudden resignation of the US ambassador around this time was suspected to be a result of Arias' strong stance. In a public ceremony, Costa Rican schoolchildren planted trees on top of the CIA's secret airfield. Most notably, Arias became the driving force in uniting Central America around a peace plan, which ended the Nicaraguan war and earned him the Nobel Peace Prize in 1987.

In 2006 Arias once again returned to the presidential office, winning the popular election by a 1.2% margin and subsequently ratifying the controversial Central American Free Trade Agreement (Cafta), which Costa Rica entered in 2009.

When Laura Chinchilla became the first female president of Costa Rica in 2010, she promised to continue with Arias' free-market policies, in spite of the divisive Cafta agreement (the referendum in 2007 barely resulted in a 'yes' vote at 51%). She also pledged to tackle the rise of violent crime and drug trafficking, on the increase due to Costa Rica's being used as a halfway house by Colombian and Mexican cartels. Ironically, a month after discussing the drug-cartel problem with the then US president Barack Obama during his visit to Costa Rica, Chinchilla herself became embroiled in a drug-related scandal over the use of a private jet belonging to a man under investigation by Costa Rican intelligence for possible links to international drug cartels.

Going Green in Costa Rica

Costa Rica has long had a reputation for being green. In 2009, the then president Arias set an over-ambitious goal: that Costa Rica would achieve carbon neutrality by the year 2021. Ten years later Environment Minister Carlos Manuel Rodríguez has revised that time frame and said he plans to combat climate change by achieving zero emissions by 2050.

Proposed changes to the energy sector include completely reforming transportation, energy, waste and land use in Costa Rica. In 2019, the nation was running on 98% renewable energy and Costa Rica's forested areas totaled 53%, after highly commendable work to counteract decades of deforestation. In 2017, Costa Rica ran without fossil-fuel-generated electricity for 300 days – a feat achieved using geothermal, hydro and wind power to produce household electricity. The next target is to achieve 100% renewable electricity by

2015	2016	2017
The International Court of Justice settles the land dispute between Costa Rica and Nicaragua in Costa Rica's favor.	Volcán Turrialba erupts, engulfing the country's major cities in a toxic ash cloud.	The government files a new case with the International Court of Justice concerning Nicaraguan military presence on its territory.

2030, and to make the majority of public transportation services electric, with full electrification projected for 2050.

According to the UN, Costa Rica's population of 4.09 million produces just 0.4% of global emissions. In 2019, the country received the UN's highest environmental honor, the 'Champions of the Earth' award for its focus on green policy and measures to combat climate change.

The Government Today

On April 1, 2018, Costa Rica elected President Carlos Alvarado Quesada, of the center-left Citizen Action Party (PAC). His second-in-command, Epsy Campbell Barr, became the first female vice president of African descent in Latin America. Alvarado took over from President Luis Guillermo Solís, also a member of PAC. Solís was Costa Rica's first president in half a century not to come from the two-party system, under which the social-democratic National Liberation Party and the center-right Social Christian Unity Party took turns holding power.

Although polls predicted the run-off would be close, it wasn't. Alvarado – a 38-year-old novelist, musician and former cabinet minister – won more than 60% of the vote, becoming the youngest serving president for a century. The decisive victory was particularly good news for progressives, environmentalists and proponents of equal rights, with same-sex marriage becoming legal in mid-2020, and proposals to become carbon-neutral by 2050.

Key challenges the president faces before the next election in 2022 include a widening national deficit; tensions between indigenous and non-indigenous peoples following the murder of Sergio Rojas, the leader of the indigenous Bribrí community, in 2019; and an escalating crime rate against tourists, resulting in the US increasing their travel advisory to Level 2 ('exercise increased caution') for US citizens in 2020. Most visits to Costa Rica are trouble-free, but this amendment is expected to affect US tourist numbers, in turn impacting the Costa Rican economy. Alvarado also plans to reduce unemployment, gaps in education, health and social disparity.

2018	**2019**	**2020**
Carlos Alvarado Quesada, 38, is elected as the country's second-youngest president ever.	Environment Minister Carlos Manuel Rodríguez plans to combat climate change by achieving zero emissions by 2050.	The ban on same-sex marriage is fully abolished in May, and joint adoption by same-sex couples becomes legal.

Rufous-tailed hummingbird

KEVIN WELLS/GETTY IMAGES ©

Costa Rica Outdoors

Whether you're hiking through the steamy jungle, riding powerful waves on the coast or zipping through the rainforest canopy, Costa Rica is an adrenaline-pumping destination. Families will appreciate mellower rafting expeditions and short hikes in the country's national parks, while experienced adventurers get their kicks in Costa Rica's varied and untamed wildernesses.

Hiking & Trekking

Hiking opportunities around Costa Rica are seemingly endless. With extensive mountains, canyons, dense jungles, cloud forests and two coastlines, this is one of Central America's best and most varied hiking destinations.

Hikes come in an enormous spectrum of difficulty. At tourist-packed destinations, shorter trails are clearly marked and sometimes paved. This is fantastic if you're traveling with kids or aren't confident about route-finding. For long-distance trekking, there are many more options throughout the country.

Opportunities for moderate hiking are typically plentiful in most parks and reserves. For the most part, you can rely on signs and maps for orientation, though it helps to have

Hiking (p234), Parque Nacional Volcán Arenal

DUDAREV MIKHAIL/SHUTTERSTOCK ©

some navigational experience. Good hiking shoes, plenty of water and confidence in your abilities may enable you to combine several shorter day hikes into a lengthier expedition. Tourist-information centers at park entrances are great resources for planning your intended route.

Costa Rica's top challenges are scaling Cerro Chirripó (p118) and traversing Corcovado (p132), both of which normally take at least two days of hiking. In these cases, lodges in the parks mean that camping is not required. While Chirripó can be undertaken independently, local guides are required for Corcovado.

Make It Happen

If you're planning your trip around long-distance trekking, it's best to visit during the dry season (December to April). Outside this window, many rivers become impassable and trails (and roads) are prone to flooding. In the highlands, journeys become more taxing in the rain, and the bare landscape offers little protection.

Costa Rica is hot and humid: hiking in these tropical conditions, harassed by mosquitoes, can really take it out of you. Wear light clothing that will dry quickly. Overheating and dehydration are the main sources of misery on the trails, so be sure to bring plenty of water and take rest stops. Make sure you have sturdy, comfortable footwear and a lightweight rain jacket.

Unfortunately, people have been known to be robbed while on some of the more remote trails. Although this rarely happens, it is always advisable to hike in numbers for added

Ghost crab, Parque Nacional Marino Ballena (p152)

SILVIA COZZI/ALAMY STOCK PHOTO ©

★ Top Five for Wildlife

Parque Nacional Corcovado (p132)

Parque Nacional Tortuguero (p72)

Parque Nacional Marino Ballena (p152)

Monteverde & Santa Elena (p214)

Parque Nacional Manuel Antonio (p168)

safety. Hiring a local guide is another excellent way to enhance your experience, avoid getting lost and learn an enormous amount about the flora and fauna around you.

Some of the local park offices have maps, but this is the exception rather than the rule. If you are planning to do independent hiking on long-distance trails, be sure to purchase your maps in San José in advance.

A number of companies offer trekking tours in Costa Rica:

Costa Rica Trekking Adventures (⏏2771-4582; www.chirripo.com) Offers multiday treks in Chirripó, Corcovado and Tapantí.

Osa Aventura (⏏2735-5670, 8372-6135; www.osaaventura.com; 1-/2-day Corcovado hikes US$105/350) ✐ Specializes in treks through Corcovado.

Osa Wild (p135) Offers a huge variety of hikes in the Osa, in partnership with a sustainability organization.

Surfing

Point and beach breaks, lefts and rights, reefs and river mouths, warm water and year-round waves make Costa Rica a favorite surfing destination. For the most part, the Pacific coast has bigger swells and better waves during the latter part of the rainy season, but the Caribbean cooks from November to May. Basically, there's a wave waiting to be surfed at any time of year.

For the uninitiated, lessons are available at almost all of the major surfing destinations – especially popular towns include Jacó, Dominical, Sámara and Tamarindo on the Pacific coast. Surfing definitely has a steep learning curve, and it can be dangerous if the currents are strong. With that said, the sport is accessible to children and novices, though it's advisable to start with a lesson. Always inquire locally about conditions before you paddle out.

Throughout Costa Rica, waves are big (though not massive), and many offer hollow and fast rides that are perfect for intermediates. As a bonus, Costa Rica is one of the few places on the planet where you can surf two different oceans in the same day. Advanced surfers with plenty of experience can contend with some of the world's most famous waves. The top ones include Ollie's Point and Witch's Rock, off the coast of the Sector Santa Rosa of the Área de Conservación Guanacaste (featured in *Endless Summer II*); Mal País and Santa Teresa (p193), with a groovy scene to match the powerful waves; Playa Hermosa (p192), whose bigger, faster curls attract a more determined (and experienced) crew of wave chasers; Pavones, a legendary long left across the sweet waters of the Golfo Dulce; and the infamous Salsa Brava (p82) in Puerto Viejo de Talamanca, for experts only.

Make It Happen

Some international airlines accept surfboards, though usually only shortboards. Although some will take longboards (meticulously check luggage allowances for board lengths before you book). Boards must be properly packed in a padded board bag. Transporting surfboards is getting harder and pricier in the age of higher fuel tariffs. Domestic airlines offer more of a challenge: they will accept surfboards for an extra charge, but the board must be under 2.1m (6.68ft) in length. On full flights, there's a chance your board won't make it on because of weight restrictions.

An alternative is to buy a new or used board in Costa Rica and then sell it before you leave. Great places to start your search include Jacó, Mal País and Santa Teresa, and Tamarindo. It's usually possible to buy a cheap longboard for about US$250 to US$300, and a cheap shortboard for about US$150 to US$200. Some surf shops will buy back your board for about 50% of the price you paid.

Outfitters in many of the popular surf towns rent all kinds of boards, fix dings, give classes and organize excursions. Jacó, Tamarindo, Pavones and Puerto Viejo de Talamanca are good for these types of activities.

Caribbean Surf School (p83) Based in Puerto Viejo de Talamanca, Hershel is widely considered to be one of the best teachers on the Caribbean side.

Costa Rica Surf Camp (p161) Excellent teachers with safety certification and low teacher-student ratios.

Dominical Surf Adventures (p161) An excellent source of surf lessons in Dominical.

Pura Vida Adventures (p193) An excellent women-only surf-and-yoga camp at Playa El Carmen.

Wildlife-Watching & Birding

Costa Rica's biodiversity is legendary, and the country delivers unparalleled opportunities for birding and wildlife-watching. Most people are already familiar with the most famous, yet commonly spotted, animals. You'll recognize monkeys bounding through the treetops, sloths clinging to branches and toucans gliding beneath the canopy. Young children, even if they have been to the zoo dozens of times, typically love the thrill of spotting creatures in the wild. Keeping checklists is a fun way to add an educational element to your travels.

A quality pair of binoculars is highly recommended and can really make the difference between far-off movement and a veritable face-to-face encounter. Most guides carry a spotting scope, which they will set up when they sight a bird or creature, so that clients can get a good look and even take photographs.

Make It Happen

Costa Rica is brimming with wildlife at every turn, but sometimes it takes an experienced guide to help you notice it.

Aratinga Tours (www.aratinga-tours.com; tours from US$1900) ⚑ Some of the best bird tours in the country are led by Belgian ornithologist Pieter Westra.

Birding Eco Tours (📱in USA 937-238-0254; www.birdingecotours.com; 9-day tours around US$4000) An international bird-tour company with highly entertaining and qualified guides in Costa Rica.

Tropical Feathers (📱2771-9686; www.costaricabirdingtours.com; 10-day tours from US$3900) Local owner and guide Noel Ureña has two decades of experience leading birding tours.

Kayaking, Parque Nacional Manuel Antonio (p168)

★ Top Five for Rafting & Kayaking

Río Pacuare (p86)

La Virgen (p256)

Parque Nacional Manuel Antonio (p168)

Parque Nacional Tortuguero (p72)

Bahía Drake (p142)

White-Water Rafting & Kayaking

White-water rafting has remained one of Costa Rica's top outdoor pursuits since the '80s. Ranging from family-friendly Class I riffles to nearly unnavigable Class V rapids, the country's rivers offer highly varied experiences.

First-time runners are catered for year-round, while seasoned enthusiasts arrive en masse during the wildest months from June to October. There is also much regional variation, with gentler rivers located near Manuel Antonio along the central Pacific coast, and world-class runs along the Río Pacuare near Turrialba in the Central Valley. Since all white-water rafting in Costa Rica requires the presence of a certified guide, you will need to book trips through a reputable tour agency. No matter the run, you'll get totally soaked and tossed about, so bring your sense of adventure, but no fancy clothes or jewelry.

The tiny village of La Virgen in the northern lowlands is the unofficial kayaking capital of Costa Rica and the best spot to hook up with other paddlers. The neighboring Río Sarapiquí has an impressive variety of runs that cater to all ages and skill levels.

With 1228km of coastline, two gulfs and plentiful mangrove estuaries, Costa Rica is also an ideal destination for sea kayaking. This is a great way for paddlers to access remote areas and catch glimpses of rare birds and wildlife. Access varies considerably, and is largely dependent on tides and currents.

Make It Happen

June to October are considered peak season for river rafting and kayaking, though some rivers offer good runs all year. Government regulation of outfitters is shoddy, so ask lots of questions about your guide's water safety, emergency and medical training.

River kayaking can be organized in conjunction with white-water-rafting trips if you are experienced; sea kayaking is popular year-round.

Aguas Bravas (p255) Near Chilamate, this is the top outfitter on Costa Rica's best white water.

Exploradores Outdoors (p77) This outfit offers one- and two-day trips on the Ríos Pacuare, Reventazón and Sarapiquí.

Green Rivers (p255) A young and fun Sarapiquí-based outfit working out of the Posada Andrea Cristina.

H2O Adventures (p174) Arranges two- and five-day adventures on the Río Savegre.

Pineapple Tours (p161) Exciting half-day kayaking trips go through caves and mangrove channels.

Ríos Tropicales (p87) Multiday adventures on the Río Pacuare and two days of kayaking in Tortuguero.

Diving & Snorkeling

The good news is that Costa Rica offers body-temperature water with few humans and abundant marine life. The bad news is that visibility is low because of silt and plankton, and soft corals and sponges are dominant. However, if you're looking for fine opportunities to see massive schools of fish, as well as larger marine animals such as turtles, sharks, dolphins and whales, then jump right in.

The Caribbean Sea is better for snorkeling, with the beach towns of Manzanillo and Cahuita particularly well suited to youngsters. Along the Pacific, Islas Santa Catalina and Murciélago near Playa del Coco, and Isla del Caño near Bahía Drake are excellent options for those with solid diving experience.

Isla del Coco, a remote island floating in the deep Pacific, is regarded by veteran divers as one of the best spots on the planet. To dive the wonderland of Coco, you'll need to visit on a liveaboard and have logged some serious time underwater.

Make It Happen

Generally, visibility isn't great during the rainy months, when rivers swell and their outflow clouds the ocean. At this time, boats to offshore locations offer better viewing opportunities. The water is warm – around 24°C (75°F) to 29°C (84°F) at the surface, with a thermocline at around 20m below the surface where it drops to 23°C (73°F). If you're keeping it shallow, you can skin-dive.

Drake Divers (p139) This operation in Bahía Drake takes divers to Isla del Caño.

Rich Coast Diving (☏2670-0176; www.richcoastdiving.com; 2-tank dives from US$95, Open Water courses US$575; ◷7am-6pm) One of several dive outfits in Playa del Coco and nearby Playa Hermosa.

Undersea Hunter (☏2228-6613, in USA 800-203-2120; www.underseahunter.com) Get in touch with this liveaboard operation to plan a trip to Isla del Coco.

Diving, Isla del Coco

Mountain Biking & Cycling

Although the winding, potholed roads and aggressive drivers can be a challenge, cycling is on the rise in Costa Rica. Numerous less-trafficked roads offer plenty of adventure – from scenic mountain paths with sweeping views to rugged trails that take riders through streams and past volcanoes.

The best long-distance rides are along the Pacific coast's Interamericana, which has a decent shoulder and is relatively flat, and on the road from Montezuma to the Reserva Natural Absoluta Cabo Blanco on the southern Península de Nicoya.

Mountain biking has taken off in recent years and some tour operators can organize guided rides, including **Ecoaventuras** (☑8868-3938, 2556-7171; www.ecoaventuras.co.cr; Calle 6; white-water rafting from US$70, mountain biking Turrialba Valley from US$70) in Turrialba, Aventuras del Sarapiquí (p254) in Chilamate, and Green Rivers (p255) in Puerto Viejo de Sarapiquí.

Near Arenal, there are trail networks at:

Arenal 1968 (Map p231; ☑2462-1212; www.arenal1968.com; El Castillo-La Fortuna road; trails US$15, mountain-bike park US$15; ☺7am-10pm) A private network of trails sits along the original 1968 lava flow next to the entrance of Parque Nacional Volcán Arenal.

Río Perdido (☑2673-3600, in USA 888-326-5070; www.rioperdido.com; San Bernardo de Bagaces; day pass adult/child US$40/30, spa treatment US$55-95) Has an extensive network of biking trails on its gorgeous grounds near Volcán Miravalles.

Sky Adventures (p247) Trails combine with high-altitude thrills (hanging bridges, ziplines and tree climbing) in El Castillo.

Make It Happen

Some international airlines will fly your bike as a piece of checked baggage for an extra fee. Pad it well, because the box is likely to be roughly handled.

Alternatively, you can rent mountain bikes in almost any tourist town, but the condition of the equipment varies greatly. For a monthly fee, **Trail Source** (www.trailsource.com) can provide you with information on trails all over Costa Rica and the world.

Outfitters in Costa Rica and the US can organize multiday mountain-biking trips. If you want to tour Costa Rica by bicycle, be forewarned that the country's cycling shops are decidedly more geared toward utilitarian concerns. Bring any specialized equipment (including a serious lock) from home.

Handmade Sarchí oxcarts (p285)

The Tico Way of Life

Blessed with natural beauty and a peaceful, army-less society, it's no wonder Costa Rica is known as the Switzerland of Central America. The country is certainly challenged by its eco-conscious goals and modern intercontinental maladies (such as border control and drug trafficking), but the Tico (Costa Rican) attitude remains sunny and family-centered, with a good work-life balance.

The Pura Vida

Pura vida – pure life – is more than just a slogan that rolls off the tongues of Ticos and emblazons souvenirs. In the laid-back tone in which it is constantly uttered, the phrase is a bona fide mantra for the Costa Rican way of life. Perhaps the essence of the pure life is something better lived than explained, but hearing *'pura vida'* again and again while traveling across this beautiful country – as a greeting, a stand-in for goodbye, 'cool,' and an acknowledgment of thanks – makes it evident that the concept lives deep within the DNA of this country.

The living seems particularly pure when Costa Rica is compared with its Central American neighbors such as Nicaragua and Honduras; there's little poverty, illiteracy or political tumult, the country is crowded with ecological jewels, and the standard of living is high. What's more, Costa Rica has flourished without an army for the past 60 years. The sum of the parts is a country that's an oasis of calm in a corner of the world that has been continuously degraded by warfare. And though the Costa Rican people are justifiably proud hosts, a compliment to the country is likely to be met simply with a warm smile and an enigmatic two-word reply: *pura vida*.

Daily Life

With its lack of war, long life expectancy and a relatively sturdy economy, Costa Rica enjoys the highest standard of living in Central America. Most Costa Ricans live fairly affluent and comfortable lives, even by North American standards.

As in many places in Latin America, the family unit in Costa Rica remains the nucleus of life. Families socialize together and extended families often live near each other. When it's time to party it's also largely a family affair; celebrations, vacations and weddings are a social outlet for rich and poor alike, and those with relatives in positions of power – nominal or otherwise – don't hesitate to turn to them for support.

Given this mutually cooperative environment, it's no surprise that life expectancy in Costa Rica is slightly higher than in the US. In fact, most Costa Ricans are more likely to die of heart disease or cancer as opposed to the childhood diseases that plague many developing nations. A comprehensive socialized health-care system and excellent sanitation systems account for these positive statistics, as do tropical weather, a healthy, varied diet and a generally stress-free lifestyle – the *pura vida*.

Still, the divide between rich and poor is evident. The middle and upper classes largely reside in San José, as well as in the major cities of the Central Valley highlands (Heredia, Alajuela and Cartago), and enjoy a level of comfort similar to their economic brethren in Europe and the US. City dwellers are likely to have a maid and a car or two, and a lucky few have a second home on the beach or in the mountains.

The home of an average Tico is a one-story construction built from concrete blocks, wood, or a combination of both. In the poorer lowland areas, people often live in windowless houses made of *caña brava* (a local cane). For the vast majority of *campesinos* (farmers) and *indígenas* (people of indigenous origin), life is harder than in the cities; poverty levels are higher and standards of living are lower than in the rest of the country. This is especially true in indigenous reservations, and along the Caribbean coast, where the descendants of Jamaican immigrants have long suffered from lack of attention from the federal government. However, although poor families have few possessions and little financial security, every member assists with working the land or contributing to the household, which creates a strong safety net.

As in the rest of the world, globalization is having a dramatic effect on Costa Ricans, who are increasingly mobile, international and intertwined in the global economy – for better or for worse. These days, society is increasingly geographically mobile – the Tico who was born in Puntarenas might end up managing a lodge on the Península de Osa. And, with the advent of better-paved roads, cell coverage and the increasing presence of North American and European expats (and the accompanying malls and big-box stores), the Tico family unit is somewhat influenced by the changing tides of a global society.

Women in Costa Rica

Costa Rica's progressive legal stance on women's issues makes the country stand out among its Central American neighbors. A 1974 family code stipulated equal duties and rights for men and women. Additionally, women can draw up contracts, assume loans and inherit property. Sexual harassment and sex discrimination are also illegal, and in 1996

Costa Rica passed a landmark law against domestic violence that was one of the most progressive in Latin America. With women holding more and more roles in political, legal, scientific and medical fields, Costa Rica has been home to some historic firsts: in 1998 both vice presidents (Costa Rica has two) were women, and in February 2010 Arias Sánchez' former vice president, Laura Chinchilla, became the first female president. The elected vice president in 2018 was another historic milestone for the country: a woman of Afro-Costa Rican descent, Epsy Campbell Barr.

Still, the picture of sexual equality is much more complicated than the country's bragging rights might suggest. Unwanted byproducts of the legal prostitution trade include illicit underground activities such as child prostitution and the trafficking of women (despite middlemen or 'pimps' being illegal). Aside from the cultural reverence for the matriarch (Mother's Day is a national holiday), traditional Latin American machismo persists and anti-discrimination laws are rarely enforced. Particularly in the countryside, many women maintain traditional societal roles: raising children, cooking and running the home.

Marriage Equality

In 2015 a Costa Rican judge granted a same-sex common-law marriage, making Costa Rica the first country in Central America to recognize gay relationships. The previous president, Luis Guillermo Solís, expressed support for gay rights, and he even flew the rainbow flag at the presidential house.

His successor, Carlos Alvarado Quesada, continues this spirit of tolerance and in August 2018 the Supreme Court ruled that a ban on same-sex marriage was unconstitutional. The Legislative Assembly was given 18 months to change the law or it would be automatically overturned. Meaning that from May 26, 2020 same-sex marriage became legal in Costa Rica. Costa Rica is firmly on the map for the international LGBT+ community, and is slowly becoming a destination for same-sex weddings. The liberal-minded Manuel Antonio, with its gay-friendly clubs and hotels, is a hot spot for ceremonies. Adoption by same-sex couples was also made legal in May 2020.

Sport

No Costa Rican sporting venture can compare with *fútbol* (soccer). Every town has a soccer field (which usually serves as the most conspicuous landmark) where neighborhood aficionados play in heated matches.

The *selección nacional* (national selection) team is known affectionately as La Sele. Legions of Tico fans still recall La Sele's most memorable moments, including an unlikely showing in the quarterfinals at the 1990 World Cup in Italy and a solid (if not long-lasting) performance in the 2002 World Cup. More recently, La Sele's failure to qualify for the 2010 World Cup led to a top-down change in leadership and the reinstatement of one-time coach Jorge Luis Pinto, a Colombian coach who has had mixed results on the international stage. Pinto seemed to be a good fit for the team's ferocious young leaders such as record-setting scorer Álvaro Saborío, goalkeeper Keylor Navas and forward Bryan Ruiz. In fact, Pinto led the team to qualify for the 2014 World Cup in Brazil, where the team reached the quarterfinals, making them national heroes. Led by former Tico legend Óscar Ramírez as coach, the country qualified for the 2018 World Cup in Russia, but did not advance past the first round, managing just one draw in three matches.

The women's national *fútbol* team proved their mettle in 2018, though, making it to the final of the Caribbean and Central American Games.

Costa Rica by the Book

Costa Rica's history and culture have been detailed in a number of books.

Tycoon's War (Stephen Dando-Collins) A well-told tale of US business tycoon Cornelius Vanderbilt's epic struggle to maintain his economic stranglehold over the Central American isthmus.

Bananas: How United Fruit Company Shaped the World (Peter Chapman) The story of the rise and collapse of fruit company giant 'el pulpo' (the octopus).

Nation Thief (Robert Housto) A novelistic telling of William Walker's excursions into Central America.

Green Phoenix (William Allen) Details the ultimate victory of halting deforestation and establishing the Guanacaste Conservation Area.

Walking with Wolf (Kay Chornook and Wolf Guindon) Recounts the life of one of Monteverde's pioneering Quakers who preserved his adopted cloud-forest home.

With such perfect waves, surfing has steadily grown in popularity among Ticos, especially those who grow up in surf towns. Costa Rica hosts numerous national and international competitions annually that are widely covered by local media.

For a nation that values its wildlife, it may be surprising that the controversial sport of bullfighting is still popular, particularly in the Guanacaste region, though the bull isn't killed in the Costa Rican version of the sport. More aptly described, bullfighting is really a ceremonial opportunity to watch an often tipsy cowboy run around with a bull.

Arts

Literature

Costa Rica has a relatively young literary history and few works by Costa Rican writers or novelists are available in translation. Carlos Luis Fallas (1909–66) is widely known for *Mamita Yunai* (1940), an influential 'proletarian' novel that took the banana companies to task for their labor practices, and he remains very popular among the Latin American left.

Carmen Naranjo (1928–2012) is one of the few contemporary Costa Rican writers to have risen to international acclaim. She was a novelist, poet and short-story writer who also served as ambassador to India in the 1970s, and later as minister of culture. In 1996 she was awarded the prestigious Gabriela Mistral medal by the Chilean government. Her short-story collection, *There Never Was a Once Upon a Time,* is widely available in English. Two of her stories can also be found in *Costa Rica: A Traveler's Literary Companion.*

Memoirist José León Sánchez (b 1929) hails from the border of Costa Rica and Nicaragua. After being convicted for stealing from the famous Basílica de Nuestra Señora de Los Ángeles in Cartago, he was incarcerated at Isla San Lucas, one of Latin America's most notorious jails, where he clandestinely authored one of the continent's most poignant books: *La isla de los hombres solos* (called *God Was Looking the Other Way* in the translated version).

Music & Dance

San José features a regular lineup of domestic and international rock, folk and hip-hop artists, but you'll find that the regional sounds also survive, each with their own special rhythms, instruments and styles. For instance, the Península de Nicoya has a rich musical history, most of its sound made with guitars, maracas and marimbas. The common sounds on the Caribbean coast are reggae, reggaetón (a newer version of reggae mixed with hip-hop beats) and calypso, which has roots in Afro-Caribbean slave culture.

Popular dance music includes Latin dances, such as salsa, merengue, bolero and *cumbia*. Guanacaste is also the birthplace of many traditional dances, most of which depict courtship rituals between country folk. The most famous dance – sometimes considered the national dance – is the *punto guanacasteco*. What keeps it lively is the *bomba,* a funny (and usually racy) rhymed verse shouted by the male dancers during the musical interlude.

Visual Arts

The visual arts in Costa Rica first took on a national character in the 1920s, when Teodórico Quirós, Fausto Pacheco and their contemporaries began painting landscapes that differed from traditional European styles, depicting the rolling hills and lush forest of the Costa Rican countryside, often sprinkled with characteristic adobe houses.

The contemporary scene is more varied and it's difficult to define a unique Tico style. The work of several artists has garnered acclaim, including the magical realism of Isidro Con Wong, the surreal paintings and primitive engravings of Francisco Amighetti and the mystical female figures painted by Rafa Fernández. The Museo de Arte y Diseño Contemporáneo (p47) in San José is the top place to see this type of work, and its permanent collection is a great primer.

Many galleries are geared toward tourists and specialize in 'tropical art' (for lack of an official description): brightly colored, whimsical folk paintings depicting flora and fauna that evoke the work of French artist Henri Rousseau.

Folk art and handicrafts are not as widely produced or readily available here as in other Central American countries. However, the dedicated souvenir hunter will have no problem finding the colorful handmade Sarchí oxcarts that have become a symbol of Costa Rica – there are many skilled oxcart-makers in the Central Valley. Indigenous crafts, which include intricately carved and painted masks made by the Boruca indigenous people, as well as handwoven bags and linens and colorful Chorotega pottery, can also be found in San José and more readily along Costa Rica's Pacific coast.

Film

Artistically, while film is not a new medium in Costa Rica, young filmmakers have been upping the country's ante in this arena. Over the last decade or so, a handful of Costa Rican filmmakers have submitted their work for Oscar consideration, and many others have received critical acclaim for their pictures nationally and internationally. Films include the adaptation of Gabriel García Márquez' magical-realism novel *Del amor y otro demonios* (Of Love and Other Demons, 2009), directed by Hilda Hidalgo; a comedic coming-of-age story of young Ticos on the cusp of adulthood in contemporary Costa Rica in *El cielo rojo* (The Red Sky, 2008), written and directed by Miguel Alejandro Gomez; and the light-hearted story of a Costa Rican farmer who embarks on the journey to Europe to raise money to avoid losing his farm in *Maikol Yordan de viaje perdido* (Maikol Yordan Traveling Lost, 2014), also directed by Gomez. More recently, the 2016 rom-com *About Us (Entonces nosotros)*, directed by Hernan Jimenez, sees a couple trying to repair their relationship on a beach getaway, simultaneously making you laugh, cringe and somehow want to be on that beach.

A film-festival calendar has also been blossoming in Costa Rica, though dates vary year on year. Sponsored by the Ministerio de Cultura y Juventud, the Costa Rica Festival Internacional de Cine (www.costaricacinefest.go.cr) takes place in San José (check the website for current dates) and features international films fitting the year's theme. The longer-running Costa Rica International Film Festival (CRIFF; www.filmfestivallife.com) takes place annually; check the website for dates.

Monteverde (p201)

LARWIN/SHUTTERSTOCK ©

Landscapes & Ecology

Despite its diminutive size, Costa Rica has an astounding collection of habitats. On one coast are the breezy skies and big waves of the Pacific, while only 119km away lie the Caribbean's languid shores. In between are active volcanoes, alpine peaks and crisp high-elevation forests. Few places can compare with this little country's spectacular inter-action of natural, geological and climatic forces.

The Land

The Pacific Coast

Two major peninsulas hook out into the ocean along the 1016km-long Pacific coast: Nicoya in the north and Osa in the south. Although they look relatively similar from space, on the ground they could hardly be more different. Nicoya is one of the driest places in the country and holds some of Costa Rica's most developed tourist infrastructure; Osa is wet and rugged, run through by wild, seasonal rivers and rough dirt roads that are always encroached upon by the creeping jungle.

Just inland from the coast, the Pacific lowlands are a narrow strip of land backed by mountains. This area is equally dynamic, ranging from dry deciduous forests and open cattle country in the north to misty, mysterious tropical rainforests in the south.

Central Costa Rica

Move a bit inland from the Pacific coast and you immediately ascend the jagged spine of the country: the majestic Cordillera Central in the north and the rugged, largely unexplored Cordillera de Talamanca in the south. Continually being revised by tectonic activity, these mountains are part of the majestic Sierra Madre chain that runs north through Mexico.

Home to active volcanoes, clear trout-filled streams and ethereal cloud forest, these mountain ranges generally follow a northwest to southeast line, with the highest and most dramatic peaks in the south near the Panamanian border. The highest peak in the country is windswept Cerro Chirripó (3820m).

In the midst of this powerful landscape, surrounded on all sides by mountains, are the highlands of the Meseta Central – the Central Valley. This fertile central plain, some 1000m above sea level, is the agricultural heart of the nation and enjoys abundant rainfall and mild temperatures. It includes San José and cradles three more of Costa Rica's five largest cities, accounting for more than half of the country's population.

The Caribbean Coast

Cross the mountains and drop down the eastern slope and you'll reach the elegant line of the Caribbean coastline – a long, straight 212km along low plains, brackish lagoons and waterlogged forests. A lack of strong tides allows plants to grow right over the water's edge along coastal sloughs. Eventually, these create the walls of vegetation along the narrow, murky waters that characterize much of the region. As if taking cues from the slow-paced, Caribbean-influenced culture, the rivers that rush out of the central mountains take on a languid pace here, curving through broad plains toward the sea. There are smoothly paved main roads along the southern Caribbean coast, but the northern Caribbean is still largely inaccessible except by boat or plane.

Geology

If all this wildly diverse beauty makes Costa Rica feel like the crossroads between vastly different worlds, that's because it is. As it's part of the thin strip of land that separates two continents with hugely divergent wildlife and topographical character, and right in the middle of the world's two largest oceans, it's little wonder that Costa Rica boasts such a colorful collision of climates, landscapes and wildlife.

The country's geological history began when the Cocos Plate, a tectonic plate that lies below the Pacific, crashed headlong into the Caribbean Plate, which is off the isthmus' east coast. Since the plates travel about 10cm every year, the collision might seem slow by human measure, but it was a violent wreck by geological standards, creating the area's subduction zone. The plates continue to collide, with the Cocos Plate pushing the Caribbean Plate toward the heavens and making the area prone to earthquakes and volcanic activity.

Despite all the violence underfoot, these forces have blessed the country with some of the world's most beautiful and varied tropical landscapes.

Out on the Reef

Compared with the rest of the Caribbean, the coral reefs of Costa Rica are not a banner attraction. Heavy surf and shifting sands along most of the Caribbean coast produce conditions that are unbearable to corals. The exceptions are two beautiful patches of reef

Don't Disturb the Dolphins

Swimming with dolphins has been illegal since 2006, although shady tour operators who are out for a quick buck may encourage it. Research indicates that in some heavily touristed areas, dolphins are leaving their natural habitat in search of calmer seas. When your boat comes across these amazing creatures of the sea, avoid the temptation to jump in with them – you can still have an unforgettable experience by peacefully observing them without disturbing them.

in the south that are protected on the rocky headlands of Parque Nacional Cahuita and Refugio Nacional de Vida Silvestre Gandoca-Manzanillo. These diminutive but vibrant reefs are home to more than 100 species of fish and many types of coral and make for decent snorkeling and diving.

Unfortunately, the reefs themselves are in danger due to global warming, increased water temperatures and tourism (divers and snorkelers damaging the reefs with sunscreen and contact), plus pollutants like sediments washing downriver from logging operations and toxic chemicals that wash out of nearby agricultural fields. Although curbed by the government, these factors persist. Scientists are experimenting with 'reforesting' and reviving coral reefs, like those off the Península de Osa. It's a slow process and only time will tell if it's a viable solution to Costa Rica's dying coral.

Wildlife

Nowhere else are so many types of habitats squeezed into such a tiny area. Costa Rica has the world's largest number of species per 10,000 sq km – more than 615. This simple fact alone makes Costa Rica the premier destination for nature lovers.

The large number of species here is also due to the country's relatively recent appearance. Roughly three million years ago, Costa Rica rose from the ocean and formed a land bridge between North and South America. Species from these two vast biological provinces started to mingle and doubled in number.

Flora

Simply put, Costa Rica's floral biodiversity is mind-blowing – there are more than 500,000 species in total, including close to 12,000 species of vascular plant, and the list gets more and more crowded each year. Orchids alone account for about 1400 species. The diversity of habitats created when this many species mix is a wonder to behold.

Rainforest

The humid, vibrant mystery of the tropical rainforest connects acutely with a traveler's sense of adventure. These forests, more dense with plant life than any other environment on the planet, are leftover scraps of prehistoric jungles that once covered the continents. Standing in the midst of it and trying to take it all in can be overwhelming: tropical rainforests contain more than half of the earth's known living organisms. Naturally, this riotous pile-up of life requires lots of water – the forest typically gets between 5m and 6m of rainfall annually (yes, that's *meters*!).

Classic rainforest habitats are well represented in the parks of southwestern Costa Rica and in the mid-elevation portions of the central mountains. Here you will find towering trees that block out the sky, long, looping vines and many overlapping layers of vegetation. Large trees often show buttresses – wing-like ribs that extend from their trunks for added structural support. And plants climb atop other plants, fighting for a bit of sunlight. The most impressive areas of primary forest – a term designating completely untouched land that has never been disturbed by humans – exist on the Península de Osa.

Cloud Forest

Visiting the unearthly terrain of a cloud forest is a highlight for many visitors; there are amazing swaths of it in Monteverde, along the Cerro de la Muerte and below the peaks of Chirripó. In these regions, fog-drenched trees are so thickly coated in mosses, ferns, bromeliads and orchids that you can hardly discern their true shapes. These forests are created when humid trade winds off the Caribbean blow up into the highlands, then cool and condense to form thick, low-hanging clouds. With constant exposure to wind, rain and sun, the trees here are crooked and stunted.

Cloud forests are widespread at high elevations throughout Costa Rica and any of them warrant a visit. Be forewarned, though, that in these habitats the term 'rainy season' has little meaning, as it's always dripping wet from the fog – humidity in a cloud forest often hovers around 100%.

Tropical Dry Forest

Along Costa Rica's northwestern coast lies the country's largest concentration of tropical dry forest – a stunningly different scene to the country's wet rainforests and cloud forests. During the dry season, many trees drop their foliage, creating carpets of crackling, sun-drenched leaves and a sense of openness that is largely absent in other Costa Rican habitats. The large trees here, such as Costa Rica's national tree, the guanacaste, have broad, umbrella-like canopies, while spiny shrubs and vines or cacti dominate the understory. At times, large numbers of trees erupt into spectacular displays of flowers, and at the beginning of the rainy season everything is transformed with a wonderful flush of new, green foliage.

This type of forest was native to Guanacaste and the Península de Nicoya, but it suffered generations of destruction for its commercially valuable lumber. Most was clear-cut or burned to make way for ranching. Guanacaste and Santa Rosa national parks are good examples of the dry forest and host some of the country's most accessible nature hiking.

Mangroves

Along brackish stretches of both coasts, mangrove swamps are a world unto themselves. Growing on stilts out of muddy tidal flats, five species of tree crowd together so densely that no boats and few animals can penetrate. Striking in their adaptations for dealing with salt, mangroves thrive where no other land plant dares to tread and are among the world's most relentless colonizers. Mangrove seeds are heavy and fleshy, blooming into flowers in the spring before falling off to give way to fruit. By the time the fruit falls, it is covered with spiky seedlings that anchor in the soft mud of low tides. In only 10 years, a seedling has the potential to mature into an entire new colony.

Mangrove swamps play extremely important roles in the ecosystem and are protected by Costa Rican law. Not only do they buffer coastlines from the erosive power of waves but they also have high levels of productivity because they trap nutrient-rich sediment and serve as spawning and nursery areas for innumerable species of fish and invertebrate. The brown waters of mangrove channels – rich with nutrients and filled with algae, shrimp, crustaceans and caimans – form tight links in the marine food chain and are best explored in a kayak, early in the morning.

There are miles of mangrove channels along the Caribbean coast, and a vast mangrove swamp around the Río Tárcoles and on the Pacific, near Bahía Drake.

Fauna

Though tropical in nature – with a substantial number of tropical animals such as poison-dart frogs and spider monkeys – Costa Rica is also the winter home for more than 200 species of migrating bird that arrive from as far away as Alaska and Australia. Don't be surprised to see one of your familiar backyard birds feeding alongside trogons and toucans. Birds are one of the primary attractions for naturalists, who scan endlessly for birds of every color, from strawberry-red scarlet macaws to the iridescent jewels called violet sabrewings (a type of hummingbird). Because many birds in Costa Rica have restricted ranges, you are guaranteed to find different species everywhere you travel.

The extensive network of national parks, wildlife refuges and other protected areas are prime places to spot wildlife. Visitors to national parks will almost certainly see one of Costa Rica's four types of monkey or two types of sloth, but there are an additional 230 types of mammal awaiting the patient observer. More exotic sightings might include the amazing four-eyed opossum or the silky anteater, while a lucky few might spot the elusive tapir or have a jaguarundi cross their path.

If you are serious about observing birds and animals, the value of a knowledgeable guide cannot be underestimated. Their keen eyes are trained to notice the slightest movement in the forest, and they recognize the many exotic sounds. Bird guides are proficient in the dialects of local birds, greatly improving your chances of hearing or seeing these species.

No season is a bad one for exploring Costa Rica's natural environment, though most visitors arrive during the peak dry season, when trails are less muddy and more accessible. A bonus of visiting between December and February is that many of the wintering migratory birds are still hanging around. A trip after the peak season means fewer birds, but this is a stupendous time to see dry forests transform into vibrant greens and it's also when resident birds begin nesting.

Endangered Species

As expected in a country with unique habitats and widespread logging, there are numerous species whose populations are declining or in danger of extinction. Currently, the number-one threat to most of Costa Rica's endangered species is habitat destruction, followed closely by hunting and trapping.

Costa Rica's four species of sea turtle – olive ridley, leatherback, green and hawksbill – deservedly get a lot of attention. All four species are classified as endangered or critically endangered, meaning they face an imminent threat of extinction. While populations of some species are increasing thanks to various protection programs along both coasts, the risk for these *tortugas* (turtles) is still very real.

Destruction of habitat is a huge problem. With the exception of the leatherbacks, all of these species return to their natal beach to nest, which means that the ecological state of the beach directly affects that turtle's ability to reproduce. All of the species prefer dark, undisturbed beaches, and any sort of development or artificial lighting (including flashlights) will inhibit nesting.

Hunting and harvesting eggs are two major causes of declining populations. Green turtles are hunted for their meat. Leatherbacks and olive ridleys are not killed for meat, but their eggs are considered a delicacy – an aphrodisiac, no less. Hawksbill turtles are hunted for their unusual shells, which are sometimes used to make jewelry and hair ornaments. Any trade in tortoiseshell products and turtle eggs and meat is illegal, but a significant black market exists.

The ultra-rare harpy eagle and the legendary quetzal – the birds at the top of every naturalist's must-see list – teeter precariously as their home forests are felled at an alarming rate. Seeing a noisy scarlet macaw could be a birdwatching highlight in Costa

Rica, but trapping for the pet trade has extirpated these magnificent birds from much of their former range. Although populations are thriving on the Península de Osa, there are fewer than 1500 remaining in Central America and the species is now extinct in most of the region, including the entire Caribbean coast.

A number of Costa Rica's mammals are highly endangered, including the elusive jaguar and the squirrel monkey, both due to the habitat destruction. Both survive in the depths of Parque Nacional Corcovado, with the latter also found in some numbers in Parque Nacional Manuel Antonio.

Harassment and intimidation of conservationists in Costa Rica is nothing new, and although the brutal murder of 26-year-old environmentalist Jairo Mora Sandoval in Limón Province in 2013 brought the issue to international attention, those accused of his murder were initially acquitted. In 2015, seven men were accused of Sandoval's murder. Four of the men were not convicted of murder but of assault, kidnapping and aggravated robbery for a crime that took place after Mora's murder. Then in 2016, after an appeal, the not-guilty verdict was overturned. Each of the men is serving 50 years in prison, the maximum sentence in Costa Rica.

National Parks & Protected Areas

The national-park system began in the 1960s, and has since been expanded into the Sistema Nacional de Areas de Conservación (National System of Conservation Areas; Sinac), with an astounding 186 protected areas, including 27 national parks, eight biological reserves, 32 protected zones, 13 forest reserves and 58 wildlife refuges. At least 10% of the land is strictly protected and another 17% is included in various multiple-use preserves. Costa Rican authorities take pride in the statistic that more than 27% of the country has been set aside for conservation, but multiple-use zones still allow farming, logging and other exploitation, so the environment within them is not totally protected. The smallest number might be the most amazing of all: Costa Rica's parks are a safe haven to approximately 5% of the world's wildlife species.

In addition to the system of national preserves, there are hundreds of small, privately owned lodges, reserves and haciendas (estates) that have been set up to protect the land. Many belong to longtime Costa Rican expats who decided that this country was the last stop in their journey along the 'gringo trail' in the 1970s and '80s. The abundance of foreign-owned protected areas is a bit of a contentious issue with Ticos. Although these are largely nonprofit organizations with keen interests in conservation, they are private and often cost money to enter. There's also a number of animal rescue and rehabilitation centers (also largely set up by expats), where injured and orphaned animals and illegal pets are rehabilitated and released into the wild, or looked after for life if they cannot be released.

Although the national-park system appears glamorous on paper, the Sinac authority still sees much work to be done. A report from several years ago amplified the fact that much of the protected area is, in fact, at risk. The government doesn't own all of this land – many of the areas are in private hands – and there isn't the budget to buy it. Technically, the private lands are protected from development, but there have been reports that many landowners are finding loopholes in the restrictions and selling or developing their properties, or taking bribes from poachers and illegal loggers in exchange for access.

On the plus side is a project by Sinac that links national parks and reserves, private reserves and national forests into 13 conservation areas. This strategy has two major effects. First, these 'megaparks' allow greater numbers of individual plants and animals to exist. Second, the administration of the national parks is delegated to regional offices, allowing a more individualized management approach. Each conservation area has regional and subregional offices charged with providing effective education, enforcement, research and management, although some regional offices only seem to have what appear to be obscure bureaucratic roles.

Support for land preservation remains high in Costa Rica because it provides income and jobs to so many people, plus important opportunities for scientific investigation.

Environmental Issues

No other tropical country has made such a concerted effort to protect its environment, and a study published by Yale and Columbia Universities in 2012 ranked Costa Rica in the top five nations for its overall environmental performance. At the same time, as the global leader in the burgeoning ecotourism economy, Costa Rica is proving to be a case study in the pitfalls and benefits of this kind of tourism. Costa Rica has slipped in the rankings and the pressures of overpopulation, global climate change and dwindling natural resources have further illuminated the urgency of environmental protection.

Deforestation

Sometimes, when the traffic jams up around the endless San José sprawl, it is hard to keep in mind that this place was once covered in a lush, unending tropical forest. Tragically, after more than a century of clearing for plantations, agriculture and logging, Costa Rica lost about 80% of its forest cover before the government stepped in with a plan to protect what was left. Through its many programs of forest protection and reforestation, 53% of the country is forested once again – a stunning accomplishment.

Despite protection for two-thirds of the remaining forests, cutting trees is still a major problem for Costa Rica, especially on private lands that are being cleared by wealthy landowners and multinational corporations. Even within national parks, more remote areas are being logged illegally as there is not enough money for law enforcement.

Apart from the loss of tropical forests and the plants and animals that depend on them, deforestation leads directly or indirectly to a number of other severe environmental problems. Forests protect the soil beneath them from the ravages of tropical rainstorms. After deforestation, much of the topsoil is washed away, lowering the productivity of the land and silting up watersheds and downstream coral reefs.

Cleared lands are frequently planted with a variety of crops, including acres of bananas, the production of which entails the use of pesticides as well as blue plastic bags to protect the fruit. Both the pesticides and the plastic end up polluting the environment. Cattle ranching has been another historical motivator for clear-cutting. It intensified during the 1970s, when Costa Rican coffee exports were waning in the global market.

Because deforestation plays a role in global warming, there is much interest in rewarding countries such as Costa Rica for taking the lead in protecting their forests. The US has forgiven millions of dollars of Costa Rica's debt in exchange for increased efforts to preserve rainforests. The Costa Rican government itself sponsors a program that pays landowners for each hectare of forest they set aside, and for adopting sustainable land management. It also petitioned the UN for a global program that would pay tropical countries for their conservation efforts and they listened. The UN, under the REDD+ initiative, has helped begin a system for tropical forest countries to be paid for their positive actions on deforestation. Travelers interested in taking part in projects that can help protect Costa Rica's trees should look to volunteer opportunities in conservation and forestry.

Tourism

The other great environmental issue facing Costa Rica comes from the country being loved to death, directly through the passage of around two million foreign tourists a year, and less directly through the development of extensive infrastructure to support this influx. For years, resort hotels and lodges continued to pop up, most notably on formerly pristine beaches or in the middle of intact rainforest. Too many of these projects were poorly planned, and they necessitate additional support systems, including roads and countless vehicle trips, with much of this activity unregulated and largely unmonitored.

As tourism continues to become a larger piece of the Costa Rican economy, the bonanza invites more and more development. Taking advantage of Costa Rica's reputation as a green destination, developers promote mass tourism by building large hotels and package tours that, in turn, drive away wildlife, hasten erosion and strain local sewer and water systems. The irony is painful: these businesses threaten to ruin the very environment that they're selling.

It's worth noting that many private lodges and reserves are also doing some of the best conservation work in the country,

Volunteer Opportunities

Cloudbridge Nature Reserve (www. cloudbridge.org) Trail building, construction, tree planting and projects monitoring the recovery of the cloud forest are offered to volunteers, who pay for their own housing with a local family. Preference is given to biology students, but all enthusiastic volunteers can apply.

Fundación Corcovado (www.corcovado foundation.org) An impressive network of people and organizations committed to preserving Parque Nacional Corcovado.

Monteverde Institute (www.monte verde-institute.org) A nonprofit educational institute offering training in tropical biology, conservation and sustainable development.

Tropical Science Center (www.cct. or.cr) This long-standing NGO offers volunteer placement at Reserva Biológica Bosque Nuboso Monteverde. Projects can include trail maintenance and conservation work.

and it's heartening to run across the ever-increasing homespun efforts to protect Costa Rica's environment, spearheaded by hardworking families or small organizations tucked away in quiet corners of the country. These include projects to boost rural economies by raising native medicinal plants, efforts by villagers to document their local biodiversity, and resourceful fundraising campaigns to purchase endangered lands.

Sustainable Travel

Costa Rica's visitors presently account for the largest sector of the national economy and thus have unprecedented power to protect this country. How? By spending wisely, asking probing questions about sustainability claims and simply avoiding businesses that threaten Costa Rica's future.

In its purest form, sustainable tourism simply means striking the ideal balance between the traveler and their surrounding environment. This often includes being conscientious about energy and water consumption, and treading lightly on local environments and communities. Sustainable tourism initiatives support their communities by hiring local people for decent wages, furthering women's and civil rights, and supporting local schools, artists and food producers. On the road, engage with the local economy as much as possible; for example, if a local artisan's handiwork catches your eye, make the purchase – every dollar infuses the micro-economy in the most direct (and rewarding) way.

Chifrijo (rice and pinto beans with fried pork and salsa)

Food & Drink

Costa Rica is a foodie's delight. Bordered by two oceans and heavily populated with expats, Dive into an oh-so-satisfying casado, *the Ticos' staple rice-beans-and-meat platter, or feast on five-star sushi. French and Italian pastry chefs sate morning munchies while* taquerías *and American bar food tempt nocturnal nibblers. And the regional Nicoya diet is one of the healthiest in the world. Dig in!*

What to Eat

Meals

Breakfast is taken in the early morning, usually from 6am to 8am. Many hotels offer a local or tropical-style continental breakfast, usually consisting of toast with butter and jam, accompanied by fresh fruit. American-style breakfasts are also available in many eateries.

A midday lunch (served between 11:30am and 2:30pm) at most *sodas* (lunch counters) usually involves a *casado* (set meal; literally, 'married'), a cheap, well-balanced plate of rice, beans, meat, salad and sometimes *plátanos maduros* (fried sweet plantains) or *patacones* (twice-fried plantains), which taste something like French fries.

For dinner (6pm to 9pm), a *casado* is on offer at most restaurants. Upscale Tico establishments may serve *lomito* (a lean cut of steak) and dishes like *pescado en salsa palmito* (fish in heart-of-palm sauce). Some of the more forward-thinking eateries in San José may drop an experimental vegetable plate in front of you.

Local Specialties

Breakfast for Ticos is usually *gallo pinto* (literally 'painted rooster'), a stir-fry of last night's rice and beans. When combined, the rice gets colored by the beans, and the mix obtains a speckled appearance. Served with eggs, cheese or *natilla* (sour cream), *gallo pinto* is cheap, filling and sometimes downright tasty. If you plan to spend the whole day surfing or hiking, you'll find that *gallo pinto* is great energy food.

Habits & Customs

When you sit down to eat in a restaurant, it is polite to say *buenos días* (good morning), *buenas tardes* (good afternoon) or *buenas noches* (good evening) to the waitstaff and any people you might be sharing a table with – and it's generally good form to acknowledge everyone in the room this way. It is also polite to say *buen provecho,* which is the equivalent of *bon appetit,* at the start of the meal.

Considering the extent of the coastline, it's no surprise that seafood is plentiful, and fish dishes are usually fresh and delicious. While it's not traditional Tico fare, *ceviche* is on most menus, usually made from *pargo* (red snapper), *dorado* (mahi-mahi), octopus or tilapia. The fish is marinated in lime juice with some combination of chilis, onions, tomatoes and herbs. Served chilled, it is a delectable way to enjoy fresh seafood. Emphasis is on 'fresh' here – it's raw fish, so if you have reason to believe it's not fresh, don't risk eating it. Sushi is also finding a place in many towns.

Food is not heavily spiced, unless you're having traditional Caribbean-style cuisine. Most local restaurants will lay out a bottle of Tabasco-style sauce, homemade salsa or Salsa Lizano, the Tico version of Worcestershire sauce and the 'secret' ingredient in *gallo pinto*. Some lay out a tempting jar of pickled hot peppers as well.

Most bars also offer the country's most popular *boca* (snack), *chifrijo,* which derives its name from two main ingredients: *chicharrón* (fried pork) and frijoles (beans). Diced tomatoes, spices, rice, tortilla chips and avocado are also thrown in for good measure. Fun fact about *chifrijo:* in 2014 a restaurant owner named Miguel Cordero claimed he officially invented it. He brought lawsuits against 49 businesses (including chain restaurants KFC and Spoon) and demanded a cool US$15 million in damages. So far he has not been able to collect.

Caribbean cuisine is the most distinctive in Costa Rica, having been steeped in indigenous, *criollo* (Creole) and Afro-Caribbean flavors. It's a welcome cultural change of pace after seemingly endless *casados*. Regional specialties include *rondón* (whose moniker comes from 'rundown,' meaning whatever the chef can run down), a spicy seafood gumbo; Caribbean-style rice and beans, made with red beans, coconut milk and curry spices; and *patí,* the Caribbean version of an *empanada* (savory turnover), the best street food, busride snack and picnic treat.

Vegetarians & Vegans

Costa Rica is a relatively comfortable place for vegetarians to travel. Rice and beans, as well as fresh fruit, are ubiquitous, but there's a lot more than that. The Happy Cow has a handy list of veggie restaurants nationwide (www.happycow.net). Visit farmers markets to sample what's in season: Costa Rica is a growers' paradise.

Green Treats

Feria Verde de Aranjuez (p51) San José's 'green market,' and an all-around winner for breakfast, produce, smoothies – everything.

Punta Mona (www.puntamona.org; cabinas per person incl meals US$90; @) 🖉 The sprawling garden at this secluded eco-retreat near Manzanillo has one of the world's largest collections of edible tropical plants.

Costa Rica Cooking (🖉2479-1569; www.costaricacooking.com; per person full day/bocas US$125/75) Help to whip up your own meal in La Fortuna, based on local and almost entirely organic produce.

Most restaurants will make veggie *casados* on request and many places are now including them on the menu. These set meals usually include rice and beans, cabbage salad and one or two selections of variously prepared vegetables or legumes.

With the high influx of tourism, there are also many specialty vegetarian restaurants or restaurants with a veggie menu in San José and in tourist towns, and even vegans will find some options in these places. Lodges in remote areas that offer all-inclusive meal plans can accommodate vegetarians with advance notice.

Gluten-free, macrobiotic and raw-food-only travelers will have a tougher time, as there are fewer outlets accommodating those diets, although this is slowly changing. If you intend to keep to your diet, it's best to choose lodgings where you can prepare food yourself. Many towns have *macrobióticas* (health-food stores), but the selection varies. Fresh vegetables can be hard to come by in isolated areas and are often quite expensive, but farmers markets are cropping up throughout the country.

What to Drink

Coffee

Coffee is probably the most popular beverage in the country, and wherever you go, someone is likely to offer you a *cafecito*. Traditionally, it is served strong and mixed with hot milk to taste, also known as *café con leche*. Purists can get *café negro* (black coffee); if you want a little milk, ask for *leche al lado* (milk on the side). Many trendier places serve espresso drinks.

Fruit Drinks

For a refresher, nothing beats *batidos* – fresh fruit shakes made either *al agua* (with water) or *con leche* (with milk). The array of available tropical fruit can be intoxicating and includes mango, papaya, *piña* (pineapple), *sandía* (watermelon), *melón* (cantaloupe), *mora* (blackberry), *carambola* (starfruit), *cas* (a type of tart guava), *guanábana* (soursop or cherimoya) and *tamarindo* (fruit of the tamarind tree). If you are wary about the condition of the drinking water, ask that your *batido* be made with *agua enbotellada* (bottled water) and *sin hielo* (without ice), though water is generally safe to drink throughout the country.

Pipas are green coconuts that have had their tops hacked off with a machete and then been spiked with a straw for drinking the coconut water inside – super refreshing when you're wilting in the tropical heat. If you're lucky enough to find it, *agua dulce* is sugarcane water, a slightly grassy, sweet juice that's been pressed through a heavy-duty, hand-cranked mill.

On the Caribbean coast, look for *agua de sapo* (literally 'toad water'), a beautiful lemonade laced with fresh ginger juice and *tapa de dulce* (brown sugar; also known as *tapa dulce*). *Resbaladera*, found mostly in the Guanacaste countryside, is a sweet milk – much like *horchata* (the Mexican rice drink) – made from rice, barley, milk and cinnamon. Other local drinks you may encounter include *linaza* (a flaxseed drink said to aid digestion) and *chan* (a drink made from chia seed and lemon) – which can be an acquired taste due to its slimy (yum!) texture.

Beer

The most popular alcoholic drink is *cerveza* (beer; aka *birra* locally), and there are several national brands. Imperial is the most popular – either for its smooth flavor or for the ubiquitous merchandise emblazoned with the eagle-crest logo – and Pilsen is also popular; both are tasty pilsners. Bavaria produces a lager and Bavaria Negro, a delicious, full-bodied dark beer; this brand is harder to find. A most welcome burgeoning craft-beer scene, with microbreweries popping up around the country, is increasing the variety of Costa Rican beers and broadening local palates.

Guaro

After beer, the poison of choice is *guaro*, which is a colorless alcohol (most similar to *aguardiente*) distilled from sugarcane and usually consumed as a sour or by the shot, often with hot sauce and lime juice. This spicy concoction is called a *chili guaro*, and in the last few years it has become a staple in San José and certain beach towns. *Guaro* goes down mighty easily but leaves one hell of a hangover.

Rum

As in most of Central America, the local rums are inexpensive and worthwhile, especially the Ron Centenario, which recently shot to international fame. And at the risk of alienating the most patriotic of Ticos, it would be remiss not to mention the arguably tastier Flor de Caña from Nicaragua (pause for rotten tomatoes). The most popular rum-based tipple is a *cuba libre* (rum and cola), which hits the spot on a hot, sticky day, especially when served with a fresh splash of lime. Premixed cans of *cuba libre* are also available in stores, with a hint of aluminum.

Tree boa, Bosque Nuboso Monteverde (p204)

VACLAV SEBEK/SHUTTERSTOCK ©

Survival Guide

Directory A–Z

Accessible Travel

Independent travel in Costa Rica is difficult for anyone with mobility constraints. Although Costa Rica has an equal-opportunity law, the law applies only to new or newly remodeled businesses and is loosely enforced. Therefore, some hotels and restaurants have features specifically suited to wheelchair use. However, many don't have ramps, and room or bathroom doors are rarely wide enough to accommodate a wheelchair.

Streets and sidewalks are potholed and poorly paved, making wheelchair use frustrating at best. Public buses don't have provisions to carry wheelchairs, and most national parks and outdoor tourist attractions don't have trails suited to wheelchair use. Notable exceptions include Parque Nacional Carara and Parque Nacional Manuel Antonio (both of which have a wheelchair-accessible trail) and Parque Nacional Poás Volcano.

The hearing-impaired will find most museums have signs and info boards explaining exhibits. However, at most museums, these will be in Spanish only. Audio guides are available at few museums for the visually impaired.

Download Lonely Planet's free Accessible Travel guide from https://shop.lonely planet.com/categories/accessible-travel.

Accommodations

Accommodations come at every price and comfort level: from luxurious ecolodges and sparkling all-inclusive resorts and backpacker palaces to spartan rooms with little more than a bed and four cinder block walls. The variety and number of rooms on offer, coupled with online booking, means that advance booking is usually not required, except in the peak of high season and Christmas, New Year and Easter (Semana Santa) holidays.

Note: the term *cabina* (cabin) is a catchall that can define a wide range of prices and amenities, from very rustic to very expensive.

Climate

San José

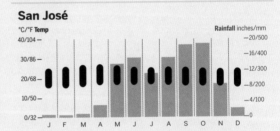

Puerto Limón

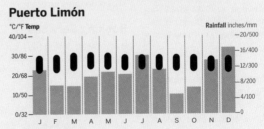

Puntarenas

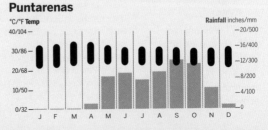

Book Your Stay Online

For more accommodation reviews by Lonely Planet authors, check out http://hotels.lonely planet.com/costa-rica. You'll find independent reviews, as well as recommendations on the best places to stay. Best of all, you can book online.

Hotels

● It's always advisable to ask to see a room – including the bathroom – before committing to a stay, especially in budget lodgings. Rooms within a single hotel can vary greatly.

● Some pricier hotels will require confirmation of a reservation with a credit card. Before doing so, note that some top-end hotels require a 50% to 100% deposit up-front when you reserve. This rule is not always clearly communicated.

● In most cases reservations can be canceled and refunded with enough notice. Ask the hotel about its cancellation policy before booking. It is often easier to make the reservation than to unmake it.

● Many hotels charge a hefty service fee for credit-card use.

● Have the hotel email you a confirmation. Hotels often get overbooked, and if you don't have a confirmation, you could be out of a room.

● To compete with online booking services, some hotels offer a discount if you book direct, or if you pay in cash.

● Walk-ins are usually given a discount.

Pricing

Many lodgings lower their prices during the low (rainy, aka 'green') season, from May to November. Prices change quickly and many hotels charge per person rather than per room – read rates carefully and always check ahead.

US dollars are the preferred currency for listing rates in Costa Rica. However, colones are accepted everywhere and are usually exchanged at current rates without an additional fee. Paying with a credit card sometimes incurs a surcharge and cash discounts are sometimes on offer.

Booking Services

Book ahead during the high season; this is especially important during the Christmas, New Year and Easter (Semana Santa) holidays. Prices skyrocket during those weeks, too. Some lodgings close during the months of September and October, or even longer, especially in the Península de Osa and the Golfo Dulce.

Lonely Planet (www.lonely planet.com/costa-rica/hotels) Independent reviews and recommendations.

Costa Rica Innkeepers Association (www.costa ricainnkeepers.com) A non profit association of B&Bs, small hotels, lodges and inns.

Escape Villas (www.villas costarica.com) High-end accommodations across Costa Rica – most near Parque Nacional Manuel Antonio – that are suitable for families and honeymooners looking for luxury.

Go Visit Costa Rica (www. govisitcostarica.com) Lots of information to help you plan your trip, including booking hotels, ecolodges and vacation rentals around the country.

Customs Regulations

● All travelers over the age of 18 are allowed to enter the country with 5L of wine or spirits and 500g of processed tobacco (roughly 400 cigarettes or 50 cigars).

● Camera gear, binoculars, and camping, snorkeling and other sporting equipment are readily allowed into the country.

● Dogs and cats are permitted entry providing they have obtained both general-health and rabies-vaccination certificates.

● Pornography and illicit drugs are prohibited.

Electricity

While Costa Rica uses a 110V/60Hz power system that is compatible with North American devices, power surges and fluctuation are frequent.

Type A
120V/60Hz

Health

Travelers to Central America need to be vigilant about food- and mosquito-borne infections. The majority of the illnesses most frequently caught while on holiday here are not life threatening, but they can certainly ruin your trip. Besides getting the proper vaccinations, it's important to use a good insect repellent and exercise care in what you eat and drink.

Before You Go

Health Insurance

High-risk adventure activities or water sports such as diving are not covered on all travel policies, so make sure you pay for the appropriate level of insurance coverage. Yours may cover basic activities, such as walking, but not ziplining or surfing. If diving, some companies may only cover you up to a certain number of dives or a certain depth. If unsure, check with your insurer before leaving your home country.

A list of medical-evacuation and travel-insurance companies can be found on the US State Department (www.travel.state.gov) website under the International Travel 'Before You Go' tab.

Recommended Vaccinations

○ Get necessary vaccinations four to eight weeks before departure.

○ Ask your doctor for an International Certificate of Vaccination (otherwise known as the 'Yellow Card'), which will list all the vaccinations you've received. This is mandatory for countries that require proof of yellow-fever vaccination upon entry (Costa Rica only requires such proof if you are entering from a country that carries a risk of yellow fever – check if your country of origin has a risk of yellow fever before you travel).

In Costa Rica

Availability & Cost of Health Care

○ Good medical care is available in most major cities but may be limited in rural areas.

○ For an extensive list of physicians, dentists and hospitals, visit https://cr.usembassy.gov and look under 'U.S. Citizen Services /Medical Assistance/ Medical Practitioners List.'

○ Most pharmacies are well supplied and a handful are open 24 hours. Pharmacists are licensed to prescribe medication. If you're taking any medication on a regular basis, make sure you know its generic (scientific) name, since many pharmaceuticals go under different names in Costa Rica.

Infectious Diseases

Chikungunya virus The newest mosquito-borne viral disease was accidentally introduced to Costa Rica from Africa, and carried from *Aedes albopictus* (Tiger mosquitoes). The symptoms are similar to those of dengue fever (high fever, joint inflammation, a skin rash, headache, muscle aches, nausea), and so are the treatments – replace fluids, reduce fever and wait it out. Unlike dengue, it's very unlikely to be fatal, and once you get it you'll probably develop an immunity. The best prevention is to cover up with long sleeves and DEET.

Dengue fever (breakbone fever) Dengue is transmitted by *Aedes aegypti* mosquitoes, which often bite during the daytime and are usually found close to human habitations, often indoors. Dengue is especially common in densely populated urban environments. It usually causes flu-like symptoms including fever, muscle aches, joint pains, headaches, nausea and vomiting, often followed by a rash. Most cases resolve uneventfully in a few days. There is no treatment for dengue fever except taking analgesics such as acetaminophen/paracetamol (Tylenol) and drinking plenty of fluids. Severe cases may require hospitalization for intravenous fluids and supportive care. There is no vaccine. The key to prevention is taking insect-protection measures.

Hepatitis A The second most common travel-related infection (after traveler's diarrhea). It's a viral infection of the liver that is usually acquired by ingestion of contaminated water, food or ice, though it may also be acquired by direct contact with infected persons. Symptoms may include fever, malaise, jaundice, nausea, vomiting and abdominal pain. Most cases resolve without complications, though hepatitis A occasionally causes severe liver damage. There is no treatment. The vaccine for hepatitis A is extremely safe and highly effective.

Leishmaniasis This is transmitted by sand flies. Most cases occur in newly cleared forest or areas of secondary growth; the highest incidence is in Talamanca. It causes slow-growing ulcers over exposed parts of the body. There is no vaccine. To protect yourself from sand flies,

follow the same precautions as for mosquitoes.

Malaria Malaria is very rare in Costa Rica, occurring only occasionally in rural parts of Limón Province. It's transmitted by mosquito bites, usually between dusk and dawn. Taking malaria pills is not necessary unless you are making a long stay in the province of Limón (not Puerto Limón). Protection against mosquito bites is most effective.

Traveler's diarrhea Tap water is safe and of high quality in Costa Rica, but when you're far off the beaten path it's best to avoid tap water unless it has been boiled, filtered or chemically disinfected (with iodine tablets). To prevent diarrhea, be wary of dairy products that might contain unpasteurized milk and be highly selective when eating food from street vendors. If you develop diarrhea, be sure to drink plenty of fluids, preferably with an oral rehydration solution containing lots of salt and sugar. If diarrhea is bloody or persists for more than 72 hours, or is accompanied by fever, shaking chills or severe abdominal pain, seek medical attention.

Typhoid Caused by ingestion of food or water contaminated by a species of salmonella known as *Salmonella typhi*. Fever occurs in virtually all cases. Other symptoms may include headache, malaise, muscle aches, dizziness, loss of appetite, nausea and abdominal pain. Possible complications include intestinal perforation, intestinal bleeding, confusion, delirium or (rarely) coma. A pre-trip vaccination is recommended.

Zika virus At the time of research, there was no evidence of Zika virus, which has been linked to microcephaly, a birth defect that affects a baby's brain development. Zika is primarily transmitted by mosquitoes, but it can also be transmitted by a man to his sexual partner or by a woman to her fetus. Be aware that symptoms are usually mild in adults, and many people may not realize that they are infected.

For a full list of potential risks, see the CDC website's Costa Rica page at https://wwwnc.cdc.gov/travel/destinations/traveler/none/costa-rica.

Environmental Hazards

Animal bites Do not attempt to pet, handle or feed any animal. Any bite or scratch by a mammal, including bats, should be promptly and thoroughly cleansed with large amounts of soap and water, and an antiseptic such as iodine or alcohol should be applied. Contact a local health authority in the event of such an injury. Rabies cases are rare but do happen.

Poison dart frogs They are very colorful and maybe tempting to touch, but don't. These colors serve as a warning. Their skin secretes toxins and may cause swelling, nausea and even muscular paralysis, and sometimes death, depending on the species of the frog.

Snakes When trekking in thick forest terrain wear long pants (trousers) and closed-toed shoes to help prevent encounters with camouflaged snakes on grass and tree branches.

Insect bites No matter how much you safeguard yourself, getting bitten by mosquitoes is part of every traveler's experience here. The best prevention is to stay covered up – wear long pants, long sleeves, a hat and shoes, not sandals. Invest in a good insect repellent, preferably one containing 20% DEET. Apply to exposed skin and clothing (but not to eyes, mouth, cuts, wounds or irritated skin). Compounds containing DEET should not be used on children under the age of two and should be used sparingly on children under 12 years. Invest in a bug net to hang over beds (along with a few thumbtacks or nails with which to hang it). Many hotels in Costa Rica don't have windows (or screens), and a cheap little net will save you plenty of nighttime aggravation. The mesh size should be less than 1.5mm. Dusk is the worst time for mosquitoes, so take extra precautions then.

Sun Stay out of the midday sun, wear sunglasses and a wide-brimmed hat, and apply sunblock with SPF 15 or higher, with both UVA and UVB protection and reapply often, especially if getting in the sea or rivers. Drink plenty of fluids and avoid strenuous exercise when the temperature is high.

Tap Water

- It's generally safe to drink tap water in Costa Rica, except in the most rural and undeveloped parts of the country. However, if you prefer to be cautious, buying bottled water is your best bet.

- If you have the means, vigorous boiling for one minute is the most effective means of water purification. At altitudes greater than 2000m, boil for three minutes.

- Another option is to disinfect water with iodine pills: add 2% tincture of iodine to 1L of water (five drops to clear water, 10 drops to cloudy water) and let stand for 30 minutes. If the water is cold, longer times may be required.

- Alternatively, carry a SteriPen that destroys most bacteria, viruses and protozoa with UV light or a purifying water bottle or straw.

Insurance

It's vital that travelers purchase the right type of travel insurance before coming to Costa Rica. Basic insurance tends to cover medical expenses, baggage loss, trip cancellation, accidents and personal liability, but it's worth spending extra to make sure you're covered in the event of natural disasters. If you intend to take part in adventure sports, make sure that those particular sports are covered by your policy; for divers, some policies only cover you up to a certain depth.

Worldwide travel insurance is available at www.lonelyplanet.com/travel-insurance. You can buy, extend and claim online anytime – even if you're already on the road.

Internet Access

- The number of internet cafes in Costa Rica has greatly decreased with the advent of smartphones, and wi-fi in restaurants and cafes.

- Expect to pay US$1 to US$2 per hour at internet cafes in San José and tourist towns.

- Wi-fi is common in all midrange and top-end hotels, and in the vast majority of cafes, budget hotels and hostels. Some hostels still have computers for guest use and/or wi-fi.

Legal Matters

- If you are arrested, your embassy can offer limited assistance. Embassy officials will not bail you out, but can contact a lawyer on your behalf. You are subject to Costa Rican laws, not the laws of your own country.

• The use of recreational substances other than tobacco and alcohol is illegal in Costa Rica and punishable by imprisonment.

LGBT+ Travelers

Costa Rica is miles ahead in terms of tolerance, compared with other Central American countries, and some areas of the country – particularly Quepos and Parque Nacional Manuel Antonio – have been gay vacation destinations for two decades. Homosexual acts are legal, and in 2015 Costa Rica became the first country in Central America to recognize gay relationships. On May 26, 2020, same-sex marriage became legal. Same-sex couples are unlikely to be the subject of harassment, though same-sex affection is rarely seen in smaller towns and might attract unwanted attention, as some cultural attitudes remain behind the times.

The undisputed gay and lesbian capital of Costa Rica is Manuel Antonio; visit www.gaymanuelantonio. com for info on the scene.

Center of Investigation & Promotion of Human Rights in Central America (CIPAC; ☏2280-7821; www.cipacdh. org) The leading gay activist organization in Costa Rica.

Toto Tours (☏USA 773-274-8686; www.tototours.com)

Gay-travel specialist that organizes regular trips to Costa Rica, among other destinations.

Maps

Detailed maps are hard (but not impossible) to come by in Costa Rica, so for ease it's best to purchase one online before your trip.

• The excellent, water-resistant 1:350,000 *Costa Rica Adventure Map* published by National Geographic also has an inset map of San José. Available online or in various book and gift shops in San José.

• Another quality option is the 1:330,000 *Costa Rica* sheet produced by International Travel Map, which is waterproof and includes a San José inset.

• Few national-park offices or ranger stations have maps for hikers.

• *Waterproof Travel Map Of Costa Rica* by Toucan Maps is a robust overview map of the country, with detailed 4WD seasonal roads marked, plus highlighted beaches, national parks and attractions. It also has zoomed-in maps of Arenal, Monteverde and Manuel Antonio. Available online.

• **Instituto Geográfico Nacional** (IGN; ☏2202-0777; www.registronacional.go.cr/instituto_geografico/index.htm; Ruta 215, San Gerardo, Zapote District; ☽8:30am-3:30pm

Mon-Fri) in San José has topographical maps available for purchase.

• Incafo formerly published the *Mapa-Guía de la Naturaleza Costa Rica*, an atlas that included 1:200,000 topographical sheets, as well as English and Spanish descriptions of Costa Rica's natural areas. Used copies can be purchased online.

Money

• The Costa Rican currency is the colón (plural colones), named after Cristóbal Colón (Christopher Columbus).

• Bills come in 1000, 2000, 5000, 10,000, 20,000 and 50,000 colón notes, while coins come in denominations of 5, 10, 20, 25, 50, 100 and 500 colones.

• Paying for things in US dollars is common, and at times is encouraged, since the currency is viewed as being more stable than the colón.

• In US-dollar transactions the change will usually be given in colones.

• Newer US dollars are preferred throughout Costa Rica; if your note has a rip in it, it may not be accepted.

• When paying in US dollars at a local restaurant, bar or shop the exchange rate can be unfavorable.

ATMs

ATMs are ubiquitous, typically dispensing colones; many dispense US dollars. They are not as easily found in rural and remote areas.

Changing Money

All banks will exchange US dollars, and some will exchange euros and British pounds; other currencies are more difficult. Most banks have excruciatingly long lines, especially at the state-run institutions (Banco Nacional, Banco de Costa Rica, Banco Popular). Make sure the bills you want to exchange are in good condition or they may be refused.

Credit Cards

- Cards are widely accepted at midrange and top-end hotels, as well as at top-end restaurants and some travel agencies; they are less likely to be accepted in small towns and in remote areas.

- A transaction fee (around 3% to 5%) on all international credit-card purchases is often added.

- Holders of credit and debit cards can buy colones in some banks, though expect to pay a high transaction fee.

- All car-rental agencies require drivers to have a credit card. It's possible to hire a car with just a debit card, but only on the condition that you pay for full insurance and leave a large

Dollars Versus Colones

While colones are the official currency of Costa Rica, US dollars are virtually legal tender. Case in point: most ATMs in large towns and cities will dispense both currencies. However, it pays to know where and when you should be paying with each currency.

In Costa Rica you can use US dollars to pay for hotel rooms, midrange to top-end meals, admission fees for sights, tours, domestic flights, international buses, car rental, private shuttle buses and big-ticket purchases. Local meals and drinks, domestic bus fares, taxis and small purchases should be paid for in colones.

deposit for traffic violations (check with the car-rental company ahead of time).

Exchange Rates

Australia	A$1	₡435
Canada	C$1	₡462
Euro zone	€1	₡711
Japan	¥100	₡580
New Zealand	NZ$1	₡406
UK	£1	₡786
USA	US$1	₡606

For current exchange rates, see www.xe.com.

Tipping

Guides Tip guides US$5 to US$20 per person per day. Tip the tour driver about half of what you tip the guide.

Hotels Tip the bellhop/porter US$1 to US$5 per service and the housekeeper US$1 to US$2 per day in top-end hotels; less in budget places.

Restaurants Bills usually include a 10% service charge. If

not, you might leave a small tip.

Taxis Tip only if special service is provided.

Opening Hours

These are high-season opening hours; hours will usually shorten in the shoulder and low seasons. Generally, sights, activities and restaurants are open daily.

Banks 9am–4pm Monday to Friday, sometimes 9am–noon Saturday

Bars and clubs 8pm–2am

Government offices 8am–5pm Monday to Friday; often closed 11:30am–1:30pm

Restaurants 7am–9pm; upscale places may open only for dinner, and in remote areas even the small *sodas* (inexpensive eateries) might open only at specific meal times

Shops 9am–6pm Monday to Saturday

Public Holidays

Días feriados (national holidays) are taken seriously in Costa Rica. Banks, public offices and many stores close. During these times, public transportation is tight and hotels are heavily booked. Many festivals coincide with public holidays.

New Year's Day January 1

Semana Santa Holy Week; March or April. The Thursday and Friday before Easter Sunday is the official holiday, though most businesses shut down for the whole week. From Thursday to Sunday bars are closed and alcohol sales are prohibited; on Thursday and Friday buses stop running.

Día de Juan Santamaría April 11. Honors the national hero who died fighting William Walker in 1856; major events are held in Alajuela, his hometown.

Labor Day May 1

Día de la Madre Mother's Day; August 15. Coincides with the annual Catholic Feast of the Assumption.

Independence Day September 15

Día de la Raza Columbus Day; October 12

Christmas Day December 25. Christmas Eve is also an unofficial holiday.

Last week in December The week between Christmas and New Year is an unofficial holiday; businesses close and beach hotels are crowded.

Safe Travel

Costa Rica is a largely safe country, but petty crime (bag snatchings, car break-ins etc) is common and muggings do occur, so it's important to be vigilant.

○ Many of Costa Rica's dangers are nature-related: riptides, earthquakes and volcanic eruptions are among them.

○ Predatory and venomous wildlife can also pose a threat, so a wildlife guide is essential if trekking in the jungle.

Smoking

Smoking is banned in all public places, restaurants, bars and casinos and on public transport. There are no separate 'smoking areas.' Some hotels in Costa Rica are nonsmoking only.

Telephone

○ To call Costa Rica from abroad, use the country code (506) before the eight-digit number. Costa Rica has no area codes.

○ Due to the widespread popularity of internet-based services, such as Skype, WhatsApp and iChat, calls with a smartphone or tablet can be free over wi-fi (or cheapest using a local internet provider) and are the easiest way to call internationally.

○ SIM cards are available at large supermarkets and phone shops; providers include Kolbi (state-owned), Claro, Movistar and TuYo. Some networks have better coverage than others. Top-ups are easy and possible with numerous recharge services in English online.

○ To buy an internet package SIM you may need your passport to register. Your phone will also need to be unlocked before you arrive in Costa Rica.

○ Cell (mobile) service now covers most of Costa Rica and nearly all of the country that is accessible to tourists.

○ Public phones are slowly being retired, but if you search they can still be found around Costa Rica. Chip phone cards are available from local shops. Payphones cannot receive international calls.

○ Chip cards are inserted into the phone and scanned. Colibrí cards (more common) require you to dial a toll-free number (199) and enter an access code. Instructions are provided in English or Spanish.

○ Cheap international calls from Costa Rica can be direct-dialed using a phone card. To make international calls, dial '00' followed by the country code and number.

Time

Costa Rica is six hours behind GMT, so Costa Rican time is equivalent to Central Time in North America. There is no daylight saving time.

Toilets

● Public restrooms are rare, but most restaurants and cafes will let you use their facilities, sometimes for a small charge – never more than 500 colones.

● Bus terminals and other major public buildings usually have toilets, also at a charge.

● Don't flush your toilet paper. Costa Rican plumbing is often poor and has very low pressure.

● Dispose of toilet paper in the rubbish bin inside the bathroom.

Tourist Information

● The government-run Costa Rica Tourism Board, the ICT (www.ict.go.cr/en), has an office in the capital; English is spoken.

● The ICT can provide you with free maps, a master bus schedule, information on road conditions in the hinterlands and a helpful brochure with up-to-date emergency numbers for every region.

● Consult the ICT's English-language website for information.

Visas

Passport-carrying nationals from the following countries are allowed 90 days' stay with no visa: Argentina, Australia, Brazil, Canada, Chile, Ireland, Israel, Japan, Mexico, New Zealand, Panama, South Africa, UAE, USA and most Western European countries.

Some visitors from other nations require a visa from a Costa Rican embassy or consulate.

For the latest info on visas, check the websites of the ICT (www.ict.go.cr) or the Costa Rican embassy (www.costarica-embassy.org).

Women Travelers

Most female travelers experience little more than a *'mi amor'* ('my love') or an appreciative glance from the local men. But, in general, Costa Rican men consider foreign women to have looser morals and to be easier conquests than Ticas (female Costa Ricans). Men will often make flirtatious comments to single women, particularly blondes, and women traveling together are not exempt. The best response is to do what Ticas do: ignore it completely. Women who firmly resist unwanted verbal advances from men are normally treated with respect.

● In small highland towns, the dress is usually conservative. Women rarely wear shorts, but belly-baring tops are all the rage. Bathing suits are common on public beaches; topless and nude bathing is not allowed.

● We don't recommend hitchhiking. There have been cases of solo women being attacked when hitchhiking.

● Assaults on women by unlicensed taxi drivers have taken place. Travelers should avoid unlicensed 'pirate' taxis where possible (licensed taxis are red and have medallions).

● Some travelers have reported that their drinks have been spiked in bars. It's advisable for travelers to keep a watchful eye on open drinks, and don't leave them unattended or with strangers, or accept drinks from strangers. There have been recent reports of spiked drinks in touristy places such as Jacó.

Transport

Getting There & Away

Costa Rica can be reached via frequent, direct international flights from the US and Canada and from other Central American countries. You can also cross a land border into Costa Rica from Panama or Nicaragua. Flights, cars and tours can be booked online at lonelyplanet.com/bookings.

Air

Costa Rica has two international airports, served by several major international airlines. It's especially well connected to the US, plus other Central and South American countries.

Airports & Airlines

Aeropuerto Internacional Juan Santamaría (Map p103; ☎2437-2400; www.fly2sanjose. com) International flights arrive here, 17km northwest of San José, in the town of Alajuela.

Aeropuerto Internacional Daniel Oduber Quirós (LIR; ☎2666-9600; www.lircr.com) This airport in Liberia also receives international flights from the USA, the Americas and Canada. It serves a number of American and Canadian airlines and some charters from London, as well as regional flights from Panama and Nicaragua.

Avianca (www.avianca.com) Part of the Central American airline consortium Grupo TACA, this Colombian-owned airline is regarded as the national airline of Costa Rica and flies to the USA, plus Central and Latin America.

Sea

Cruise ships stop in Costa Rican ports and enable passengers to make a quick foray into the country. Typically, ships dock at either the Pacific ports of Caldera, Puntarenas, Quepos and Bahía Drake, or the Caribbean port of Puerto Limón.

It is also possible to arrive in Costa Rica by private yacht.

Getting Around

Air

○ Costa Rica's domestic airlines are **Sansa** (☎2290-4100, in USA 877-767-2672; www.flysansa.com), Aerobell (www.aerobell.com) and Skyway (https://skywaycr.com), plus a new carrier named Green Airways (www.costaricagreenair.com).

○ Airlines fly small passenger planes; check your luggage allowance, as some only allow around 12kg.

○ Space is limited and demand is high in the dry season, so reserve and pay for tickets in advance.

Charter Flights

○ Travelers on a larger budget or in a larger party should consider chartering a private plane, which is by far the quickest way to travel around the country.

Climate Change & Travel

Every form of transportation that relies on carbon-based fuel generates CO_2, the main cause of human-induced climate change. Modern travel is dependent on aeroplanes, which might use less fuel per kilometer per person than most cars but travel much greater distances. The altitude at which aircraft emit gases (including CO_2) and particles also contributes to their climate change impact. Many websites offer 'carbon calculators' that allow people to estimate the carbon emissions generated by their journey and, for those who wish to do so, to offset the impact of the greenhouse gases emitted with contributions to portfolios of climate-friendly initiatives throughout the world. Lonely Planet offsets the carbon footprint of all staff and author travel.

○ It takes under 90 minutes to fly to most destinations, though weather conditions can significantly speed up or extend travel time.

○ Charter companies in the country include Carmon Air (www.carmonair.com), and Aero Caribe Air Charter (www.aerocaribecr.com). Flights can be booked directly through the company, a tour agency or some high-end accommodations.

○ Luggage space on charters is extremely limited.

Bicycle

With an increasingly large network of paved secondary roads and heightened awareness of cyclists, Costa Rica is emerging as one of Central America's most exciting cycle-touring destinations.

In the Central Valley highlands, there's a burgeoning road biking scene and visitors are likely to see Lycra-clad cyclists climbing and zooming down the attractive winding roads, taking in the epic scenery. That said, many roads are narrow, potholed and winding and there are no designated cycle lanes, so there's an element of risk involved.

Bikes, mostly mountain bikes and beach cruisers, can be rented in towns with a significant tourist presence for US$10 to US$20 per day. A few companies organize bike tours around Costa Rica.

Boat

○ In Costa Rica there are some regular coastal services, and safety standards are generally good.

○ Ferries cross the Golfo de Nicoya, connecting the central Pacific coast with the southern tip of the Península de Nicoya.

○ The **Coonatramar** (☑2661-1069; www. coonatramar.com; adult/ child/bicycle/motorcycle/car US$2/1/4/6/18) ferry links the port of Puntarenas with Playa Naranjo several times daily. The ferry **Naviera Tambor** (☑2661-2084; www. navieratambor.com; adult/ child/bicycle/motorcycle/car US$1.50/1/4/6/20) travels between Puntarenas and Paquera frequently each day, for a bus connection to Montezuma.

○ On the Golfo Dulce a daily passenger ferry links Golfito with Puerto Jiménez on the Península de Osa. On the other side of the Península de Osa, water taxis connect Bahía Drake with Sierpe.

○ On the Caribbean coast there are various bus and boat services that run several times a day, linking Cariari and Tortuguero via La Pavona, while another links Parismina and Siquirres (transfer in Caño Blanco).

○ Boats ply the canals that run along the coast from Moín to Tortuguero; although no regular service exists, tourists can prebook water taxis to transport them around these water-ways. Costa Rica and Nicaragua have disputed the San Juan as territory, so take your passport if you want to explore these waters. You can try to arrange boat transportation for Barra del Colorado from Tortuguero.

Bus (Shuttle)

The tourist-van shuttle services (aka gringo buses) are a pricier alternative to the standard intercity buses. Services are provided by the following:

Easy Ride (☑8812-4012, in USA 703-879-2284; www.easyride-costarica.com)

Gray Line (☑2220-2126, in USA 800-719-3905; www.grayline-costarica.com)

Interbus (☑6050-6500, 4100-0888; www.interbusonline.com).

Monkey Ride (☑2787-0454; www.monkeyridecr.com)

Tropical Tours (☑2640-1900; www.tropicaltourshuttles.com)

○ All five companies run overland transportation from San José to the most popular destinations, as well as directly between other destinations (see the websites for the comprehensive list).

○ These services will pick you up at your hotel, and reservations can be made online or through local travel agencies and hotel owners.

○ Popular destinations include Quepos/Manuel Antonio, Monteverde/Santa Elena, Jacó, Dominical, Uvita, Puerto Jiménez, Arenal, Montezuma and Mal País.

○ Easy Ride offers international services directly from Jacó, Tamarindo and Liberia to Granada and Managua in Nicaragua and from Monteverde to Managua.

Car & Motorcycle

○ Foreign drivers in Costa Rica are required to have a valid driver's license from their home country. Many places will also accept an International Driving Permit (IDP), issued by the automobile association in your country of origin. After 90 days, however, you will need to get a Costa Rican driver's license.

○ Gasoline (petrol) and diesel are widely available, and 24-hour service stations are along the Interamericana. At the time of research, fuel prices averaged around US$1.10 per liter.

○ In more remote areas, fuel will be more expensive and might be sold at the neighborhood *pulpería* (corner store).

○ Spare parts may be hard to find, especially for vehicles with sophisticated electronics and emissions-control systems.

○ If you have an accident, call the police immediately to make a report (required for insurance purposes).

○ Leave the vehicles in their places until the report has been made and do not make any statements except to members of law-enforcement agencies.

Rentals & Insurance

○ There are car-rental agencies in San José and in popular tourist destinations on the Pacific coast.

○ All of the major international car-rental agencies have outlets in Costa Rica, though you can sometimes get better deals from local companies.

○ Due to road conditions, it's necessary to invest in a 4WD unless travel is limited to the Interamericana.

○ Many agencies will insist on 4WD in the rainy season, when driving through rivers is a matter of course.

○ To rent a car you'll need a valid driver's license, a major credit card and a passport. The minimum age for car rental is 21 years. It's possible to rent with a debit card, but only if you agree to pay full insurance and leave a deposit for traffic violations (check with your agency ahead of time).

○ Carefully inspect rented cars for minor damage and make sure that any damage is noted on the rental agreement. If your car breaks down, call the rental company. Don't attempt to get the car fixed yourself – most companies won't reimburse expenses without prior authorization.

○ Prices vary considerably; on average you can expect to pay more than US$250 per week for a standard SUV, including *kilometraje libre* (unlimited mileage). Economy cars are much cheaper upwards of US$150 a week (prices are not including mandatory local insurance).

○ Costa Rican insurance is mandatory, even if you have insurance at home. Expect to pay about US$10 to US$40 per day. Many rental companies won't rent you a car without it. The basic insurance that all drivers must buy is from a government monopoly, the Instituto Nacional de Seguros. This insurance does not cover your rental car at all, only damages to other people and their car or property. It is legal to drive with this insurance only, but it can be difficult to negotiate with a rental agency to allow you to drive away with just this minimum standard. Full insurance through the rental agency can be up to US$60 a day.

○ Some roads in Costa Rica are rough and rugged, meaning that minor accidents or car damage are common.

○ Note: if you pay basic insurance with a gold or platinum credit card, the card company may take responsibility for damage to the car, in which case you can forgo the cost of the full insurance. Make sure you verify this with your credit-card company ahead of time.

○ Most insurance policies do not cover damage caused by flooding or driving through a river, so be aware of the extent of your policy.

○ Rental rates fluctuate wildly, so shop around. Some agencies offer discounts for extended rentals. Note that rental offices at the airport charge an extra fee in addition to regular rates.

○ Thieves can easily recognize rental cars. Never leave anything in sight in a parked car – nothing! – and remove all luggage from the trunk overnight. If possible, park the car in a guarded parking lot rather than on the street.

○ Motorcycles (including Harley-Davidsons) can be rented in San José and Escazú, but considering the condition of the roads it's not recommended.

Road Conditions & Hazards

○ The quality of roads varies, from the quite smoothly paved Interamericana

to the barely passable, bumpy, potholed, rural back roads. Any can suffer from landslides, sudden flooding and fog.

○ Many roads are single lane and winding; mountain roads have huge gutters at the sides and lack hard shoulders; other roads are rock-strewn, dirt-and-mud affairs that traverse rivers.

○ Drive defensively and expect a variety of obstructions, from cyclists and pedestrians to broken-down cars and cattle. Unsigned speed bumps are placed on some stretches of road.

○ Roads around major tourist areas are adequately marked; all others are not.

○ Always ask about road conditions before setting out, especially in the rainy season, when a number of roads become impassable.

Road Rules

○ There are speed limits of 100km/h to 120km/h or less on highways; limits will be posted. The minimum driving speed on highways is 40km/h. The speed limit is 60km/h or less on secondary roads (in urban areas, the speed limit is usually 40m/h).

○ Traffic police use radar, and speed limits are sometimes enforced with speeding tickets.

○ Tickets are issued to drivers operating vehicles without a seat belt.

○ It's illegal to stop at an intersection or make a right turn on a red.

○ At unmarked intersections, yield to the car on your right.

○ Drive on the right. Passing is allowed only on the left.

○ If you are issued with a ticket, you have to pay the fine at a bank; instructions are given on the ticket. If you're driving a rental car, the rental company may be able to arrange your payment for you – the amount of the fine should be on the ticket.

○ Police have no right to ask for money, and they shouldn't confiscate a car unless: a) the driver cannot produce a license or ownership papers/rental agreement, b) the car lacks license plates, c) the driver is drunk or the driver has been involved in an accident causing serious injury.

○ If you're driving and see oncoming cars with headlights flashing, it often means that there is a road problem or a radar speed trap ahead. Slow down immediately.

Taxis

In San José, taxis have *marías* (meters) and it's illegal for drivers not to use them. Outside San José, most taxis don't have meters and fares tend to be agreed upon in advance. Bargaining is acceptable.

Language

Spanish pronunciation is not difficult as most of the sounds are also found in English. You can read our pronunciation guides below as if they were English and you'll be understood just fine. And if you pronounce 'kh' in our guides as a throaty sound and remember to roll the 'r,' you'll even sound like a real Costa Rican.

To enhance your trip with a phrasebook, visit **lonelyplanet.com**. Lonely Planet iPhone phrasebooks are available through the Apple App store.

Basics

Hello
Hola   *o·*la

How are you?
¿Cómo está? (pol)   *ko·*mo es·*ta*
¿Cómo estás? (inf)   *ko·*mo es·*tas*

I'm fine, thanks.
Bien, gracias.   byen *gra·*syas

Excuse me (to get attention)
Con permiso   kon per·*mee·*so

Yes/No
Sí/No   see/no

Thank you
Gracias   *gra·*syas

You're welcome/That's fine
Con mucho gusto   kon *moo·*cho *goo·*sto

Goodbye/See you later
Adiós/Nos vemos   a·*dyos*/nos *ve·*mos

Do you speak English?
¿Habla inglés? (pol)   *a·*bla een·*gles*
¿Hablas inglés? (inf)   *a·*blas een·*gles*

I don't understand.
No entiendo.   no en·*tyen·*do

How much is this?
¿Cuánto cuesta?   *kwan·*to *kwes·*ta

Can you reduce the price a little?
¿Podría bajarle el   po·*dree·*a ba·*khar·*le
el precio?   el *pre·*syo

Accommodations

I'd like to make a booking.
Quisiera reservar   kee·*sye·*ra re·ser·*var*
una habitación.   *oo·*na a·bee·ta·*syon*

Do you have a room available?
¿Tiene una habitación?   *tye·*ne *oo·*na a·bee·ta·*syon*

How much is it per night?
¿Cuánto es por noche?   *kwan·*to es por *no·*che

Eating & Drinking

I'd like ..., please.
Quisiera ..., por favor.   kee·*sye·*ra ... por fa·*vor*

That was delicious!
¡Estuvo delicioso!   es·*too·*vo de·*lee·*syo·so

Bring the bill/check, please.
La cuenta, por favor.   la *kwen·*ta por fa·*vor*

I'm allergic to ...
Soy alérgico/a al ... (m/f)   soy a·*ler·*khee·ko/a al ...

I don't eat ...
No como ...   no *ko·*mo ...
  chicken   *pollo*   *po·*yo
  fish   *pescado*   pes·*ka·*do
  (red) meat   *carne (roja)*   *kar·*ne (*ro·*kha)

Emergencies

I'm ill.
Estoy enfermo/a. (m/f)   es·*toy* en·*fer·*mo/a

Help!
¡Socorro!   so·*ko·*ro

Call a doctor!
¡Llame a un doctor!   *ya·*me a oon dok·*tor*

Call the police!
¡Llame a la policía!   *ya·*me a la po·lee·*see·*a

Directions

Where's a/the ...?
¿Dónde está ...?   *don·*de es·*ta* ...
  bank
  el banco   el *ban·*ko
  ... embassy
  la embajada de ...   la em·ba·*kha·*da de ...
  market
  el mercado   el mer·*ka·*do
  museum
  el museo   el moo·*se·*o
  restaurant
  un restaurante   oon res·tow·*ran·*te
  toilet
  el baño   el *ba·*nyo

Behind the Scenes

Acknowledgements

Climate map data adapted from Peel MC, Finlayson BL & McMahon TA (2007) 'Updated World Map of the Köppen-Geiger Climate Classification', Hydrology and Earth System Sciences, 11, 163344.

Cover photograph: Volcán Arenal, Nick Ledger/AWL Images ©

This Book

This 3rd edition of Lonely Planet's *Best of Costa Rica* guidebook was researched and written by Jade Bremner, Ashley Harrell, Brian Kluepfel and Mara Vorhees. The previous edition was written by Ashley, Jade and Brian. This guidebook was produced by the following:

Senior Product Editors Sandie Kestell, Martine Power

Product Editors Ronan Abayawickrema, Katie Connolly

Senior Cartographer Corey Hutchison

Book Designer Ania Bartoszek

Assisting Editors Gemma Graham, Kristin Odijk, Gabrielle Stefanos

Cover Researcher Brendan Dempsey-Spencer

Thanks to Melanie Dankel, Karen Henderson, Kate Kiely, Amy Lynch, Amy Lysen, Anne McGuire, Genna Patterson, Tamara Sheward

Send Us Your Feedback

We love to hear from travelers – your comments keep us on our toes and help make our books better. Our well-traveled team reads every word on what you loved or loathed about this book. Although we cannot reply individually to postal submissions, we always guarantee that your feedback goes straight to the appropriate authors, in time for the next edition. Each person who sends us information is thanked in the next edition, the most useful submissions are rewarded with a selection of digital PDF chapters.

Visit lonelyplanet.com/contact to submit your updates and suggestions or to ask for help. Our award-winning website also features inspirational travel stories, news and discussions.

Note: We may edit, reproduce and incorporate your comments in Lonely Planet products such as guidebooks, websites and digital products, so let us know if you don't want your comments reproduced or your name acknowledged. For a copy of our privacy policy visit lonelyplanet.com/privacy.

Index

Symbols & Map Key

Look for these symbols to quickly identify listings:

- ◉ Sights
- ✈ Activities
- ◉ Courses
- ◉ Tours
- ◉ Festivals & Events
- ✖ Eating
- ◉ Drinking
- ✦ Entertainment
- ◉ Shopping
- ◉ Information & Transport

These symbols and abbreviations give vital information for each listing:

- 🌿 Sustainable or green recommendation
- **FREE** No payment required

- ☎ Telephone number
- ☺ Opening hours
- Ⓟ Parking
- ☺ Nonsmoking
- ❊ Air-conditioning
- @ Internet access
- ☎ Wi-fi access
- ☰ Swimming pool

- ▢ Bus
- ☰ Ferry
- ☰ Tram
- ☰ Train
- ◉ English-language menu
- ✎ Vegetarian selection
- ✦ Family-friendly

Find your best experiences with these Great For... icons.

 Art & Culture

 Beaches

Budget

 Cafe/Coffee

Cycling

Detour

 Drinking

 Entertainment

 Events

Family Travel

Food & Drink

 History

Local Life

 Nature & Wildlife

 Photo Op

 Scenery

Shopping

 Short Trip

 Sport

 Walking

 Winter Travel

Sights

- ◉ Beach
- ◉ Bird Sanctuary
- ◉ Buddhist
- ◉ Castle/Palace
- ◉ Christian
- ◉ Confucian
- ◉ Hindu
- ◉ Islamic
- ◉ Jain
- ◉ Jewish
- ◉ Monument
- ◉ Museum/Gallery/ Historic Building
- ◉ Ruin
- ◉ Shinto
- ◉ Sikh
- ◉ Taoist
- ◉ Winery/Vineyard
- ◉ Zoo/Wildlife Sanctuary
- ◉ Other Sight

Points of Interest

- ◎ Bodysurfing
- ◎ Camping
- ◎ Cafe
- ◎ Canoeing/Kayaking
- ◎ Course/Tour
- ◎ Diving
- ◎ Drinking & Nightlife
- ◎ Eating
- ◎ Entertainment
- ◎ Sento Hot Baths/ Onsen
- ◎ Shopping
- ◎ Skiing
- ◎ Sleeping
- ◎ Snorkelling
- ◎ Surfing
- ◎ Swimming/Pool
- ◎ Walking
- ◎ Windsurfing
- ◎ Other Activity

Information

- ◉ Bank
- ◉ Embassy/Consulate
- ◉ Hospital/Medical
- @ Internet
- ◉ Police
- ◉ Post Office
- ◉ Telephone
- ◉ Toilet
- ◉ Tourist Information
- ● Other Information

Geographic

- ◉ Beach
- ⋈ Gate
- ◉ Hut/Shelter
- ◉ Lighthouse
- ◉ Lookout
- ▲ Mountain/Volcano
- ◉ Oasis
- ◉ Park
-)(Pass
- ◉ Picnic Area
- ◉ Waterfall

Transport

- ◉ Airport
- Ⓑ BART station
- ◉ Border crossing
- Ⓣ Boston T station
- ◉ Bus
- ╂◉╂ Cable car/Funicular
- ◉ Cycling
- ◉ Ferry
- Ⓜ Metro/MRT station
- ◉ Monorail
- Ⓟ Parking
- ◉ Petrol station
- Ⓢ Subway/S-Bahn/ Skytrain station
- ◉ Taxi
- ╂◉╂ Train station/Railway
- ⋯ Tram
- Ⓤ Underground/ U-Bahn station
- ● Other Transport

Brian Kluepfel

Brian lived in three states of America and seven different residences by the time he was nine, and just kept moving, making stops in Berkeley, Bolivia, the Bronx and the 'burbs further down the line. His journalistic work across the Americas has ranged from the Copa America soccer tournament in Paraguay to a poi farm on Maui, to an accordion festival in Quebec. Brian's titles for Lonely Planet include *Venezuela, Costa Rica, Belize & Guatemala, Bolivia* and *Ecuador*. Look for his stuff in Lonely Planet's *Secret Marvels of the World* and *Global Chocolate Tour*. Brian is an avid birder and musician and dabbles in both on the road; his singing has been tolerated at open mics from Sámara, Costa Rica to Beijing, China.

Our Story

A beat-up old car, a few dollars in the pocket and a sense of adventure. In 1972 that's all Tony and Maureen Wheeler needed for the trip of a lifetime – across Europe and Asia overland to Australia. It took several months, and at the end – broke but inspired – they sat at their kitchen table writing and stapling together their first travel guide, *Across Asia on the Cheap*. Within a week they'd sold 1500 copies. Lonely Planet was born.

Today, Lonely Planet has offices in Tennessee, Dublin, Beijing and Delhi, with a network of over 2000 contributors in every corner of the globe. We share Tony's belief that 'a great guidebook should do three things: inform, educate and amuse'.

Our Writers

Mara Vorhees

Mara Vorhees writes about food, travel and family fun around the world. Her work has been published by *BBC Travel, Boston Globe, Delta Sky, Vancouver Sun* and more. For Lonely Planet, she regularly writes about destinations in Central America and Eastern Europe, as well as New England, where she lives. She often travels with her twin boys in tow, making her an expert in family travel. Follow their adventures and misadventures at www.havetwinswilltravel.com.

Jade Bremner

Jade has been a journalist for more than 15 years. She has lived in and reported on four different regions. It's no coincidence many of her favourite places have some of the best waves in the world. Jade has edited travel magazines and sections for *Time Out* and *Radio Times* and has contributed to *The Times, CNN* and *The Independent*. She feels privileged to share tales from this wonderful planet we call home and is always looking for the next adventure. @jadebremner

Ashley Harrell

After a brief stint selling day spa coupons door-to-door in South Florida, Ashley decided she'd rather be a writer. She went to journalism grad school, convinced a newspaper to hire her, and starting covering wildlife, crime and tourism, sometimes all in the same story. Fueling her zest for storytelling and the unknown, she traveled widely and moved often, from a tiny NYC apartment to a vast California ranch to a jungle cabin in Costa Rica, where she started writing for Lonely Planet. From there her travels became more exotic and further flung, and she still laughs when paychecks arrive.

More Writers

STAY IN TOUCH LONELYPLANET.COM/CONTACT

IRELAND Digital Depot, Roe Lane (off Thomas St), Digital Hub, Dublin 8, D08 TCV4, Ireland

USA 230 Franklin Road, Building 2B, Franklin, TN 37064
☎ 615 988 9713

 twitter.com/
lonelyplanet

 facebook.com/
lonelyplanet

 instagram.com/
lonelyplanet

 youtube.com/
lonelyplanet

 lonelyplanet.com/
newsletter